Telling the Barn Swallow

EMILY GROSHOLZ, Editor

Telling the Barn Swallow

POETS ON THE POETRY
OF MAXINE KUMIN

University Press of New England | *Hanover and London*

University Press of New England, Hanover, NH 03755
© 1997 by University Press of New England
All rights reserved
Printed in the United States of America   5   4   3   2   1
CIP data appear at the end of the book

Contents

JUL -- 1999

vi | Contents

Acknowledgments

I would like to thank Virginia McFarland for her generous support of the project represented by this volume and for her love and encouragement over the years. Her friendship has become as important to me as it once was to my mother. I would also like to thank Eleanor Wilner for her many kindnesses, especially for her substantial editorial help when I was out of the country. My thanks also go to Ansie Baird for her support, in this and other poetic endeavors, and to the staff of the New Hampshire Writers and Publishers Project for their administrative help.

Charles Scribner's Sons & Co. gave permission to reprint Hilda Raz's essay, and W. W. Norton & Co. gave permission to reprint from *Women, Animals, and Vegetables* and *Looking for Luck* on generous terms. All other poems by Maxine Kumin are reprinted by permission of Curtis Brown, Ltd., which is gratefully acknowledged. Philip Pochoda and the staff at University Press of New England welcomed the book enthusiastically from its inception and produced it in a timely and professional way. I am grateful for this support.

Finally, my deepest gratitude remains with my husband, Robert R. Edwards, and our children, Benjamin, Robert, William Jules-Yves, and Mary-Frances, for their love and liveliness.

May 1996   E.G.

Editor's Introduction

Maxine Kumin's poetry deserves its popularity, for it is hopeful without being sentimental, formal without being contrived, and deliberative without being doctrinaire. Over the past four decades it has consistently and increasingly won a loyal readership, and Kumin is widely recognized as one of the leading women of letters in this country. Yet the critical response to her poetry has not been proportionate to the importance of her art and acclaim, perhaps because her life's geography has removed her from the cultural capitals where poetic reputations are invented.

One of the few members of the generation of Lowell, Plath, Sexton, and Berryman to survive and thrive, Kumin moved with her husband from Boston to rural New Hampshire twenty years ago, to live on a farm that they had already owned for more than a decade. In rural New England, training horses and raising vegetables, Kumin discovered a new source of poetic topics that referred back to predecessors like Thoreau and Frost and across to contemporaries like Wendell Berry, Robert Morgan, and A. R. Ammons. But her treatment of these topics was that of a woman conscious of issues generated by feminism and by new concerns for the environment raised by writers like Rachel Carson. Thus, in Kumin's poetry the perspective is at once cosmopolitan and local, urban and rustic, human and female. Her subjects are as likely to be her grandchildren as the exigencies of art, the cruelty of barn cats as the follies of her countrymen, the weather afflicting her farm as street fighting in Paris or Jerusalem.

This volume is an attempt to extend and deepen the conversation of poets, literary critics, and lovers of poetry about the work of Maxine Kumin. The editor and all the contributors hope to encourage more people to read, memorize, consider, and talk about Kumin's poems and to understand better the complex view of wild and human nature they compose, as well as their place in the literature of this country and century.

The essays fall roughly into two sections dealing with form and content, though this division must be artificial insofar as poetic form and content cannot be disentangled. The first five allow the reader to consider Kumin's poetry in structural terms: her phonemic patterns (Wilner), metrical strategies (Finch), diction and vocabulary (Taylor), and choice of tropes (Grosholz emphasizes tropes of unity; Bowers, tropes of difference).

The last seven essays take up thematic issues. Long essays by Ostriker and Raz provide thematic overviews, one external and one internal, both informed by American feminism. Ostriker locates Kumin's work in the nineteenth- and twentieth-century tradition of American nature writing; Raz also treats Kumin as an exemplary nature writer but uses the occasion to track the unfolding of Kumin's career in chronological order. The interposed essay by Mark Jarman reminds the reader that great poetry engages and yet surpasses any particular political interest, as the wisdom of the heart eludes the categories of the intellect. The final four essays explore four thematic topoi that recur in Kumin's poetry: animals (McNair), the body (Becker), tools (Burns), and gardens (Oles).

Many of these essays testify that Kumin's structural allegiance to traditional form is linked to her attraction to human mortality as a theme. As Wilner writes, "The awareness of our small place in large things, the sanity and sense of proportion in all her work, is intimately related to the existential facing of limits, which is inextricably linked to her use and mastery of prosodic form." Yet the common perception of this linkage plays itself out as a series of debates among the essays, that is, as places where further conversation may take root. What is more significant, Kumin's allegiance to traditional form or her experiments in the distortion or loosening of that form? Is her insistence on mortality the austere restraint of a twentieth-century puritan or the robust affirmation of earthly paradise? Is her poetry marked by a rejection or evasion of transcendence, or does transcendence reappear in the guise of myth and dream?

The poems that make up the final section of the book are the homage of poets to both the work of Maxine Kumin and the poet herself. In some of them the writer directly addresses Kumin, in others the address is indirect or by analogy, and in some the poem simply testifies to Kumin's influence. But all the poems express a respect that is personal as well as poetic and an affection that is poetic as well as personal. Maxine Kumin combines the divine madness of poetry with a healthy and unpretentious sanity that is very compelling at this end of the century, on this island Earth becalmed in the sea of space.

Note on References

References in each essay will be given to Maxine Kumin's books first by title and thereafter by the following abbreviations.

Poems:
Halfway   HW
The Privilege   TP
The Nightmare Factory   NF
Up Country   UC
House, Bridge, Fountain, Gate   HBFG
The Retrieval System   RS
Our Ground Time Here Will Be Brief   GT
The Long Approach   LA
Nurture   N
Looking for Luck   LL
Connecting the Dots   CD

Essays:
To Make a Prairie   MP
In Deep   ID
Women, Animals, and Vegetables   WAV

Full bibliographic information is given at the end of the book. It was compiled by Hilda Raz, with the help of her graduate student at the University of Nebraska, Sherrie Flick.

Note on Poems

"Floating Farm" and "A Marriage" from *Giacometti's Dog*, by Robin Becker, © 1990. Reprinted by permission of the University of Pittsburgh Press.

"Chicory" © 1996 Wendell Berry. First published in *The Sewanee Review*.

"The Dive" from *The Islanders* by Philip Booth. Copyright 1952, 1956, 1957, 1958, 1959, 1960, 1961 by Philip Booth. Used by permission of Viking Penguin, a division of Penguin Books USA Inc.

"Another Language" © 1996 Neal Bowers.

"Zaraf's Star" © 1996 Annie Finch.

"Sidonie" from *Eden*, by Emily Grosholz, © 1992. Reprinted by permission of the Johns Hopkins University Press.

"Parents' Pantoum" from *Harping On*, by Carolyn Kizer, © 1996. Reprinted by permission of Copper Canyon Press and the author.

"The Puppy" and "Why We Need Poetry" © 1996 Wesley McNair. First published in *Poetry Northwest*.

"Small Poem of Thanks" reprinted by permission of Louisiana State University Press from *The Deed*, by Carole Simmons Oles. Copyright © 1988, 1991 by Carole Simmons Oles. First published in *Prairie Schooner*.

"Mid-February" © 1996 Alicia Ostriker.

"Family" from *What Is Good* by Hilda Raz © 1989. Reprinted by permission of the author.

"Postscript" from *Sarah's Choice*, by Eleanor Wilner, © 1989. Reprinted by permission of the author. First published in *Feminist Studies*.

Telling the Barn Swallow

The Wedding of Meaning and Measure: Kumin and the Poetics of Finitude

A graduate student friend wrote me not long ago about "Postscript," the self-parodying poem that appears in the last section of this volume, a poem I wrote to honor the work of Maxine Kumin, whose virtues as a poet seemed to throw my own excesses into high relief, for which reason the writing of the poem was itself that other kind of relief—confession, which is currently mistaken for honesty. For what my correspondent[1] detected was that, though it had at first reading "taken her in," "the poem ultimately affirms the poet's own poetics, even as it . . . mocks them." I want to speak to that observation, as it gives me a chance to consider how that might be true and how at the same time the praise of Maxine Kumin both stands and is sharpened in the light of our difference.

At one of her readings I remember Max saying that there are some (or many) poems we labor and labor over and others, which she called by the French name, *la donnée*, that are just "given." They appear, they seem to pour out like molten lava, shaping themselves as they go. "Postscript" is such a poem. It came out at white-hot speed as it stands. So figuring out its intentions is as after-the-fact for me as for any reader. I too was entirely taken in by the confessional tone of the speaker (the poem depends on this), was carried away by it, and took great joy in the demonstration and expiation of my flaws, both poetic and personal, in this self-parody that was also one of my few chances to get away with self-dramatization. For isn't self-dramatization an ingredient of public confession? Which is also, though it is not nice to say so, often at least a little bit hilarious.[2]

Of course, the point about Maxine Kumin is that she does not dramatize herself, and thus her personal poems remain admirable—exemplary, really. Her poems never call attention to herself but to the world seen through her eyes. They are personal without being exposés; she guards her privacy with all the skill of her craft, the revelatory concealments of metaphor, and the clear knowledge that, though there is nothing to hide, there is plenty to protect.

I think that when my poem's speaker sees herself as a potentially disastrous publicizer of the private spaces, in using words like "mad striptease of art," she is pointing toward the current confusion between nakedness and truth, between display and candor. For among the requirements that personal poetry makes of the writer, the chief of them is probably what used to be called character, and character expresses itself in style and in craft. "Postscript," then, would seem to contain an implicit argument about *three* kinds of poetry, and the one I am parodying and also covertly endorsing because it's what I do provides the fun but is not strictly the point of the exercise. The real point, as Dürer's gesture illustrates, is to honor Maxine Kumin's personal poetics, her études of finitude—the courage to face mortality solo but accompanied by the restraint and craft to point to where it hurts, to say what needs to be said to save what can be saved. And in honoring her artful accuracy, to distinguish her work from that *other* kind of ubiquitous personal poetry that is solipsized and/or exhibitionist, frequently without ear or form—dull or banal or sensational, or all three at once.

The poetry of Maxine Kumin is a corrective to the all too pervasive poetry of tin-ear diarists who, believing that the personal authenticates the genuine, merely confess, telling only what they already know—these plaintiffs of the arbitrarily broken line, minions of the morning after, who, lacking a larger perspective, their vision steamy and clouded from stewing in their own juice, seem so unaware of the rest of humanity and history as to fail to recognize the privilege involved in taking the self as the primary object of gaze and who reduce poetry's subject to what Zbigniew Herbert called "a small broken soul with a great self-pity."

The awareness of our small place in large things, the sanity and sense of proportion in all her work, is intimately related to the existential facing of limits, which is inextricably linked to her use and mastery of prosodic form. There is currently much talk about "neoformalism," which is mainly just the time-ripened truth that what was once experimental and inventive is by now conventional and, moreover, that open forms of poetry were first propagated by poets already imbued with and unerringly informed by older, prescribed forms; while today, as with third- or fourth-generation photocopies, younger poets are too far from the originals to have any but the most blurred image of what deep music the modernist poets were roughing up. Which has left much of our poetry without even a muffled drum to accompany its own funeral cortège.

But neoformalism, to my mind, also sometimes refers to one kind of nearly mechanical resuscitation of the prescribed forms of English prosody, which bear something in common with the stiff neoclassicism of the French painter David, whose late-eighteenth-century work seems to have petrified living bodies in hopes of somehow mathematically making them appear immortal. And yet these unnaturally immobile figures are lit with the harsh light of change, a theatrical intensity that reveals the strain under which reason labored when faced with real bodies and the maelstrom of historical events. Needless to say, the formalism in the work of Kumin is not in the least neo-, neither in the sense of a neoformalism that barely disguises its mechanical hopes to dominate its unruly material nor in the sense of being a rediscovery of a lost music. Her use of form has been perennial and is, over and over, intrinsically part of the lesson that her practice of poetry tries again and again to learn. It is, quite simply, the one grievous and needful truth that all our traditional Western systems seem constructed to deny—mortality.

This is why, and not just for the ring of the phrase, I called her poems "études of finitude." An étude in music is fundamentally an exercise designed to hone a technical skill, like arpeggios or scales. It was Chopin who turned it from an exercise to an art in itself: a short virtuoso piece suggesting the intrinsic relation between technique and expressive power, between practice and accomplishment. The mortal exercise that Kumin's études enact, time after time, creates her particular art—one that combines technical virtuosity with the existential learning of the skill of living within limits, consciously inhabiting a natural system that draws its living energy out of the continuous death of its creatures. Thus is the practice of poetry equally the learning to live with finitude and of how to carry, with some grace and lightness, the cargo stored in the hold of such a word.

Her work, as both poet and country dweller, makes irrelevant, almost laughable, theologies, Platonism, occultism, transcendence in all its forms —all the ultimate hopes and outside chances of those systems that blind us to the little moves of life as it is, drown out the cries of mortal danger: "the small mayday alarms of chilled cicadas. / They are almost done" (*Up Country* 80). Her poems never appeal to some abstract design or absent authority in hopes of mitigation of the sentence. Not "Thy will be done" but rather, "They are almost done," they *will* be done. Her speakers here are a sign of her sense of proportion, her lack of dramatics; there is a playful pathos in the notion of this "May Day" alert against winter—to whom is such a futile call made? The parallel with our own outcries against the inevitable is made not only by assigning the cicadas our historical vocabulary of panic but by having her own loss throughout the poem accompanied and articulated by all the small creatures (bees, midges, moths) of the country as chorus—a far cry from the Mormon Tabernacle Choir. Addressed to and written out of longing for someone an ocean away, the poem suddenly bursts out: "I am tired of this history of loss! / What drum can I beat to reach you?" And to this she answers in the poem's final lines:

> Now let the loudest sound I send you
> be the fuzzheads of ripe butternuts
> dropping tonight in Joppa like
> the yellow oval tears of some rare dinosaur
> dropping to build up
> the late September ground.
> (*UC* 83)

The poem comes full circle back to the ground of its title, "September 22nd," which set its limit from the start—the inescapable fall that is not biblical but seasonal. The way her imagery and its echoic diction brings that home is artful enough to be in itself a mitigation, a play of language and surprising similitude that marry accuracy to delight. Underneath these lines with their rich internal assonance and open form is a broken pentameter, which provides a ground bass. Her six irregular lines can be recombined to form five pentameter lines, the first line a perfect iambic pentameter: "now let the loudest sound I send you be."

Even as she both carries and breaks the metric pattern, so the line announces both intention and frustration with the *ow*'s of "now," "loud," "sound," and then she allows meaning to mute those notes in the next line, the way such messages are muted by the realities of distance, loss, and change: first come the muffled *u*'s of "fuzz" and "butternuts," then the soft thuds of "dropping" and "Joppa" in the next line, a sound prepared in the preceding words by the consonantal run of *d, p, b, t*; and then comes the surprise of the simile. The "yellow oval"—with *oh* in the middle that ends one word and begins the next, its doubling lengthening the vowel's duration—suggests an egg even as it becomes a magnified tear, huge because of the eye that drops it, some long-lost dinosaur, a creature known both for its size and its extinction. Thus, the magnitude of that sorrow (enhanced by the echoing modulations of "tears," "rare," "-saur," "-ember") is earned by the literal, even as we feel its weight magnified by her longing and by her accompanying knowledge of all that is always being lost. She gets away with such an unhatchable egg and such an amplitude of dampness by the wit of her invention—making it so unexpected, so almost comical, so self-mockingly aware of how our own longing uselessly enlarges itself: this huge extinct beast weeping its yellow tears.

All this "dropping" is also functioning to "build up / the late September ground," a rather cold comfort, but like it or not, one thing builds on the loss of another to make our common ground. Even so, we live off the death of other creatures: "I cross on snowshoes / cunningly woven from / the skin and sinews of / something else that went before" (*UC* 43). She never pretends that we find any of this constant plowing under quite bearable; thus, the need to play, and to play the études again and again. In "Cellar Hole in Joppa" (*UC* 49–51), which digs down through nature's decay into the cellar hole of some lost human habitation, it becomes clear how hard it is to be

> Bearing in mind the way
> the earth takes back into itself each year
> half an inch or so of rot,
> digesting amiably enough deer
> droppings, splinters of dead birds, the splay
> of struck trees and what-
> ever man has left behind, . . .
>
> (*UC* 49)

The characteristic Kumin touch here is that light arpeggio that ripples over a dark theme, such as "digesting amiably enough deer / droppings." Even the way the lineation makes an enormous meal of deer turn, at the line's turn, into mere "deer droppings" is part of her method of constantly and playfully tugging the poems away from the tragic and into the larger view, where natural things are as they are, and the joke's on us who dream it otherwise. This poem is, remarkably, an apostrophe to her skeleton: "*o my dear skeleton*"—the skeleton that is both the support on which we rely and the memento mori, the very emblem of our mortality. Built into this doubleness is a crucial reason why the études of mortality must be played, why we cannot, for the sake of our desire for preservation, devalue the little life we have, the limits that end us being equally the forms on which we depend. The poem begins with the apostrophe above, then adds to it a question, "*o my dear skeleton / what is to be preserved and why?*" Then, repeating the apostrophe, adds a second question, "*is there a word to keep you by?*"

The answer closes the poem: "No document of that outcry. / *o my dear skeleton / no word to keep you by*" (*UC* 51). No document, no word. In this closure is the foreclosure of another inherited hope—the long hope of Shakespeare's sonnets, written at that moment when the old beliefs were beginning to seem a cracking veneer over a void, when "Like as the waves make toward the pebbled shore, / So do our minutes hasten to their end. . . . And nothing stands but for [Time's] scythe to mow, And yet,"—and here is that other immortality, of art, to which the Renaissance anchored itself— "to times in hope, my verse shall stand, / Praising thy worth, despite his cruel hand" (Sonnet LX). It is part of the proportion she keeps that she forgoes this vaunted literary ambition as well. She is too concerned with family, animals, farming, writing and teaching writing, and the interplay of them all to cast glances over her shoulder at Posterity, that capricious darling on whom so many seem to count and in whose imagined eyes they bask, unable to note how little actual daylight filters through their fears of being forgotten.

She plays with this foolish notion of making an indelible name in "Revisiting the MacDowell Colony" (*Our Ground Time Here Will Be Brief* 33), where she had gone to visit years before. Above the hearth is a plaque bearing the names of those in the "club" of a momentary recognition, "names of the early-great and almost-great." Because "too many pale ones [have] gone to smudges," she gives advice on perpetuation, advice that melts like a snowflake on the tongue: "Use a penknife, I advise my friend, / then ink each letter for relief / —as if a name might matter / against the falling leaf." The images here are code, speaking of the need for accurate vision with its unerring cutting edge, the hard work of etching the material, the ink that is the writer's medium, and her characteristic message in the turn of "relief" into "falling leaf"—the nearly exact, rhyming repetition an echoing closure in the ear. These lines, then, are less about fame (which is finally beside her point) and more about the act and art of naming that is poetry; and embodied in this image is a little *ars poetica* naming the method and tools of her craft, the driving need for relief, the *as if* that keeps us at it, and the end that, in her work, is kept ever in sight.

The imagining of the end is the subject of "Thinking of Death and Dogfood," a poem of direct address to her horse, Amanda, on whom she rides "dead center, bareback / on the intricate harp of your spine." As she rides she imagines, in tandem, both her own death and that of the horse, herself one day cremated, "a pint of potash spoor. I'm something to sweeten the crops / when the clock hand stops," even as her horse will make food for another much loved creature, the dog. And here, in another context, the issue of what we leave behind is raised in a different light, in relation to writing—almost as a credo:

> May I leave no notes behind
> wishful, banal or occult
> and you, small thinker in
> the immensity of your frame,
> may you be caught and crammed
> midmouthful of the best grain
> when the slaughter's bullet slams
> sidelong into your brain.
> (*House, Bridge, Fountain, Gate*, in *GT* 140)

The blissfully unsuspecting end she imagines for her mare is our nightmare. The price paid for the relief and compassion of imagining the horse's dumb luck in such an ending is to suffer our own awareness in yet another rehearsal of the violence of the world, for the strong language of that "slaughter's bullet slams / sidelong" makes us experience what the horse misses, for we are seldom taken so unawares, and the flesh does not fall as gently as the "fallen leaf." This chilling and authentic "happy ending" manages to undo the fairy tale plot we were raised with, and, especially as women, were so suckered by. A poetry that does not turn away from this sight, refuses its mitigation with myth, and does not blush to find rhyming form for the exact imagining of such an end is precisely an expression of her credo—to write so as to leave behind nothing "wishful, banal or occult."

The existential practice of mortality, this limbering up for loss, the outwitting of ambush (to paraphrase Emily Dickinson), the way in which limits are set to everything both as the shape and the price of life, are constantly served by her practice of a formal poetry, a reciprocal discipline of set limits that are equally a living form, encouraging the unexpected that prescribed form often invites in surreptitiously. In a poem about marriage as a game of tennis, the unexpected hard turn at the end brings us back to her leitmotif, as the poem closes with an image of the wedding of measure and mortality: "the dividing line / you toe against, limbering for your service, / arm up, swiping the sun time after time, / and the square I live in, measured out with lime" ("Prothalamium," *The Privilege*, in *GT* 202). It is hard to read that "measured out with lime" without a shudder.

The resemblance of her art to living form that depends on a hidden structure is in the natural, almost casual spoken voice of so many of her poems, which, on closer scrutiny, turn out to be heavily determined forms. The Cellar Hole poem, for all its seeming informality, is really built of three sonnet-like parts, fourteen lines each with a sestet and two quatrains—rhyming *abcbac, deed, fggf*—interspersed with the apostrophe lines as refrains. Growing ever more marked in its patterning as it moves toward closure, it ends with a seven-line strophe that combines the refrains and verse lines with a highly patterned, alternating *ababababa* rhyme scheme, as well as the use of anaphora: "Not the spoon . . . Not the chimney . . . not the black . . . No document . . . no word . . ." At the poem's finale, where it faces finality, she drops the enjambment with its syntactical burying of its own line-defining end-rhymes; the repetition of long *i* sounds makes an audible cry, one that neither "pen" nor "Amen" can amend:

> *what is to be preserved and why?*
> Not the spoon fingers that dipped the pen.
> Not the chimney maker, not the black sky
> full of wind that spoke Amen.
> No document of that outcry.
> *o my dear skeleton*
> *no word to keep you by.*
>
> (*UC* 51)

Though I dislike the reductionism of today's biographical creeping back into the nursery, as if poetry (like the bogeyman) were something that was simply waiting for a simple explanation to make it go away, I couldn't help making one connection with Kumin's past as a possible contributing cause to the obsessive recurrence in her poems, early and late, of the knowledge that we can't keep what we have, that at any moment it may be taken away, the awareness that (in this metaphoric shift she makes from airline lingo to mortal truth) "our ground time here will be brief." Though her themes and subjects are many, as are her moods, it is striking, when looking retrospectively through the pages of her oeuvre, to see in how many poems there appears a memento mori, how often she worries about when the other shoe will drop.

In an early poem, "The Pawnbroker," she writes tenderly about her late father, about growing up "under the sign of those three gold balls," and says: "Every good thing in my life was secondhand. / It smelled of having been owned before me by / a redcap porter whose ticket / ran out." That she had childhood nightmares about the porter's revenge is hardly surprising in a business where the meaning of redemption is getting your own back. Nor is it strange that her conscience was tenderized by what must have been the helpless knowledge that your luck meant somebody else's misfortune— a subject she often returns to and a truth about privilege from which the privileged young are generally more insulated than she was. Above all, a sense of justice combined with such clear-sighted knowledge of what produces the surplus we call wealth, may have honed her sense that there is "no word to keep you by," that everything is on loan, potentially in hock— everything, including, and especially, life itself. It is not the redeeming but the running out of the ticket that defines the conditions given by nature, where, without malice or intention, life feeds on the defeat of life.

One of the most hateful things about conventional religion, to which she returns again and again, is the monstrosity in believing in a moral directing agency in a world of cruel chance as well as a human world of calculated cruelty. Her humor sharpens the cutting edge of a deeply ethical iconoclasm:

> Now angels, God's secret agents,
> I am assured by Billy Graham,
> circulate among us to tell
> the living that they are not alone.
> On twenty-four-hour duty, angels
> flutter around my house and barn
> blundering into the cobwebs,
> letting pots boil over
> or watching the cat torture
> a chipmunk. When my pony,
> filching apples, rears and catches
> his halter on a branch and hangs
> himself all afternoon, I like
> to think six equine angels fan
> the strangling beast
> until his agony is past.
> ("Address to the Angels,"
> *The Retrieval System* 47)

Imagine, implies this poem, such beings who would be forced to look on, hour after hour, the noninterventional witnesses of such terminal suffering (the "fan" brings just enough compassion to sharpen the awful scene), who would be condemned to watch the proliferation of torture that comes by chance to the world's innocent creatures. (Actually, watching television nowadays is not unlike being in the role of these angels.) And imagine the Billy Grahams who market to the miserable these divinely indentured voyeurs.

"Who gets Rapture?" she asks in another poem ("After the Harvest," *The Long Approach* 78) Who indeed? But being ethically clear-eyed, she sees the danger of being smug about her unbelief in popular mythology, which, though it rests on what her poems argue is a saner ethic, may also be a privilege of a relatively protected life, one neither circumstantially nor temperamentally called to the terrible verge of extremity where faith and atrocity meet. In the poem "In the Absence of Bliss," written on the occasion of visiting the Museum of the Diaspora in Tel Aviv and contemplating the powerful madness of faith of those who died in agony rather than recant their Judaism, she pulls the rug out from under whatever pride she might take in her own position:

> Bliss is belief,
> agnostics always say
> a little condescendingly
> as befits mandarins who function
> on a higher moral plane.
>   (*LA* 39)

The implied suggestion is that the zealot has not had what she designates as the "mandarin" luxury of doubt and presumably may live in such misery and single-minded hope born of despairing outrage that it is preferable to "die cherishing the fond / certitude of a better life beyond." Knowing that she would not die "for Yahweh, Allah, Christ, / those patriarchal fists / in the face," she asks "what would I die for and reciting what? / . . . would / I die to save a child? Rescue my lover? Would / I run into the fiery barn / to release animals?" In short, she asks whether she would have the courage to die for what she has lived for. She doesn't know. She knows "[o]nly questions," and the last of these is the leveling one: "where's the higher moral plane I roost on?" (*LA* 40–41). Notice that in the surprising choice of verb, that "roost," she reminds us once more of our place in the animal world and that any position, whatever its moral plane, is merely a resting place, a temporary roost.

In her latest book, with a poem called "The Green Well," she is still playing her études, never the same twice, the subject deepening with time, the reciprocal mastery of the techniques of supple form, both fluid and finite, showing an increase in the subtlety of skills honed by years of writing, by the births and deaths of so many animals in her barn or her pastures, the children growing and gone, the longevity of love, the losses and separations, the rhymes still holding their lines while the past leaves its images, its rich strata of mulch for some future garden, the same inexhaustible "green well of losses, a kitchen midden // where the newly dead layer by layer / overtake the long and longer vanished / Gone . . ." (*Looking for Luck* 32).

In the "green well" of the American tradition of nature poetry, in which Thoreau is indisputably her primary ancestor and Frost her nearer forebear,[3] it is perhaps instructive to consider Kumin's departure from these forefathers in whose line she is clearly descended. Like Thoreau, she turns from the world of acquisition, sham convention, and accumulation to an active rural life that includes nature's cultivation, its contemplation, and transformation into art. But her poetics of finitude is also contrary to his line; for all his attention to nature, it is what is extratemporal that he is finally after: "Time is but the stream I go a-fishing in. I drink at it; but while I drink I see the sandy bottom and detect how shallow it is. Its thin current slides away, but eternity remains. I would drink deeper; fish in the sky. . . ."[4] Such sentiments are alien to Kumin's work, whose gaze is everywhere earthward, her lines time-drenched. Though she hews her material with as fine a craft and tunes her life and lyrics to the rural seasons with the same labor and loving attention to detail as Thoreau, yet she is proof against the weightless glamour of the Eternal, the Transcendentalist side of her literary ancestor that continues, in the Puritan line, to read the solid world as a reflection of a divine, invisible one. She sees this as a form of magic, revealing both its childishness and the mechanism by which the invisible becomes the invincible in her poem "A Distant Grandchild Listens to Farm Sounds": "He is waiting for Grandpa / to step out of the cassette. . . . // This is it, this nonappearance. This is how gods are made" (*LA* 15–16).

That a sane intelligence will not wish to steal energy from life to fuel the soul-searing flame at the altar of the unknowable is a fundamental tenet of her poetry. In one of her earliest published poems she writes of her childhood, of memory mixing up the convent and the madhouse between which their family's house stood: "the plain song and the bedlam hung / on the air and blew across / into the garden where I played" (*Halfway*, in *GT* 211). Between these two often indistinguishable madnesses is the livable place where this poem explicitly (and many others implicitly) suggests that we must find our way. Repeatedly in her work, from early to late, images appear that reverse or undo the old patterns of belief: rather than seeing what *is* as an image of what *isn't* there, she is constantly winning back the old images of religion and immortality to the living and frequently animal body of the world. In "The Green Well," for example, the field appears "with an aura. Gnats form an ectoplasmic cloud / over the bruised bathtub, over the salt lick // hollowed out by tongues, like medieval stairs / petitioners' feet have worn, looking for truth. / I hold truth in a Nine Lives can twice / weekly for the cats" (*LL* 32). Truth in a can of cat food (Nine Lives, no less) is again her wit at play, doing its trickster work on the pretentions and platitudes of our conventional Judeo-Christian heritage.

Hers is a deciduous offshoot (and growing tip) of the family tree of American nature poetry, completely non-Transcendental, shed of even a

Romantic shadow. I particularly choose to write "non-" rather than "anti-," for she is so far from the sublimating tendencies in those earlier, eternity-hungry poets (British and American) as to constitute a negation by in-difference to precedents no longer relevant. For just as antiheroes require the old image of the hero against which to measure their diminishment, so an anti-Romantic would have to strike a counterposture to counteract an influence still feelingly present. But there is none of this in the work of Maxine Kumin—no trace of the sublime, no hangover of regret for lost theological privilege (whether God's chosen or Empress of Calvary), no fear of sentiment nor any loud insistence on what the tradition before her had failed to value—in fact, no postures at all.

Her other radical difference from Thoreau, the nature-loving and at the same time ethical Puritan strain he represents, is her at-homeness in our animal nature. Though, as we shall see, morality is very central to her work, and the Puritan work ethic drives both her art and her rural hus-bandry. She is a passionate devotee of just those generative forces in nature to which Thoreau articulates his antipathy in this passage from *Walden*, which he gets in part from his Puritan background, in part from his read-ing of ascetic Hindu doctrine:

The generative energy, which, when we are loose, dissipates and makes us unclean, when we are continent invigorates and inspires us. Chastity is the flowering of man; and what are called Genius, Heroism, Holiness and the like, are but various fruits which succeed it. Man flows at once to God when the channel of purity is open. By turns our purity inspires and our impurity casts us down. He is blessed who is assured that the animal is dying out in him day by day, and the divine being estab-lished. (P. 268)

Of course, Thoreau was at Walden more than twenty years before Darwin published his *Origin of Species* and made us totemists again, kin and kind of the fauna, this time with the blessings of science. That is one difference that the times themselves made in conceiving the human relation to the animal world. The deepening of that relation from the original horror and sense of comedown (still alive in the creationists) to the notion of a kind of blessed connectedness with our less neurotic animal brethren is fully realized in the poetry of Maxine Kumin, whose life has been spent in the intimate nurturing of animals. And in the love of animals, horses in particular, there is a celebration and embrace of our own instinctive, generative nature, which Thoreau despises. A poem like "The Retrieval System" makes it ex-plicit that, for her, animals revive us—and more, carry into a fresh life, by the sheer exuberant energy of their resemblance, the irreplaceably lost: "A boy / I loved once keeps coming back as my yearling colt, / cocksure at the gallop, racing his shadow / for the hell of it. He runs merely to be. / A boy who was lost in the war thirty years ago / and buried at sea" (*RS* 1).

It is the practice of nurturing, a compassionate and hands-on connection with nature's body—a bond experienced as actual and internal rather than external and philosophical, nature felt as affinity rather than seen as correspondence—that also sets her apart from her other and more immediate ancestor in the nature poetry line, Robert Frost. The tie between their work as poets seems inescapable: the common locale and the poetic transformation of that rural New Hampshire; the way in which prescribed form and meter comprise the necessary bottle to the genie of their art (to borrow Richard Wilbur's metaphor); the use of the language and syntax of everyday discourse, with its clearly identified subjectivity and accessible content; their twinned sense of poetry, in Frost's phrase, as "mortal play," with the recurrent subject, named in his often quoted line, that "nothing gold can stay."

Yet to read a Kumin poem is to feel that we are in a different New Hampshire and that the poetic territory she is staking out is quite other from his. In the attempt to uncover that difference, it might be useful to place two poems side by side: Frost's "The Woodpile," a poem that embodies many of his attitudes to nature and to his own art, and a well-known poem of hers, "Splitting Wood at Six Above." [5] Both poems have art as their subtext, an art produced by a similar action in both poems—by, in Frost's words, "the labor of his ax."

The narrative line of Frost's "The Woodpile," written in blank verse, goes like this: A man, the first-person speaker, is "[o]ut walking the frozen swamp one gray day"; he pauses, then decides to "go on farther—and we shall see." He describes the walk, its details shimmer with double meanings—the hard snow that "held him," the view through "tall slim trees" that's "all in lines," a place hard to identify except as "just far from home." "A small bird" flies before him, a shy and rather paranoid creature, who disappears "to make his last stand" behind the woodpile, the discovery of which is the poem's destination and epiphany:

> It was a cord of maple, cut and split
> And piled—and measured, four by four by eight.
> And not another like it could I see.
> No runner tracks in this year's snow looped near it.
> And it was older sure than this year's cutting,
> Or even last year's or the year's before.
> The wood was gray and the bark warping off it
> And the pile somewhat sunken. Clematis

> Had wound strings round and round it like a bundle.
> What held it, though, on one side was a tree
> Still growing, and on one a stake and prop,
> These latter about to fall. I thought that only
> Someone who lived in turning to fresh tasks
> Could so forget his handiwork on which
> He spent himself, the labor of his ax,
> And leave it there far from a useful fireplace
> To warm the frozen swamp as best it could
> With the slow smokeless burning of decay.[6]

The last pair of lines is quintessential Frost—the task as futile as the language is memorable: the best of a man's craft, "not another like it," "cut and split / and piled—and measured," "handiwork on which / He spent himself, the labor of his ax," its only use, besides offering a fort to hide the shy spirit of the singer, to contribute to the general decay of that swamp through which only winter freeze permits his passage, "save where now and then / One foot went through." Here is the horror of being drawn into the swamp—that traditional emblem of the fecundity of nature and generation, of the earth whose continuous creation includes the swallowing back of what it generates—and the irony of being drawn to contribute to that very work by one's own desire to make anew, to live "in turning to fresh tasks." The horror that embitters the irony is sounded in the extended duration, the awful patience of the words themselves—the open, long *o*'s of what modifies burning, the way the mouth lingers over the paired consonants in "the slow smokeless burning of decay." This is nature poetry in extremis, if you will, one of the bleakest portraits of a life in art imaginable.

In the Kumin poem "Splitting Wood at Six Above," it is also winter, and the speaker, who is clearly the poet herself, is splitting wood as an act of mourning for her recently dead friend; the poem's opening line is itself an opening, but one that is hard-won, for it is her own grief, her attempt to realize the loss, that she is driving home, a task so hard that it takes more than an ax; it takes both wedge and "eight-pound sledge" to open her material:

> I open a tree.
> In the stupefying cold
> —ice on bare flesh a scald—
> I seat the metal wedge
> with a few left-handed swipes
> then with a change of grips
> lean into the eight-pound sledge.
>
> (*RS* 47)

The poem is an act of love, of grieving connection, even as it is a liberation of sorts—a far cry from the man alone contemplating the decaying bundle of wood of another solitary maker. Rather than a defensive woodpile to hide a bird-self behind, her splitting open of the wood provides a release for "the tiny voice / of a bird cry . . . and then all in a rush, / all in a passionate stammer" the broken-open wood speaks, and "[t]he papery soul of the beech / released by wedge and hammer / flies back into the air." The splitting of wood both opens her to grief and makes way for the soul of the broken life to speak in its passage, a speaking that is beyond what words can articulate—it is "cry," "puppet-squeak," and "passionate stammer." There is no distance here from nature, as in Frost. Rather than a walk across a frozen swamp through a linear, alien landscape to nowhere in particular, here is the experienced pain of that "six above"—winter and the "stupefying cold" of grief: "ice on bare flesh a scald." And here too is the whole person under strain in the poem, the observant mind and the active body: the felt heft of the sledge against the metal wedge. The identification throughout the poem of her own heart wound, the truncated life of the dead friend and the cut-down tree (it is "a tree" she opens at the start, not that denatured, unliving thing, "wood") is overt; as she opens the tree, she opens herself to the death of her friend, which is announced and faced in a stoic direct address: "You are four months dead. / The beech log comes apart. . . ."

The correspondence is exact. In the poem where Frost makes his most companionable address to a tree, in his rather pat "Tree at My Window," he speaks of fate having put their "heads together"—"Your head so much concerned with outer, / Mine with inner, weather" (p. 276). It is his seeing the treetop, its head as it were, that makes the bond, and his connection with it is both mental and based on division: one head is inside his window, the other head in its own and other realm. With Kumin's tree, it is "heartwood" that will be opened, heartwood at the tree's center—the hardest wood to work and the most enduring; there is everywhere in her work an inside to the world, an embodied interior of which an attached and feeling consciousness informs us. Kumin's poetry expresses an intimacy with nature that is always also mindful. She humanizes nature in a special way—I would almost say domesticates it, making it warmly familiar in her particular kind of metaphoric invention, which a few examples may suggest: "rain / steeping the dust / in a joyous squelch the sky / standing up like steam / from a kettle of grapes" ("Continuum: A Love Poem," *GT* 15); "the new leaves are now unpacking, / still wearing their dimestore lacquer" ("May 10th," *TP* in *GT* 207); "Now the moon sits / on the windowsill, one hip / humped like an

Odalisque" ("Whippoorwill," *UC* 39). This bringing of distant things near, bringing even astral things down to earth, is far from Frost's estranged world of fright, which just underlies his seeming pastorale, like that frozen swamp a foot occasionally breaks through. The mud world of spring, when the New England earth makes itself visible kin to the swamp, is imaged as "the mother" in the Kumin poem "Mud," which ends, memorably:

> Meanwhile the mother is sucking.
> Pods will startle apart,
> pellet be seized with a fever
> and as the dark gruel thickens,
> life will stick up a finger.
> (*UC* 27)

Her ability to make familiar through metaphor and playful tone what might otherwise be estranged is expressed in "Splitting Wood" in the way the conversation with the dead is managed with a fine, lightly joking tone that characterizes their intimacy as friends. The poem ends still in that playful direct address and with images that display her ability to humanize the natural while naturalizing the human, bringing down to earth an elevated and too vaunted imagery and diction traditionally connected with the notion of soul:

> your small round
> stubbornly airborne soul,
> that sun-yellow daisy heart
> slipping the noose of its pod,
> scooting over the tightrope,
> none the worse for its trip,
> to arrive at the other side.
>
> It is the sound
> of your going I drive
> into heartwood. I stack
> my quartered cuts bark down,
> open yellow-face up.

The final dozen lines are all hard end-stopped, mainly on monosyllables and hard consonants: *t, d, p,* and *k,* echoing finality. The lineation of the poem is, throughout, more truncated than is usual for her, mostly strong-stressed dimeter and trimeter, the making of the poem paralleling the cutting and opening of the wood that is its literal and metaphoric subject. Here, outside the precincts of any established religion, an old religious ritual is reinvented, using the tools of the rural log-splitter and the poetic craftswoman—the physical and metaphorical enactment of the freeing of the soul of someone loved and lost. And seeing the body as a pod, and that pod as "a noose" from which the flower-soul slips free and becomes mobile in its passage over the border, is not only an original borrowing for human use from the vocabulary of bloom in nature but in making present the warmth and brightness of that "sun-yellow heart" is also a celebration of life and of a life that made its escape from that "pod" whose once protective enclosure had become nothing but a suffocating darkness—images that try to understand what drove her friend to suicide.

What this poem and so many of her poems remind us about, bursting open with images of birth, of growth, flourishing in the face of mortality or in the midst of decay, "everywhere on this planet, birth," is that the need to keep mortality a presence, to accept death as a condition of life, is precisely to value and protect and celebrate that life. Even as she writes of life consuming life, so she also honors the way life produces new life from within itself, all creatures sharing in this continuous act of generative creation. Staying in the barn with a mare about to foal she writes:

> What we say to each other in cold black
> of April, conveyed in a wordless yet perfect
> language of touch and tremor, connects
> us most surely to the wet cave we all
> once burst from gasping, naked or furred,
> into our separate species.
> ("Sleeping with Animals," *Nurture* 21)

While Frost's speaker is estranged from the very nature of which he writes and feels keenly its indifference, which mirrors his own (see "The Most of It"), Kumin feels the pain of mortality so keenly because she is so embedded in and so much a part of the world of generation, a person who can, at times, live and write as she swims in this early poem:

> I hung my bathrobe on two pegs.
> I took the lake between my legs.
>
> Invaded and invader, I
> went overhand on that flat sky.
>
> Fish twitched beneath me, quick and tame.
> In their green zone sang my name
>
> And in the rhythm of the swim
> I hummed a two-four-time slow hymn. . . .
>
> My bones drank water; water fell
> through all my doors. I was the well
>
> that fed the lake that met my sea
> in which I sang "Abide With Me."
> ("Morning Swim," *TP* in *GT* 191.)

This poem may bring to mind, in its subject matter, another of our current "nature poets," Mary Oliver, even as, just as immediately, its tone and cool easiness, its metrical playfulness, set it apart from her. The distinction between them is instructive in its suggestion of how many ways "nature poetry" can play and how much difference the term can grass over. Oliver's reconnection with nature has more deeply had to struggle with the Western religious and philosophical disaffection from the natural world, the mind divided from what the body is experiencing, and what she calls the hoofprint of "forever" planted early in the middle of her mind, branding and defacing present joy. Her poetry's entrance into the natural, the apprenticeship of the imagination to the swamp, has been in her case informed by a mystical bent, an immersion in nature to find the light that was traditionally connected with worship in the church. She is, in so many ways, as Kumin is not, a Romantic and a mystic, though hers is a mysticism of sensuality and immanence and not, like that of her forebears, of transcendence. The ecstatic in Oliver's poetry is not temperamentally in the scale range of Kumin's instrument, nor was Kumin, raised in a skeptical Jewish home, ever infected with the Christian "forever" and so brings none of that fervor into its rejection. Finally, Oliver, though in a changed, sacred/sensual relation with nature, is alone with it, much as her forebears were and as many of America's poets remain. Seldom does she write, by her own admission, about what she calls "the peopled kingdoms," neither the personal facts of her own autobiography nor the historical world in which our time is embedded.

And one of the constants and powers of Kumin's poetry is precisely the way the personal facts of her family, of her rural and fortunate life, are constantly read in the balance of what she calls "Out There" (the title of the second section of her book *The Long Approach*). Public historical events are not banished from this realm, for she is a poet who travels the world, and the world, in any case, leaks in daily through letters, the newspaper, the media, and an alert and necessarily troubled conscience. It is not against the eternal or some ideal realm that her daily world is measured but in the balance of other lives, correspondent but so often incommensurate. "Pulling the garden I always think / of starving to death, of how it would be," of lands "where thousands, displaced, / unwanted, diseased, are awash in despair," of the way the misery of one creature augurs well for another: "My good luck running in / as his runs out." Or "At MIT on the oval / my students stretch out like corpses / this day of budded maples. / Like the dead of Beirut in the sun. / Here everything is hopeful / because unconsidered."

As this last pair of lines suggests, the poetry of Maxine Kumin, while at times a poetry that celebrates the gracious sufficiency of her life, is not a poetry of hopefulness. As we have seen, she is too pragmatic and skeptical and perhaps too Puritan for hope. She considers everything and cares fiercely about it all. She is a pessimist in love with life.

And though the atrocities of our century shadow her own green pastures, as do the casual slaughters of nature that no one who lives a truly rural life can fudge, still she avoids what she calls, after viewing a sadistic period-piece film, "this prurient close / examination of pain, fanaticism, terror." Too many poets have fixed their eyes on images of horror and been corrupted by what they intend to condemn; too few have called the game, asked, rhetorically, as she does: "What does it profit us?" Her language deepens her point by its biblical echo: "Counsels of despair profit nothing."

Writing in the American Puritan grain, she brings to the language of profit and loss, as to the working of the land, a moral interpretation, but for her contemporary and connected sensibility the ethical measure is always one instance of the real balanced against another. Whatever "clouds of glory" may have enthralled her forebears, the realities of country life have dissipated, as illusion melts into the sparkling light of day and into the grief of real loss that cannot be argued away, the winter of encroaching age, and she "loving this poor place, / wanting to stay on." Speaking of the rural property she and her husband took on years ago, she says: "Victims of the romantic fervor to get away from it all and find harmony in nature, we did not then know that what we secretly longed for was thirty years of hard labor" (*Women, Animals, and Vegetables* 23). The country work of harrowing, growing, harvesting, and turning over again; of constantly rebuilding, reclaiming, and burying; of breeding and training and living with horses— it is this devotion to work, these well-loved and absorbing tasks, that inform the poetry as well, even as the craft of her poetry is another labor of love. In a world of phantom work, of paper shuffling and button pushing, of actions abstracted from their consequences, of living as "the ghost in the machine," Kumin's non-Romantic at-homeness in both an embodied language and a genuinely rural life are among the deep and rare pleasures her poetry offers us.

Nature in her work is neither emblematic nor backdrop for lonely musers nor landscape framed and measured by the single human gaze. It is not even "Nature" in the old sense of something distinct from humans and culture. It is simply habitat, the living place of a hardworking, conscious, and caretaking animal among other animals, brought to fresh and meaningful life for her readers by the attached awareness, the nurturing intelligence, that both inhabit and shape it. The poems cling always to the actual, moving between the celebration of the luck of a good life and all that shadows it—from its own brevity to the massive unfairness of the way abundance and privilege are apportioned both by chance (*Looking for Luck* is the title of her 1992 book of poems) and by design ("men kill for this" says her father in "Appetite," as he spoons up fresh raspberries and cream). But in relation to her own good fortune, a lifetime of unremitting hard work in writing and in the nurturing of family and of horses, and the cultivating of New England land has overcome the shame that characterized her child self; while, of course, she knows that we don't get what we deserve or ever deserve our good luck, at least she can see a clear relation between what she has and her own labor. The taking of the actual on its own terms characterizes all that she writes; things have their own real weight, their specific gravity, and are not made weightier or flimsier by comparison with or absorption into some abstract idea or system. Nor is she afflicted by the current angst about language, perhaps because it never occurred to her to insist that language be other or more than it is—the instrument by which we accompany and signify our lives.

One of my favorites of her poems is the title poem of the book I named above, "The Long Approach," in which the flying horse Pegasus, whose ancient hoofs once opened the spring of the Muses, is given a fresh and literal incarnation. For here those horses that are so much at the center of her life and art appear, like her, airborne, trying to keep their footing in the hold of an airplane. Here, as everywhere in her work, things are given their true and mortal weight at the same time as metaphor extends their meaning by the ways in which we share their condition. In this poem the poet, after one of her many trips to do readings and residencies, is heading home, lighthearted as any horse returning to its stable.

> Last week leaving Orlando in a steep climb
> my seatmate told me flying horses must be loaded
> facing the tail of the plane so they may brace
> themselves at takeoff. Otherwise you run
> the risk they'll panic, pitch over backwards
> smash their hocks. Landing, said the groom,
> there is little we can do for them except
> pray for calm winds and ask the pilot
> to make a long approach.
>
> (*LA* 80)

There is a position implicit in this quotation—the maintenance of grace, of a precarious balance, while bringing our poetry down to earth. Her work is a kind of touchstone for touching down, completing the work of return to our common ground, which may be the central imaginative task of the poetry of our age—the poetry, at any rate, that is something more than symptomatic, that is clear-eyed and sane about the value of life in the face of its finitude—this mortal world, "the green well of losses," which "does not end with us, not yet, though end it will."

Notes

1. The graduate student is Constance Merritt, first-rate poet and poetry critic, currently at the University of Nebraska, Lincoln.

2. One of the qualities that made Anne Sexton's confessional poems superior to many that follow her in the autobiographical mode is precisely her sense of the hilarious side of self-dramatizing confession, the mocking humor that reaches its apogee in her delicious, kitsch-serious fairy tale send-ups, *Transformations*.

3. I exclude Emily Dickinson from these New England nature poet forebears because she seems alien, if not antithetical, to Kumin, light years away in her metaphysical concerns, her idiosyncratic romanticism, and her posture of renunciation as Empress of Calvary, a role made all the more piercingly dramatic by the modern doubt that accompanies it.

4. Henry David Thoreau, *Walden and other Writings*, edited by J. Krutch (New York: Bantam, 1962), p. 178.

5. I owe to Hilda Raz the discovery that my poem "Postscript," with its tree-cutting imagery, had very much in the back of its mind this Kumin poem, "Splitting Wood at Six Above."

6. *The Poems of Robert Frost* (New York: Modern Library/Random House, 1946), pp. 112-13.

✿ A N N I E   F I N C H

A Rock in the River: Maxine Kumin's Rhythmic Countercurrents

Clearly, Maxine Kumin stands out among poets of her generation in her facility with iambic pentameter. Less obviously, she is also rare among contemporary poets—of any generation—because of the strength and eloquence of the passages in triple meter that also occur consistently in her work. Important passages in Kumin's poetry are enriched, lulled, or counterpointed by a dactylic rhythm embodying a highly charged cluster of themes and images.* Kumin's dactylic passages often express appreciation for female power and sometimes a generalized sense of nature's raw mystery. While iambic pentameter is still important in Kumin's poetry, in the years from *The Privilege* (1965) to *Looking for Luck* (1992), the dactylic passages—and occasional lines of trochaic and anapestic meter—have come to occupy a more and more central place in her work.

Trochees and dactyls—the "falling" meters—have served as the alter ego, the underbelly, of iambic meter throughout the history of accentual-syllabic verse in English. As early as the first century after the establishment of iambic meter as the English poetic norm, the trochaic beat of the witches' song counterpoints the iambic pentameter of *Macbeth*: "Double, double, toil and trouble, / Fire burn and cauldron bubble." The meter of the witches' song, like the meter of much noniambic verse from Blake's "The Tyger" to Poe's "The Raven," embodies powerful energies alien to the dominant meter and the dominant worldview (the anomalous or prescient American epic *Evangeline* may be one of the exceptions that proves this rule). But metrical connotations are not static. In my book *The Ghost of Meter: Culture and Prosody in American Free Verse*, I describe the metrical code, a way to read metrical patterns in free verse—where they can be seen

---

*Following the precedent established in *The Ghost of Meter*, I will call these passages generally "dactylic" for convenience's sake and because I hear in them a clear falling rhythm, although some readers may prefer to scan some of them as primarily anapestic. For a fuller discussion of this strategy, please see *The Ghost of Meter: Culture and Prosody in American Free Verse* (Ann Arbor: University of Michigan Press, 1993), 39–40, 69.

interacting with other metrical patterns—as encoding changing attitudes toward literature and culture. When read in terms of the metrical code, Kumin's dactylic passages show an acceptance of some of the very connotations that were so threatening to free-verse poets of the nineteenth and early twentieth centuries: spontaneity, nature, the irrational, and at times the feminine.

Of course, free verse from Whitman on has often incorporated dactylic rhythms; indeed, it is my opinion that an intense hunger for the dactylic rhythm, incompatible with the dominance of iambic meter, was a major factor in the development of free verse. But Kumin's achievement of a consistent and nonambivalent iambic meter, especially in her poems to women, contributes, along with Carolyn Kizer's dactylic passages and those of younger poets like Audre Lorde, to a significant shift in the sound of American poetry. If the metrical code is any indication, this rhythmic shift also embodies a shift in sensibility.

Kumin's noniambic rhythms occur sometimes alone but often, especially in the earlier books, in counterpoint or opposition to an iambic rhythm. The lyric "Morning Swim," which opens the 1965 collection *The Privilege*, describes a transcendent experience in iambic meter tempered only once by a trochaic beat:

> And in the rhythm of the swim
> I hummed a two-four time slow hymn.
>
> I hummed "Abide With Me." The beat
> Rose in the fine thrash of my feet,
>
> Rose in the bubbles I put out
> Slantwise, trailing through my mouth.
>   (*TP*, in *Our Ground Time*
>   *Here Will Be Brief* 191)

The passage is purely iambic except for the trochaic substitutions in the first and third feet of the line "Rose in the fine thrash of my feet," which lay the ground for the fully trochaic line "Slantwise, trailing through my mouth." The "slantwise" trochaic meter in this line hints at a metrical possibility that perhaps offers more of a chance for authentic self-expression than the iambic meter. Perhaps these trochaic bubbles are closer to the speaker's real voice than the iambic meter she has appropriated from the hymn she sings; certainly the physical description of the process of breathing, as the speaker "puts out" bubbles through her mouth, is more direct and immediate than the rest of the account of hymn singing in the poem.

The Privilege carries the disturbing epigraph "But you are afraid of yourself; of the inseparable being forever at your side—master and slave, victim and executioner." On one level the quote suggests that the iambic meter of poems like "Morning Swim" is not an entirely reliable rhythmic vehicle. The metrical code indicates that the privileged and powerful iambic meter, as opposed to the triple rhythms of popular tradition, has inspired ambivalence in American poets since at least the nineteenth century; it would not be surprising if the Kumin of the early 1960s—particularly as a woman poet—found this meter problematic, a slave that was also, with all its burden of male-dominated literary history, an executioner.

Kumin's earlier poems orient themselves primarily to iambic meter and control dactylic or trochaic expression carefully. Yet even as early as *The Privilege*, a sustained passage in dactylic meter hints at a metrical possibility other than the iambic. In the second poem in the book, Kumin sets up an alternative mode of transcendence, expressed in a dactylic rhythm explicitly opposed to the iambic meter. "The Habits of Childhood," told from the perspective of a child playing a game of hide-and-seek, sets out a clear opposition between the speaker's child-self and the outside world. The poem is structured in three parts, the first and last of which are rhymed, six-line stanzas of iambic pentameter and the middle section of which is in a loose dactylic rhythm. As if to underscore the freedom the dactylic rhythm offers the poet, the central section is not rhymed:

> I knew all of the closets and closets built into closets. . . .
> I leaned at the curve of the stairs with my legs lapped over the newel . . .
> Under the attic dormers, past boxes of knickers and jodhpurs,
> I courted the laces of spiders, the dust buds of dead grandparents.
> There in the dawdle of childhood I hid in the gardener's tool shed;
> I hid on an island of leafplates under the copper beech tree. . . .
>
> (*TP* 7–8)

Just at the moment when the child's dactylic freedom brings her to a point of merging with nature, the reverie ends abruptly, the iambic pentameter order is restored, and the poem moves to a controlled conclusion:

> And "All-ee-all-ee-in-free!" they called then
> While parents called from porches, and the night
> Fell up the summer sky where I sat tight
> In the skin of my secret, last out, when,
> Eyes shut behind my fingers, I could sense
> The seekers, come to find out my defense.

Only a trace of the dactylic rhythm remains in this final passage; it informs the lingering memory of the "skin of my secret" with a haunting

echo of freedom before that freedom is closed off, finally, by the conclud-
ing couplet.

In the nearly thirty years between the publication of *Privilege* and that
of the recent collection *Looking for Luck* (1992), Kumin's use of the dactylic
rhythm has stayed consistent with her earlier vision in its connotations
but has also developed greatly in its range. In "The Habits of Childhood,"
the freedom expressed by the dactylic rhythm is carefully contained, sand-
wiched between iambic passages and confined to the realm of memory. In
poem after poem of *Looking for Luck*, the dactylic rhythms have strength-
ened, enriched their connotations, and come to play a central role in the
thematics of the collection. Kumin still uses iambic pentameter to deal with
difficult situations, and the iambic meter is arguably still the touchstone or
foundation of the book; yet the dactylic meter, which builds in frequency
as the book progresses, embodies the final vision of *Looking for Luck*.

The most memorable and obvious role of the dactylic rhythms in *Look-
ing for Luck* is their celebration of femaleness in a variety of forms. The
structure of "Praise Be" is characteristic; the poem opens in primarily
iambic free verse, describing in plain language the birth of a foal. At the
end, however, it breaks out into dactylic rhythm to close with a lyrical
prayer for the female animals and their young:

> Let them prosper, the dams and their sucklings.
> Let nothing inhibit their heedless growing.
> Let them raise up on sturdy pasterns. . . .
> *(LL 23)*

"The Confidantes," a tribute to Dorothy Harbison, a ninety-year-old
woman who loves horses, also saves the dactylic rhythm until the end. Most
of the poem is in a bouncy anapestic tetrameter, which oddly distances us
from the situation, almost as if the speaker is embarrassed by her feelings
about Dorothy Harbison:

> It's the year of the Crash. I'm almost four.
> My father is riding a horse for hire
> in the manicured parkland at Valley Green.
> When he clops into sight the trees take fire. . . .
> *(LL 84)*

At the end, however, the poem shifts abruptly into two lines of dactylic
rhythm that allow a moment of deep and serious appreciation, broken only
by Dorothy Harbison's matter-of-fact iambic speech, to close the episode:

> Leaving, Dorothy Harbison
> speaks to the foal in a lilting croon:

> *I'll never wash again, I swear.*
> *I'll keep the smell of you in my hair,*
> and stumps out, fiercely young on her cane.
>
> (*LL* 84)

Brief dactylic tributes to women also occur at the end of "Remarkable Women: An Apostrophe," which closes a straightforward, detailed free-verse description of three admirable women with the generalized lyric statement, "I salute you all, I take you with me wherever / I go to fire me with your fevers." In "Falling Asleep to the Sound of Waves," the pattern is reversed; the first line of the poem—the only one that specifically refers to the pregnant woman herself in this fantasy on prenatal experience—is the dactylic line: "How it was in the womb when she walked." Though the structure of this poem differs from that of most of Kumin's poems, since it moves away from instead of toward the lyric appreciation of femaleness, the principle is the same: the dactylic rhythm, a countercurrent in contrast to free verse or iambic verse, lends power and mystery to such tributes to the female.

Kumin's triple rhythm is not only confined to the ends of poems; a dactylic beat suffuses the whole of two more poems in *Looking for Luck* that pay tribute to and celebrate women—"The Chambermaids in the Marriott in Mid-Morning" and "The Nuns of Childhood." Though the dactylic rhythm is rarely sustained for an entire line in "The Chambermaids in the Marriott in Mid-Morning," it surfaces often, several times in each stanza, creating a clear countercurrent to the free verse. Like a rock in a river, the dactylic rhythm creates eddies around itself, slowing and changing the flow of the free verse whenever it appears:

> calling across the corridors in their rich contraltos
> while luffing fresh sheets in the flickering gloom
> of the turgid passionate soaps they follow from room to room....
>
> The funerals, weddings and births, the quarrels, the fatal gunshots,
> happen again and again, inventively reenacted,
> except that the story is framed by ads and coming attractions....
>
> (*LL* 79)

"The Nuns of Childhood," Kumin's tribute to her early teachers in a convent school, uses the dactylic rhythm even more consistently for its ironic but deeply affectionate celebration of these women's mystery and strength. A premonition of the fully developed rhythmical form of this poem can be seen in the early poem on the same subject, "Mother Rosarine," whose free verse is shot through with distinct dactylic passages:

Next-door Mother Rosarine
of the square white front and black buckram
tugged up the morning with cinches of keys,
rode through The Mass, a bristle-chinned queen,
jingling the tongues that unlocked the linens,
the larder, the gym suits that luffed at the knees
of the boarders, and swung on the door to His Kingdom.

(*TP* 13)

In the slightly more ambivalent tribute, "Voices from Kansas," Kumin
again uses a triple rhythm to address a lyrical closing to the women the
poem has described: "As the grassland is rooted, so too are the Wichita
women. / No absence among them may go unmarked into sleep. / Like
wind in the wheat, the boundary blurs but keeps" (*LL* 50). Unlike most of
Kumin's other dactylic passages, the closing of "Voices from Kansas" can
scan easily as iambic pentameter; the last line, in particular, has a strong
iambic counterrhythm. Such a passage reveals that, in spite of the many
strong dactylic passages in *Looking for Luck*, the book is still fundamentally
rooted in the iambic meter. The dactylic rhythm may be strong enough to
carry many poems through lyric heights, but it is perhaps still not a "root"
rhythm for Kumin. Just as the dactylic escape in "The Habits of Child-
hood" was enabled by the fact that the other children and the certainty of
the closing iambic pentameter passage would end the speaker's idyll, so the
dactylic flight in "Voices from Kansas" is rooted, finally, in iambic pen-
tameter.

The dactylic rhythm may be Kumin's rhythm of choice for assertions
of the integral self, lyric flights, and triumphant paeans in *Looking for Luck*,
but iambic pentameter remains the book's touchstone, to which the poems
return in order to process difficult situations and resolve crises. Only a pen-
tameter couplet, for example, can bring the poem "Taking the Lambs to
Market," a tribute to a butcher as "artist," to a satisfying conclusion. The
poem progresses through a series of six stanzas that begin in free verse and
move closer and closer to iambic pentameter, until it resolves the tension
of the animal-raising, meat-eating speaker's guilt in a strict heroic couplet:
"a decent man who blurs the line of sight / between our conscience and our
appetite" (*LL* 37). Here iambic pentameter turns a difficult experience into
a tidy epigram, much as Amos, the butcher himself—in the speaker's grate-
ful account—wraps a creature that was once "living, breathed, furred" into
tidy packages of "white butcher paper." Though Kumin may elsewhere be
ambivalent about iambic pentameter, here the meter's very bloodlessness,
its inherited and formidable power, is just what enables it satisfactorily to
resolve such difficult subject matter.

In "The Porch Swing" iambic pentameter similarly serves to relieve anxiety and bring a poem on a difficult subject to a conclusion. The poem, which focuses on the speaker's relationship with her brother, opens with the phrase "we embarrass each other." It goes on to explore difficult territory in the relationship: how the speaker is her brother's "none too secret mortification" and how now, middle-aged, they both "look death straight / in its porcelain teeth" (*LL* 85). After a series of childhood memories the poem, which has been all in free verse to this point, concludes in an off-rhymed couplet, similar to the concluding couplet of "Taking the Lambs to Market": "We bask once more in our private sun, / the known astonishments of what has been" (*LL* 86). Because its first line is an iambic tetrameter, this couplet is more ragged, less stringent and overwhelming than the other; but nonetheless, the meditation that began in uncertainty has reached a resolution, however temporary, through the iambic pentameter.

In the sonnet sequence "Saga," an account of the habits and fate of a poor family named the Scutzes, iambic pentameter serves a slightly different function as an embodiment of the norm of poetry and perhaps, by implication, the norm of respectable people. The off-rhyme in the final couplet—the most monotonously regular couplet in all the sonnets—is inevitable; it stands in for the bad end predicted for the Scutzes' unfortunate children: "It all works out the way we knew it would. / They'll come to no good end, the Scutzes' kids" (*LL* 36). The monosyllabic words and end-stopped lines contribute to this relentless passage's sense of inescapable spoiling; a perfectly rhymed iambic pentameter couplet such as that which ends "Taking the Lambs to Market" is a ghost presence here, the norm from which the whole sonnet sequence's "bad end" has, horribly, fallen.

The connotations and uses of dactylic rhythm and iambic pentameter are so clearly differentiated in *Looking for Luck* that it is possible to trace the exact function of each on a small scale, for instance within the single couplet that ends the meditation "On Visiting Flannery O'Connor's Grave." Perhaps in acknowledgment of the solemnity of the occasion, this poem incorporates much more iambic pentameter than is typical in the book. The final couplet, which serves a similar function to the couplet at the end of "Taking the Lambs to Market," answers the speaker's need to come to some strongly satisfactory resolution when faced with the problem of the writer's death. Although this couplet ends in a resounding iambic pentameter, its first line is not iambic at all but dactylic: "Flannery lies unadorned except by name / who breathed in fire and fed us on the flame" (*LL* 47). In these two lines, the dactylic function of paying tribute to female power joins with the iambic pentameter function of resolving difficulty, bringing the poem to a close by two simultaneous rhythmical strategies.

In the several other poems in *Looking for Luck* that combine the iambic pentameter and dactylic rhythm, the dactylic rhythm carries a more complex set of connotations than simply female power. For Kumin, as for many of her predecessors in free verse, the dactylic rhythm associates generally with wildness, with unprocessable experience, and with untamed unconscious energy. Her ambivalence, however, is significantly less than that of the nineteenth- and early-twentieth-century poets whose work I discuss in *The Ghost of Meter*. In "Hay," a nostalgic yet ceremonial tribute containing perhaps more lines of iambic pentameter than any poem except "On Visiting Flannery O'Connor's Grave," Kumin saves the dactylic rhythm almost entirely for the poem's dark, ambiguous closing, following an extended passage of luminous blank verse:

> Allegiance to the land is tenderness.
> The luck of two good cuttings in this climate.
> Now clean down to the alders in the swale,
> the fields begin an autumn flush of growth,
> the steady work of setting roots, and then
> as in a long exhale, go dormant.
>
> (*LL* 29)

In associating iambic pentameter with traditionally sanctioned, socially valued productivity ("the steady work" of rooting) and the dactylic rhythm with dormancy (worthless on the surface, though mysteriously and deeply productive), Kumin works within the traditions of connotations these two meters have developed in American free verse over the past century and a half. But dormancy is at worst a mildly subversive state; the dactylic rhythms in Kumin never carry the truly problematic aura that they can convey in the work of Whitman, Crane, Eliot, or even Charles Wright.

For some poets, ambivalence toward the dactylic meter is most likely to reveal itself when a dactylic passage occurs immediately next to a line of iambic pentameter. Such an instance does occur in Kumin's *Looking for Luck*, in two lines near the end of "Waking to Moonlight," a poem concerning the horrible noises of porcupines coupling: "This was not murder in the underbrush / but Eros, dipped in the flaming vat of estrus" (*LL* 59). These two lines are, again, consistent with the traditional connotations of the two meters; they move from a clichéd pop culture interpretation of the noises in iambic pentameter to a melodramatic evocation of archetypal sensuality and mysteriousness that scans easily in dactyls and carries an irrefutable falling rhythm. Kumin here brings the connotative clusters of these two meters into direct juxtaposition and contrast, as does Whitman in the lines, "no poem proud I chanting bring to thee, / but a cluster containing night's darkness and blood-dripping wounds." But Kumin's purposes are less serious than Whitman's as she balances the implications of each meter against those of the other; at the climax of her darkly humorous poem, these lines verge on the parodic, defusing whatever serious threatening imagery the line may carry.

Even when Kumin uses another meter to counteract potentially disturbing dactylic connotations, the opposition is not as severe as it would have been for her predecessors. In Kumin's "Noah, at Six Months," the dactylic rhythm is opposed yet balanced with an anapestic rhythm—a subtler opposition than that between the dactylic rhythm and iambic pentameter (anapestic meter, which rises like iambic meter, occasionally takes on some of the connotations of iambic meter in free verse). The first line of "Noah, at Six Months," like several passages in T. S. Eliot's *The Waste Land*, describes rain in dactyls: "While, this rainy summer of 1990 . . ." Contrasting dactylic rain with desperate drought, *The Waste Land* uses the iambic pentameter to write about the desert's dryness. But Kumin's poem uses a less starkly opposed image and a less starkly opposed meter to deal with the summer rain: an ark works in adaptive harmony with water, and the anapestic rhythm of Kumin's last line does not oppose the dactylic rhythm so much as transform it: "Today in the rain our world is cupped in his ark."

The dactylic rhythm is a strong presence throughout most of *Looking for Luck*; the first lines of the Prologue and of the book proper both carry a triple rhythm, as do the closing lines of the last poem in the book. But the book's third and final section, with its several tributes to women, has by far the strongest concentration of dactylic passages. The last poem in the second section, foreshadowing the dactylic passages of the third section, ends with a metaphorical acknowledgment of the strength and persistence of the dactylic rhythm. The end of "The Geographic Center" focuses on a bittersweet vine—described in dactyls—that flourishes in spite of the speaker's iambic pentameter determination to get rid of it: "glint against the flourishing bittersweet / we say we should but never will rip out" (*LL* 67).

During the last section of *Looking for Luck*, Kumin develops a stronger role for the dactylic rhythm than it has carried previously in the book. The last section contains fewer lines of iambic pentameter than earlier sections, and the dactylic passages are more likely than earlier to occur without a counterpointing iambic rhythm. At the end of the Epilogue, a poem called

"The Rendezvous," the iambic pentameter and dactylic patterns that have interacted throughout *Looking for Luck* reach a resolution that promises a new direction. In an old legend, the poem says, a bear ran away, afraid, from a woman when she took off her clothes. The speaker of the poem encounters a bear, and as she takes off her blouse and skirt, the bear his teeth and fur, the dactylic and iambic rhythms are in close contact: the dactylic rhythms describe their common animality; the iambic, the possibility that he might run away. Then, as might have been expected from the course of the book, the "new legend" that they create in the last line is a dactylic one, and the deep irrational power that has been building throughout the book holds the last of its words:

> He smells of honey
> and garlic. I am wet
> with human fear. How
> can he run away, unfurred?
> How can I, without my clothes?
>
> How we prepare a new legend.
>   (*LL* 92)

🦬 HENRY TAYLOR

Remembering Where Everything Is:
The Poetry of Maxine Kumin

It is often startling to consider a poet's beginning efforts. In a widely distributed audiotape, Maxine Kumin speaks fondly of a couple of early mentors but adds that she was discouraged from writing poetry when she got to college. She continues:

I stopped writing poetry for about seven or eight years and went back to writing poems when I was a married woman—a young married woman, I should add. And then I sort of wrote in the closet for a long time. I didn't have anyone to show poems to; I didn't quite know what to do with them. I began writing light verse for the slick magazines when I was pregnant with my third child. I made a little pact with myself that I would either sell something by the time this baby was born or I would give it up entirely. And I was quite fortunate; I developed quite a cottage industry and I was being published in all of the slick places like *Good Housekeeping* and *The Saturday Evening Post* and so on. And then I lucked into a poetry workshop at the Boston Center for Adult Education.*

Sure enough, several small pieces of light verse by Maxine Kumin appear in issues of *Good Housekeeping, Better Homes and Gardens*, and *The Saturday Evening Post* published in 1955 and 1956; they are earlier than anything in her first book, *Halfway*, whose contents are copyrighted from 1957 to 1961. It would be churlish to quote one or two of them to demonstrate Kumin's wisdom in having left them uncollected, but they would strongly reinforce the point she makes in the interview: that whether or not the poems are inferior to those she included in *Halfway*, they display verbal acrobatics of a kind that have been central to her production of more durable poems.

In the retrospective collections *Up Country* (1972) and *Our Ground Time Here Will Be Brief* (1982), Kumin has been conservative in selecting poems from her first book. Among those left behind is "The Gossamer," an accomplished poem beginning with recollections of having seen migrating geese and floating spiderlings in the air overhead. The poem's concluding

---

*"Maxine Kumin in Conversation with Alicia Ostriker," *Poets in Person: A Series on American Poets and Their Art*, hosted by Joseph Parisi. Chicago: Modern Poetry Association, 1991. My transcription.

stanza shows where a good poet can go from such a starting place as "I think," from which many of us depart with less thought than we should:

> I think of spiders, hardly seen,
> weavers of hinges, brails, and trusses,
> and in the last, drifters, dependers
> on air sifts to tug them over
> towns, fields, suburbs, marshes,
> even oceans they can drown in,
> over islands they can drop to,
> growing up or dying where they land.
> (*HW* 54)

There is a significant reach between two of the forces at work here. One is the affection for sonic detail that dropped "brails" into the second line with no fanfare, and the other is the dispassionate attention to the flat fact that nature seems indifferent to a particular spider's fate. "Brails," a bit of slightly unusual nautical terminology meaning roughly "lines" or "cables," helps hold the stanza to a serious playfulness as it goes on to confuse the contrast between "drown" and "land" by placing "dying" between them.

"The Heron" is another poem from *Halfway* in which Kumin looks straight and hard at the suffering that goes on in the animal world. The poem is set on a sandy beach, where the speaker and someone she loves are taking their ease, pondering the illusions that gave rise to belief in mermaids and sea monsters. From there she turns to an actual creature, "a terrible white heron" who fishes "in an absent jerky fashion."

> Only when he turned to us I saw
> his upper bill was eaten away
> by pellet or disease, and pity
> soured in my gut.
> . . . .
> This season he will starve to death
> and the rains will steam the flesh
> from his thready bones and the sand
> will lace them to grain rows we lie on.
> (*HW* 78–79)

By the time she published her second book, *The Privilege* (1965), Kumin had written a surprising number of very accomplished poems and at least one, "Morning Swim," that has become a signature piece, a poem to which she continues to turn during public readings and that is as fresh now as it was when it first appeared. The lessons learned from light verse push the poem beyond its nominal subject—the dedicated swimmer's trancelike concentration—toward the actual subject, which is the poem itself, whose tetrameter rhymed couplets gracefully skirt the edges of audible strain, as do those in Henry King's "The Exequy," one of the poems whose form this poem recalls. These are the final four couplets:

> I hummed "Abide With Me." The beat
> rose in the fine thrash of my feet,
>
> rose in the bubbles I put out
> slantwise, trailing through my mouth.
>
> My bones drank water; water fell
> through all my doors. I was the well
>
> that fed the lake that met my sea
> in which I sang *Abide with Me.*
>
> (*TP* in *GT* 191)

Unpretentious but thoroughgoing craft is evident here throughout the poem's twenty-four lines, perhaps especially in the four of them, including the fourth of those quoted, that are each a syllable short. In each of those the metrical departure is almost unnoticeable. It feels unlikely that they could have been improved in any metrically regular version.

Of Kumin's early successes in blending a personal voice and the more audible effects of formal verse, one of the most haunting is "July 5th," from the "Joppa Diary" sequence, first published in *The Privilege* and reprinted in *Up Country* (1972). Over a third of the words in the poem are taken verbatim from the headstones in an old burying ground; Kumin weaves the lines from the epitaphs into her meditation on how we sum ourselves up at the end. The first half of the poem is specific and almost gossipy in its selection of details from the epitaphs, but as the poem moves into its final two stanzas, the names come quickly, and then the poem turns outward toward us:

> God rest his soul, and rest as well
> Jimmy Evans, Rhoda Fell,
> John Timmens (drowned) and Ellen Lee
> who once took rubbings from these stones
> —*as I am now, so you will be*—
> to frame and hang, and now are gone.
>
> *Stop, passengers, as you pass by,*
> *as you are now, so once was I*
> who chiseled out the prophecy:
> *prepare for death and follow me.*
>
> (*UC* 77)

Kumin's control of a range of tones has rarely been put to work in a smaller space, but it is typical of her work that she would risk sounding, for two or three lines, like the annual New Year's greeting couplets in the *New Yorker* immediately before quoting memorial inscriptions and sounding like the hymns that influenced the inscriptions. One of the things that is often going on in a Kumin poem is some purposeful jarring of the serene surface, a reminder that these words come out of a part of the real world and, more important, become a new part of that world, a work of art that has not been there before and that quietly but firmly announces as much. As usual, the risky juxtaposition of tones here is not merely for its own sake but also to make a statement about the dailiness of death, both the slightness and the weight of an individual life.

It is in that spirit that Kumin addresses one of her most persistent themes, which is the inexorable onrush of death among people, animals, and plants. Some readers have characterized her outlook as "unflinching," but in fact she includes the flinch in some of her observations, such as "The Heron." In other poems, it might be said that she encourages her readers to flinch.

For example, "The Vealers," from *The Nightmare Factory* (1970) is easy to read as a poem in protest of barbarity among beef farmers, but the greater part of its success is in its avoidance of prescription. Very little in it instructs us directly concerning how we should act or feel about buying, cooking, or eating veal. At one point the narrow stalls confining the veal calves are called "jail," and when the slaughterer's truck is backed up to the chute the calves are "prodded to extremes." But no one, including the speaker, is free of complicity:

> . . . in our time they will come forth for good
> dead center
> wrapped and labeled in a plastic sheet,
> their perfect flesh unstreaked with blood
> or muscle, and we will eat.
>
> (*UC* 46)

The use of the first person plural and the future tense at the end of the poem is a stern stroke. The knowledge imparted earlier may sensitize a few people, but many of us will never possess it, and some of us, possessing it, will continue not to be much moved by it.

Kumin habitually takes a commonsense approach to matters that sentimentality can render impossibly complex. In a collection of essays called *In Deep: Country Essays* (1987), Kumin extols the virtues of Scotch Highland cattle. They are small, rugged, easy keepers, calm, visually appealing, easy to be around. But just when you think Kumin might be talking about some sort of pet, she has this to say: "Because of the insulating qualities of the

Highlander's hide and hair, Highland meat lacks the thick outer layer of fat common to many other breeds. The fat is evenly dispersed throughout the flesh, giving it an excellent marble. Fine-grained and tender, Highland beef graces the table of the Queen of England, who maintains a herd at Balmoral Castle and makes a practice of flying this beef in for her own meals when she travels outside her island" (*ID* 126).

In two of her best-known poems, Kumin apostrophizes a pony and a horse as they approach death or achieve it. "For a Shetland Pony Brood Mare Who Died in Her Barren Year," like "The Vealers," was first collected in *The Nightmare Factory*. It establishes that the pony had eighteen foals and then entered a summer of false pregnancy; as the season wears on, the approach of the pony's last days becomes easier to imagine, but she has one last surprise:

> But all in good time, Trinket!
> Was it something you understood?
> Full of false pride
> you lay down and died
> in the sun,
> all silken on one side,
> all mud on the other one.
>
> (*UC* 41)

There is a balance here that seems both precarious and unshakable between the kind of grace with sound that is nearly inaudible and the kind that draws attention to itself. End rhyme and internal rhyme are highly concentrated in this passage, which in other respects gives the illusion of conversational diction. It is one of many instances in which Kumin's way of saying how it was largely determines how it was.

"Thinking of Death and Dog Food" first appeared in *House, Bridge, Fountain, Gate* (1975) among several "Amanda Poems," of which seven are reprinted in *Our Ground Time Here Will Be Brief*. Amanda, a "sensible strawberry roan," gives Kumin several opportunities to compare animal and human life; in "Eyes," the agony of a close friend and the simplicity even of catastrophe among animals arouses a kind of envy; the poem ends:

> O Amanda, burn out my dark.
> Press the warm suede of your horseflesh
> against my cold palm.
> Take away all that is human.
>
> (*GT* 135)

"The Summer of the Watergate Hearings" draws a mordant parallel between dead parasitic worms, found in Amanda's droppings after she has been medicated, to the worms that "fall out of the government / pale as the parasites." Successful poems about the Watergate era are scarce and likely to remain so; this one succeeds because there is strength in both its anger and its humor.

The Amanda sequence ends with "Thinking of Death and Dog Food"; by the time we get to it, it is impossible not to hear a trace of grim humor in the title's curious juxtaposition. It is a kind of whistling in the dark, a veering away from uncontrollable sentimentality; clearly, the speaker loves this horse very deeply indeed. The poem's first two stanzas establish that Amanda will become Alpo or Gaines, and the speaker will become ash; the tone is almost cold-blooded. In the present, alone in the woods, the two for a while seem free of time—but only for a while:

> Already in the marsh
> the yearling maples bleed
> a rich onrush. Time slips
> another abacus bead.
>
> Let it not stick in the throat
> or rattle a pane in the mind.
> May I leave no notes behind
> wishful, banal or occult
> and you, small thinker in
> the immensity of your frame,
> may you be caught and crammed
> midmouthful of the best grain
> when the slaughterer's bullet slams
> sidelong into your brain.
> (*GT* 139-40)

The deeply perplexing facts of human-animal interaction make for only one of Kumin's recurring thematic concerns. While that one gradually becomes less insistent in its depictions of violence, others intensify. The body of work becomes richly complicated as the community of living beings expands and the sense of responsibility toward it is tutored by time and circumstance. The history of a child's perception of her family history changes as the child ages, and Kumin has brilliantly and patiently evoked these gradual shifts of perception. Many of the details in these family poems are autobiographical, but they are all subordinated to the forces of the individual poems, which have their own fictions to make real. Therefore, the poems do not depend for their interest on the mere possibility that this or that relationship, event, or emotional response has a basis in the poet's life.

"A Hundred Nights" is an early poem that Kumin has carried forward from *Halfway* into both of her later selections. It recounts what is reported as a frequent occurrence: the invasion of the child's room by bats and her father's fighting them with a carpet beater:

> Frozen underneath the sheets,
> I heard the bats mew when he hit.
> I heard them drop like squashing fruit.
> (*GT* 217)

The terror of those nights was constant, yet the end of the poem reveals that there were two realities in that room:

> No matter that my parents said
> it only happened twice that way
>
> and all the rest were in my head.
> Once, before my father died,
> I meant to ask him why he chose
> to loose those furies at my bed.
> (*GT* 218)

The phrasing of the last sentence is close enough to certain conversational clichés that it might be taken to say, "I had hoped, before my father died, to manage just once to ask him. . . ." But the words as they are arranged say instead, "There was a time before my father died when I meant to ask him. . . ." The difference is significant; the latter interpretation, which seems on reflection hard to get away from, suggests that the speaker has put the question aside, having come to understand that her father did not make the choice she once imagined.

In various poems throughout her ten collections, Kumin has evoked and recalled her parents and siblings in various ways. Most of the poems focus the beam on how the child perceives, or was perceiving, at the moment being recalled. Often they include a subtle revelation, like the one above, of the ways in which perceptions shift with age. Still, treatment of real trouble in the family is more ominously portrayed in Kumin's recent work—that is, the new poems in *Ground Time* and the three books since. The memories are far less harrowing than those of many a child from an apparently normal family; the point is not that Kumin has reached a stage where she can safely reveal horrors but that her understanding of how we are all troubled in this life has enlarged the humanity of her recollections.

"Spree," first collected in *The Long Approach* (1985), begins with a scene that probably has its analogue in every family history. Father paces angrily, mother sits meekly, and the reason for the anger—a sheaf of bills from clothing and department stores—is in his hand. In the first half of the poem, Kumin uses the sense of smell to link his anger with alcohol, and in the second half she reveals that her father had his ways of encouraging shopping sprees. The ending is a lucid, disturbing blend of accusation and gratitude:

> You sent to Paris for the ermine muff
> that says I'm rich. To think twelve poor
> little things had their heads chopped off
> to keep my hands unseemly warm!
> When you went fishing down the well
> for fox furs, hats with peacock plumes
> velvet evening capes, what else befell?
>
> You paid the bills, Papá. You cast the spell.
> (*LA* 11)

In "Never," the speaker is riding a horse over jumps, either in training or competition, and a voice beside her repeats "Good for you!" It might at first be some voice in the present of the poem, but it quickly becomes another:

> O heart, we are
> a pair of good girls
> hurdling the ditch
> at the bottom of the chute
> and up the other side, *good*
> *for you*! victorious
> not over fear, my lifelong boarder,
> morose skulker about the house,
> but over time. The large
> child inside leaps up
> for daddy's loud kiss,
> for daddy's lollipop.
> (*GT* 16)

The more of these family poems one reads, the clearer comes the urgency of Kumin's realization that we are both cursed and blessed with hindsight. Episodes long past are seen in a new light and newly understood, sometimes too late for both parties to share in the enlightenment. There is room for regret that time needs to pass before understanding comes, but gratitude for the understanding usually gets more space, or emphasis at least. Even in "Atlantic City 1939," a poem in which understanding brings sadness, there is a solemn celebration in the act of memorializing a mysterious incident. The poem begins with a heavy reference to an illness that, ironically, will not be central to it:

> When I was young and returning from
> death's door, I served as chaperone,
> pale as waxworks, a holiday child,
> under the bear laprobe in the back
> of my courtesy uncle's Cadillac
> careening through a world gone wild.
>   (*LA* 3)

The closeness between "Uncle Les" and the speaker's mother feels illicit, and as the speaker's understanding develops over time, it comes to a maturity expressed partly in the stately formality of the final stanza, which is more tightly rhymed than the first:

> Pink with ardor, not knowing why,
> I longed for one of them to die
> that slow September by the sea.
> He fell on the beach at Normandy.
> I never heard her say his name
> again without a flush of shame
> for my complicity.
>   (*LA* 3-4)

As noted in connection with "Morning Swim," there are instances of poetic technique in which subject, topic, and method coalesce into something beyond any one of them. The details in this relationship are only hinted at, so paraphrase describing the relationships is likely at any moment to go too far toward explicitness. What exactly was between those two adults—aside from the observing child—we shall never know. But the last line of this poem provides another kind of knowledge in its faint but audible echo of Emily Dickinson: the poet may live as the rest of us do and face difficulties as grave, but there are moments, however brief, when the words under the hand matter more than whatever prompted them. In that knowledge there is the potential for redemption.

As the years have passed, Kumin's family has increased and aged if it is fair to say that a death reduces a family less than a birth increases it; she has lost brothers and friends and has children and grandchildren now, and writing the poems that take note of this development may have had some effect on her recollections of being a child, a grandchild, and a friend. Whatever the reason, the sense of the community of all life that suffuses *Nurture* (1989) and *Looking for Luck* (1992) seems deeper and more encompassing than even this poet, famous for widely inclusive compassion, had previously shown. The courage of her realistic perceptions continues to keep her from sentimentality, to the point that some readers may wonder whether they understand what is going on in the first few poems in *Nurture*.

There is a tremendous difference between the death of an individual and the extinction of the individual's species; in the case of the human species we can find the words to denote our extinction, but it is doubtful that we are very good at imagining it. As a species, however, we have little difficulty in bringing about the extinction of others. At the beginning of *Nurture*, Kumin places a few poems that raise difficult and disturbing questions about what our duty is to the remaining members of endangered species. It is possible to argue that in "Thoughts on Saving the Manatee" she has taken the stance of "A Modest Proposal," since even that classic piece depends for its effect on what we already believe. How are we to take Kumin's suggestion that the last of the manatees ought to be eaten?

Most of Kumin's collections of poems are emotionally unified and satisfying in their arrangement of the poems. In most cases their arrangements have probably been found in that intuitive, seat-of-the-pants search for the right emotional curve that occupies every publishing poet for a while. But the first section of *Nurture*, titled "Catchment," is so tightly organized as to constitute an essay on the place of human intervention in the progress of other species. The section begins with the book's title poem and ends with the section's title poem; in between, eleven other poems turn this subject in various directions. "Nurture" is a brief consideration of the place the "wild child" of nineteenth-century France might have found in the speaker's house, where other creatures have been rescued. The poem makes it quite clear that the speaker is an easy mark for animals in trouble: "I suffer, the critic proclaims, / from an overabundance of maternal genes" (*N* 3). It ends with what could be the epigraph for the whole section:

> Think of the language we two, same and not-same,
> might have constructed from sign,
> scratch, grimace, grunt, vowel:
>
> Laughter our first noun, and our long verb, howl.
> (*N* 3)

"Thoughts on Saving the Manatee" opens with descriptions of the animal's peculiar slow grace and of a moving encounter between a manatee and a woman of the speaker's acquaintance who groomed the creature, much to its pleasure. But right in the middle of the page, there are these lines by the way:

> At one time you could order
> manatee steak in any
> restaurant in Florida.
> It was said to taste like veal.
>
> (N 7)

What the manatee's life is like now, however, has mostly to do with what humans have done to its natural surroundings. The remaining animals choke on fishing line and beer can rings and slice their insides with tab tops where they feed on sunken acorns. Many bear scars from powerboat propellers. The Audubon Society, according to the poem, has launched a program inviting people to "adopt" a manatee for a fee, to help underwrite the expense of monitoring the last few, adorned with radio collars and pet names. The poem concludes on a hard note:

> Consider my plan.
> It's quick and humane.
> Let's revert to the Catch of the Day
> and serve up the last few as steak marinara.
> Let's stop pretending we need them
> more than they need us.
>
> (N 8-9)

"Homage to Binsey Poplars" lights the problem from another angle, recounting the failure of scientists to make a safe haven for "the rare Aleutian goose." Instead of saving it, they have failed there and also extinguished the arctic fox of Kiska. Kumin quotes a couple of lines from Hopkins's "Binsey Poplars" as her epigraph: "O if we but knew what we do / When we delve or hew—" but leaves for us to find in that poem some apt others upon the earth's plight: "even where we mean / To mend her we end her." If we cannot stop killing the manatees slowly without confronting our acts, then it may well be better to kill them quickly and admit it.

"Bringing Back the Trumpeter Swan" is another variation on this theme, laying out the scheme by which trumpeter swans might be increased in number, at the expense of mute swans and snapping turtles, of which the world seems at the moment to have plenty. The section proceeds through a salute to G. B. Shaw's vegetarianism and a couple of moving poems about the trouble the speaker will take over a specific animal, to "Catchment," which depicts two instances of instinctual predatory behavior, one in the wild and one on a farm, and concludes:

> Later, watching the after-afterglow
> flush the whole sky pink, then darken,
> we can almost discuss it, good and harm.

Nature a catchment of sorrows.
We hug each other. No lesson drawn.
(*N* 24)

Despite those last three words, one thrust of this group of poems is strongly didactic, though the tone and stance are not. A life of unusually sensitive responsibility has led Kumin to a secure if sometimes troubled understanding of the continually growing community of which she is a part. The relatively brief periods of acquaintanceship with the animals on her farm and the occasional permanent partings from members of her family, bring her, at the end of the last poem in *Nurture*, to a recognition that might seem hardhearted if it were not so well informed. "A Game of Monopoly in Chavannes" recalls childhood frustrations with the game that arose from fantasies bred in the Depression and moves to a game being played now, in which the speaker's grandson has had a run of bad luck. The poem ends:

> I will deed him the Reading Railroad, the Water Works,
> the Electric Company, my hotel on Park Place.
>
> All that I have is his, under separate cover
> and we are the mortgaged nub of all that he has.
> Soon enough he will learn, buying long, selling short
>
> his ultimate task is to stay to usher us out.
> (*N* 63)

Kumin's tenth and most recent book, *Looking for Luck* (1992) greets a second grandson ("Noah, at Six Months") and notes the poet's co-survivorship with one of her four brothers ("The Porch Swing"). The community changes, but the poet's love for it seems to have grown. "A Morning on the Hill" is a superb illustration of the power of events to alter our moods. It begins with the speaker's anger at a man operating a logging skidder. The damage he is doing causes her to hate him, to wish his machine would roll on him. But when the machine does turn over, not hurting the operator but causing him to have a heart attack, she runs as well as she can in high boots over muddy fields to be as helpful as possible. She remembers a moment of fear:

> . . . I remember the way a friend's
> husband died beside her in his sleep.
> Her voice on the phone was calm but taut as rope
> that morning: *Joe is dead. Do me a favor?*
> *Call 911 for me. I've forgotten the number.*

> *Of course I'll call them. I'll come too.*
> Nobody dead up here this morning, though
> the fat man tried. Now a relentless sun
> licks the far hill alight. Its red balloon
> lifts over pastures as if nothing new
> has happened. Indeed enough comes true.
> (*LL* 30–31)

People who do not write poems often assume that the material of strong anecdote must also be material for poetry. Hearing a poet speak of an interesting experience, such people will say, with all the goodwill in the world, that they expect to see a poem on the subject someday. They might not be entirely reassured to know how much more attractive to many poets is such a technical challenge as controlling the tone in the passage above. The tension between the caller's immediate situation and that of having "forgotten the number" for 911—one dire, the other potentially humorous—is brought to maximum pitch with no apparent effort. It is the work of someone who remembers where things are.

The source of one's own best thoughts and feelings is often a place that one has come to call home; certainly Kumin has made of her farm in New Hampshire an emblematic home that nourishes her best work. In recent years, however, perhaps partly as a result of her growing fame, she has had time in other parts of the world to respond to her surroundings. This collection is particularly peripatetic, roving from Bangkok to California, with stops in Kansas, generalized Marriotts, Alaska, Georgia. The process of travel itself is sometimes more to the point than the destination, as in "Getting Around O'Hare," which compares that vast place with certain elaborate thirteenth-century visions of Heaven and makes startling but apt use of the electronic voice that says "*Look down. The walkway is ending*" (*LL* 56)

"The Porch Swing" is another delicate dance among various tones, as two surviving siblings recall the members of the family who have died and make jokes about which of them is in fact the older. There is acknowledgment of the trouble writers can sometimes cause their families:

> . . . I am his none
> too secret mortification,
> a writer, a species of liar
> thinly disguising the whereabouts,
> squabbles, sexual habits
> of people we lived with, namely
> those voices and mirrors, our family.
> (*LL* 85)

The poem ends with a couplet establishing that Kumin has located herself with rare authority and looks widely and lovingly from that vantage point upon a world of immense possibility:

> We bask once more in our private sun,
> the known astonishments of what has been.
> (*LL* 86)

Maxine Kumin's Poetry of Metamorphosis

In the title poem of *The Retrieval System*, Maxine Kumin brings together the family members who thickly populate her "tribal" poetry, and the animals, wild and domestic, who inhabit her farm and poems. Not only does she bring them together, but with the studied uncanniness of Ovid she allows them to combine, body and soul. Various critics have noticed the frequency with which Kumin writes about her family, and others have traced her practical and literary interest in animals. But in this essay I want to show that one of her most striking habits of imagination and language is to turn people into animals (and sometimes by a kind of extension, plants) and vice versa. This habit is so strange and so pervasive that it demands explanation, and any explanation will have to be as complex as Kumin's own motives for writing a poetry of metamorphosis.

Why is it that Kumin can best represent her intimates and familiars, and even herself, by changing them into other creatures? How does transformation convey her understanding of and love for them? (Kumin rarely writes out of curious indifference; she chooses as topics those whose well-being directly concerns her.) What linguistic means does she use to carry out her transformations? What explanations of this poetic habit does she herself suggest? How does it allow her to construct poems at once personal and universal, domestic and political? The answers to all these questions, some concerning form and others more substantive, are inevitably linked.

When she combines people and animals in her poems, Kumin usually avoids the markers of simile, *like* and *as*, that point to a likeness in qualities while equally insisting on a difference in substance or kind and therefore emphasize the arbitrary construction of the author. Instead, Kumin uses other tropes that present the linkage as deeper-lying, more objective: these range from the stubborn side-by-sideness of zeugma to the half-and-half combinations of synechdoche to the full, fierce identities of metaphor. For Kumin doesn't wish to present her transformations as the poet's whimsical composition. Indeed, her tropes that are stronger than simile are often reinforced by gestures toward principles that explain how the transformations are possible. There are the principles of dream (with the tangent objectivity conferred on them by Freud & Co.), of myth (Native American, Greek, Buddhist, with the objectivity of tradition), of love (which forges the bonds it imagines), and even of evolution. For one inference to be drawn from Darwin is that all animals are part of one great body stretching backward in time; we are really one flesh with our parents, and so on *ad finitum* to the Egg.

So then what is the point of so much poetic combination and fusion? On the one hand, I think it testifies to an emotional equivalence. Kumin cares as sharply about the animals, wild and domestic, that inhabit her New Hampshire farm as she does about her friends and family. The claims of animals and more generally of things that grow are no less compelling than human claims. So on the other hand, the metamorphosis has a broader import. We human beings are animals among animals, and we must not let our temperamental strangeness sever us from our fellows, from the earth.

I

The first stanza of "The Retrieval System" is a good example of the way that Kumin merges human beings and animals in complex ways. The figure of synechdoche does all the work, though it is a strange synechdoche in which parts not only represent wholes, but representative parts are embedded in other, equally representative wholes.

> It begins with my dog, now dead, who all his long life
> carried about in his head the brown eyes of my father.
> Keen, loving, accepting, sorrowful, whatever;
> they were Daddy's all right, handed on, except
> for their phosphorescent gleam tunneling the night
> which I have to concede was a separate gift.
>
> (*RS* 1)

Kumin doesn't write, "I remember my father's eyes!" so that his eyes, the windows of the soul, can stand for him. Nor does she write, "My dog came over to me, and I thought, how like my father's eyes his eyes are." What she remembers is "my dog, now dead, who all his long life / carried about in his head the brown eyes of my father." The dog's eyes are identified with (not just likened to) her father's eyes, and her father is revived by his fleshly representation in the sockets of a living, beloved household pet. The import of the trope is then that the metamorphosis is not just something she made up but something she encountered, involuntarily and with perhaps a shiver. And it happened not just once and fleetingly but during all the long life of her dog.

So the poet reports a brute, though strange fact of experience. Indeed, the word "Fact" begins the most important line of the whole poem, in the next to last stanza: "Fact: it is people who fade, / it is animals that retrieve them." Even Kumin has to admit the strangeness of her facts. "Uncannily," she writes after recording the eyes of her father, "when I'm alone these features / come up to link my lost people / with the patient domestic beasts of my life." She is also surprised by the voice of her former piano teacher blatted by her goat; the head of maiden aunts on her ponies; her lost baby sister's chin, squint, and cry in the cat; and shades of the television weatherman and her late dentist in a "resident owl." And she finds the exuberance of an old boyfriend (killed in World War II) in the antics of her colts.

> A boy
> I loved once keeps coming back as my yearling colt,
> cocksure at the gallop, racing his shadow
> for the hell of it. He runs merely to be.
> A boy who was lost in the war thirty years ago
> and buried at sea.
>
> (*RS* 1)

Here the synechdoche is even odder: there's no transposition of representative parts, but rather the whole manner of being and moving of the young horse is that of the young man: the boy *comes back*. He is a revenant, though not a ghost because he is embodied, except that the body is not his own. And while the experience is as uncanny as it is real, the poet is not frightened, for the yearling colt is warm with the pulse of life. Kumin never says that she loves the animals because they remind her of people she has loved; rather, because she already feels affection for the animals in their own right, they can embody and manifest her people.

Kumin's candidates for metamorphosis are often the loved and lost, sometimes through death, sometimes merely through distance. Daughters whose manifold departures she grieves over in poem after poem are often transformed into animals. In "Changing the Children" (*RS* 30), Kumin seems to invoke the fairy tale–folk tale tradition of the brothers Grimm, as she does in the closely related poem "Seeing the Bones" (*RS* 33). Kumin makes herself into a poetic witch, whose spells and concoctions, while fantastic, are not imaginary.

> Anger does this.
> Wishing the furious wish
> turns the son into a crow
> the daughter, a porcupine . . .
>
>   . . . the golden daughter
> all arched bristle and quill
> leaves scribbles on the tree bark
> writing how The Nameless One
> accosted her in the dark.
>
> How to put an end to this cruel spell?

The spell is cruel, and the cure no less so.

> In spring when the porcupine comes
> all stealth and waddle to feed on the willows
> stun her with one blow of the sledge
> and the entrapped girl will fly out
>
> crying Daddy! or Danny!
> or is it Darling!

I hear the lost voice of Plath in the exclamation "Daddy!" and that of Sexton in "Darling!" If that is so, then the anxiety expressed by the poet, mother, and friend here is very great, and the process of transformation itself seems dangerous. But Kumin never shrinks from the aggression and anger that are mixed up in the tenderest parental (and filial) feelings. She gives them full expression, as of course the brothers Grimm also do, with the wisdom of the folk.

A daughter is invoked and transformed by verbal yoking, a kind of zeugma not at the level of word but of stanza, in two further poems, "Telling the Barn Swallow" (*Looking for Luck*) and "The Bangkok Gong" (*Nurture*). In both poems, the animals are presented in mother-and-daughter pairs, as the poet writes about her daughter who is always leaving to go somewhere far away. Why do the animals intervene so strongly in these poems? Why does Kumin not simply elaborate on themes like, "My child is leaving, and so I am sad" or even "My child is leaving me as a bird leaves the nest"? The role of simile to decorate or even to articulate seems inadequate to the poet's purposes.

In the first poem, while her daughter plays the cello outdoors at sundown, the poet puts up strawberries, and a barn swallow flies around them.

> The sun is going down, the crows announce it.
> Only the barnswallow continues to zig zag
> between the cello's double-stops.
> She comes with a mouthful of mosquitoes

for the budvase beaks of her nestlings
banked in the overhang.
It is the same old sloppy nest.
She keeps sieving the air for them.
They are her second setting this year.

I tell the bird this is my child
fierce now in the half light
at her harmonics. I tell the bird
how this cello has crossed and recrossed
the Atlantic in its coffin and next week
will cross again, and forever.

(LL 74)

(Her daughter is about to marry and live in Europe.) Kumin is both talking
to herself and addressing the barn swallow; the four speeches she directs to
the bird make sense only if they are understood as a reminder and admon-
ishment both to herself and to the bird. This doubling in the address, as
well as the way the poems cuts abruptly back and forth between the mother
brooding over her daughter and the swallow and her brood of hatchlings,
induces an identification.

Both Kumin and the mother barn swallow will be there later, on the
occasion of other sunsets, when their children have flown. Kumin encom-
passes the bird; the bird's fate impinges directly on her own, as her own
fortunes seem to matter to the bird.

My daughter plays Bartok to the arriving fireflies.
The swallow settles over her foursome.
I tell the bird to cover well her hatch.
I tell her that this hour
must outlast the pies and the jellies,
must stick in my head like a burdock bur.

(LL 75)

"Cover well your hatch" is an appropriate thing to say to a bird, but it in-
vokes the poem's central anxiety: the daughter, whom the poet worries has
not been properly "covered." "This hour / must outlast the pies and the
jellies, / must stick in my head like a burdock bur" is a much odder thing
to say to a bird; the poet must assume that the bird shares her concerns.
The problems of maternity are not peculiar to the human race; the speaker
here is both a human and an avian mother. The fierce attachment of a bur
is something the carrier always notices, like, one imagines, a mouthful of
mosquitoes.

But the bird, or the poet addressing the bird from the inside, is a source
of solace to herself. "Fact: it is people who fade; / it is animals that retrieve

them." Later in the season, when the daughter and the little birds have departed, the homing flight of the barn swallow will be the visual equivalent of the sound of Bartok played on a lone cello at sunset. It will always bring back the music and musician, "fierce now in the half light," as Kumin's dog (even after his own demise, in the timeless hour of poem or dream) brings back the eyes of her father.

Likewise, the same daughter, now even further flown and truly in danger, comes back by metonymic association with the gift she leaves behind, the Bangkok gong. Yet the metonymy is not enough, and the gift is further metamorphosed into a mare and her colt.

> Home for a visit, you brought me
> a circle of hammered brass
> reworked from an engine part
> into this curio . . .
>
> The tone of this gong
> is gentle, haunting, but
> hard struck three times
> can call out as far
> as the back fields . . .
>
> (*N* 57)

Kumin might have left the poem there, with the invocation, "I strike the gong to call you back home." But a metal curio, however ingenious or resonant, is too inert and cold for Kumin; her figures must be alive, capable of intention and attachment and sorrow. So she transforms the gong by asserting that its reverberation is speech.

> When barely touched it imitates
> the deep nicker the mare makes
> swiveling her neck
> watching the foal swim
> out of her body.
> She speaks to it even as
> she pushes the hindlegs clear.
> Come to me is her message
> as they curl to reach each other.
>
> Now that you are
> back on the border
> numbering the lucky ones
> whose visas let them
> leave everything behind
> except nightmares, I hang
> the gong on my doorpost.
> Some days I
> barely touch it.
>
> (*N* 57-58)

The extraordinary moment of birth is at once a separation and a re-connection, since the infant willingly and instinctively turns back to its mother to nurse; then in a new and different sense they are again one body. Kumin treats this moment and double movement recurrently in her poetry and essays. Despite the pain of separation, Kumin realizes that one reason her daughter is so far away is that she is acting like her mother and reforging the bond between them. The same sense of civic justice and responsibility to the earth that leads the daughter to work for the UN, helping Cambodian refugees, leads the mother to work on a small farm in New Hampshire and record her life there for all the rest of us. The interpretations differ, but the text that governs them (something like the golden rule) remains the same.

II

Another person who is regularly subject to metamorphosis throughout Kumin's poetry is Anne Sexton, Kumin's best poetic friend, who committed suicide in the middle of her life. In "Itinerary of an Obsession" (*Our Ground Time Here Will Be Brief* 22), Sexton appears in a dream side by side with her own "lovesick dog [that] chases a car / the twin of yours and lies dead / years back in a clump of goldenrod." In "On Being Asked to Write a Poem in Memory of Anne Sexton" (*N* 36), Sexton becomes an elk and her gifts and demons the "heavy candelabrum" of antlers.

In "Progress Report" (*RS* 15), Kumin presents her friend (like her daughter) under two totemic aspects, bird and porcupine. Encountered as objects, the bird recalls Sexton's spirited, graceful, dramatic side; the porcupine, her fury. Encountered as ideas, as acts of awareness in the presence of objects, the bird and porcupine belong to Kumin as well; they manifest her great love and the anger of her bereavement.

Memory reunites us with the dead, for the vivacity of our grief at their absence brings them to life in us. (Even when we are alive, much of our being is the way we are present in other people.) But here Kumin is not content to write, "I remember and miss my friend." Animals must once again be the figural way in which the friends are reunited, in which they encounter each other. Nor does she write, "My friend was so much like that tanager." Instead, the tanager is in the poem, and the two friends are reunited in virtue of its being there, as creature and as apparition. Oddly, the tanager as creature brings back the dead friend; the tanager as apparition calls up the living.

> The same scarlet tanager
> as last year goes up, a red
> rag flagging from tree to tree,
> lending a rakish permanence to
> the idea of going on without you
>
> even though my empty times
> still rust like unwashed dogfood cans
> and my nights fill up with porcupine
> dung he drops on purpose at
> the gangway to the aluminum
> flashed willow, saying that
> he's been here, saying he'll come
> back with his tough waddle, his pig eyes,
> saying he'll get me yet. He is
> the stand-in killer I use
> to notarize your suicide
> two years after, in deep spring.
>
> (RS 15)

Although the poet knows, and writes explicitly in the midst of the poem, that her conversations with her lost friend now require her to take both parts, the poem presents Sexton in her irreducible, unmistakable otherness. The penultimate stanza of "Progress Report" relates a dream, where two of the distinctive qualities that made Sexton what she was and is, shine through: her penchant for long telephone calls and her wisdom about the human heart.

The poem "The Green Well" turns the open graves filling up with snow in the last line of "The Retrieval System" into "the green well of losses, a kitchen midden // where the newly dead layer by layer / overtake the longer and longer vanished." The poem begins on Kumin's farm, just before sunrise in early summer; the poet muses on the obvious fact of death as she removes from the top of the feed bin a squirrel freshly killed by her own cats and deposits it in the manure pile, the green well. Through a series of interpolations in that meditation, Sexton is transformed into a mare who died in childbirth. "Gone," Kumin writes,

> now to tankage my first saved starveling mare
> and the filly we tore from her in the rain.
>
> After the lethal phenobarb, the vet
> exchanged my check for his handkerchief.
> Nine live foals since and I'm still pocked with grief,
> with how they lay on their sides, half dry, half wet. . . .
>
> (LL 32)

Immediately after these lines and so without any extra transition, the quotation "Grief, sir, is a species of idleness" appears as an admonition to the poet, perhaps to stop standing there in tears and get on to the other business of the farm. But the voice is Sexton's, though it is also Bellow's.

> *Grief, sir, is a species of idleness,*
> a line we treasured out of Bellow, my
> suicided long-term friend and I.
> All these years I've fought somehow to bless
>
> her drinking in of the killer car exhaust
> but a coal of anger sat and winked its live
> orange eye undimmed in my chest
> while the world buzzed gossiping in the hive.
>
> That mare a dangerous runaway, her tongue
> thickly scarred by wire. My friend too
> fleeing her wolves, her voices those voodoo
> doctors could not still nor save her from. . . .
>
> *(LL* 33)

The interpolations run: the mare, the friend, the mare, the friend; the poem offers no words that soften the juxtaposition except the "too" in the second line of the stanza just quoted. The death of the mare at the moment of birth and of the friend at the height of her powers enclose each other in these lines, as Kumin's meditation encloses them. Only the memory of the great, warm body of the mare cooling in the rain and the poet's immediate awareness of the decomposition of bodies can provide a faithful counterpart to Kumin's feelings about, her half-understanding of, her friend.

The poem returns to its initial setting in the final stanza. But there is no cheerful reconciliation; the transformation of Sexton into mare and mare into meadow does not stand for the resurrection of the soul. Not a hint of it.

> The cats clean themselves after the kill.
> A hapless swallow lays another clutch
> Of eggs in the accessible nest. It does
> not end with us, though end it will.
>
> *(LL* 33)

There is, however, another side to this meditation in the poem that precedes it by a few pages in *Looking for Luck*, "Praise Be." An essay in *Women, Animals, and Vegetables* tells us that Praise Be is the name of the granddaughter of a saved starveling mare with a scarred tongue. The first two stanzas are the record of a successful birth, and the last stanza proclaims,

> Let them prosper, the dams and their sucklings.
> Let nothing inhibit their heedless growing.
> Let them raise up on sturdy pasterns

and trot out in light summer rain
onto the long lazy unfenced fields
of heaven.

(*LL* 23)

This heaven is the earthly paradise that we can sometimes create if we are lucky and try hard and pay attention. In another essay in the same collection, "A Horse for Fun," Kumin reminds us that a great deal of work and sympathy are required to take care of a horse properly, as well as knowledge gleaned from both experience and books. Sentiment and faith will not succeed alone, though they are also needed. Here is Kumin's benediction, on the flown daughter and the lost friend, and the Real, which disappoints us by being less than we expected and delights us by offering more than we ever dreamed of.

III

Kumin does not just turn her lost loved ones into animals (and lost loved animals into people). She also metamorphoses herself, the most intensely present person in the poems. Quite often the explanation of that metamorphosis is myth, though, of course, for Kumin the authority of myth seems to lie rather more in the human traditions that produced it than an independently existing transcendence. In "Reviewing the Summer and Winter Calendar of the Next Life" (in *Nurture*), she uses the Buddhist myth of the transmigration of souls. This myth elongates the self through time by means of the soul, as Darwin's theory elongates the self through time by means of the body. In the poem, Kumin muses that she may next be plunged in various animal bodies, depending on the season in which she dies: "If death comes in July, they'll put me down / for barn swallow"; or by contrast,

In January, I'll get to pick and choose
among the evening grosbeaks bombing the feeder
in a savage display of yellow scapulars
or return as a wild turkey, one of the brace
who come at a waddle at 10 A.M.
punctual comics, across the manure pile
for their illicit fix of feedbin corn
or join the juncos, whose job description involves
sweeping up after everybody else,
even venturing in to dust the stalls
of the barn for stray or recycled specks of grain.

(*N* 52)

A soul transmigrating in New Hampshire (halfway between Katmandu and Jerusalem) ought to go into a winged creature, the closest natural analogue we know to angels. Yet the logic of the poem is not so simple, for in the last stanza Kumin formally requests not to be brought back as a weasel and by the very urgency of the request admits a kinship with that devilish, reptilian mammal: "Rat-toothed egg-sucker, making do / like any desperate one of us." Whatever the outcome, this change will not be a change of place; all the options set forth bring the poet back home to her own farm.

In each of the three stanzas of "Reviewing" the theme of feeding recurs; Kumin notes the ceaseless struggle of all these creatures to feed themselves and their offspring. Throughout Kumin's writings a fascination with food appears at many levels, and she often uses our relentless need for it to equate human and animal bodies, as does the myth in the foregoing poem. One of the poems that lead off her *Our Ground Time Here Will Be Brief*, "Feeding Time," records her evening provisions for domestic and wild animals around the farm and then for herself and her husband and the shades of grown-up children around the dinner table. The poem makes little distinction: we are animals among animals.

Myth returns and involves the poet in the first and last poems of Kumin's most recent book of poetry, *Looking for Luck*. In the first poem, "Credo," Kumin begins by invoking an Indian legend.

> I believe in magic. I believe in the rights
> of animals to leap out of our skins
> as recorded in the Kiowa legend:
> *Directly there was a bear where the boy had been.*
>
> As I believe in the resurrected wake-robin,
> first wet knob of trillium to knock
> in April at the underside of earth's door
> in central New Hampshire where bears are. . . .
> (*LL* 15)

There may really be a boy in the bear, just as Kumin's old dog really carried the eyes of her father. Indeed, the last poem in the collection, "The Rendezvous," attests that there may really be a poet in the bear, the poet herself, and indeed a bear in the poet. The figure of speech here is perhaps chiasmus, since there is both a fusion and a mixing up of parts; it is surely not simile.

In "The Rendezvous," the poet meets a bear, and in a dance that is part magic, part love-making (which is yet another way we have of being one body with another), they prepare to merge: he is about to enter her and she is on the brink of wrapping up in a delicious, animate fur coat.

How I meet a male bear.
How I am careful not
to insult him. I unbutton
my blouse. He takes out
his teeth. I slip off
my skirt. He turns
his back and works his way
out of his pelt,
which he casts to the ground
for a rug.

He smells of honey
and garlic. I am wet
with human fear. How
can he run away, unfurred?
How can I, without my clothes?

How we prepare a new legend.
(*LL* 91-92)

In the new legend, we might recognize our animal body beneath the cloth-
ing of soul and the animal soul beneath the fur body and create a harmony
different from our present dissonance, where we shun, ignore, slaughter,
torment, and compute our animal companions.

Kumin also, inevitably, turns herself into a horse. The change works
sometimes with respect to soul, sometimes to body, sometimes without
making the distinction. The review of her poetry so far should make clear
that Kumin, on the whole, tries to avoid the distinction. When she invokes
soul, it is quite thoroughly embodied, and when she invokes body, it is
quite thoroughly ensouled. And often she reaches for a language in which
the distinction doesn't register. In the poem "Late Snow" she writes:

Inside, I hear the horses knocking
aimlessly in their warm brown lockup,
testing the four known sides of the box
as the soul must, confined under the breastbone.
(*RS* 49)

The season is early spring, and the snow, like Housman's, is also tree blos-
som, though in this case apple rather than cherry. A few lines later the
horses emerge into the fields, and the soul exults, now acknowledged as the
poet's own and, as in the lines just given, precisely housed. The horses

. . . do not know how satisfactory
they look, set loose in the April sun,
nor what handsprings are turned under
my ribs with winter gone.

(*RS* 49)

The poet's attention to her own soul requires the horses; their initial rest-
iveness and final exuberance is her expression of herself to herself.

A few pages earlier in the same section of *The Retrieval System*, the
poet's attention to her own body also requires an equine presence. During
sessions of yoga, memories of her Catholic school education (which bore
oddly upon a young Jewish girl) and echoes of the Old Testament come
back to her, and the poem "Body and Soul: A Meditation" concludes:

> Body, Old Paint, Old Partner
> in this sedate roundup we ride,
> going up the Mountain in
> the meander of our middle age
> after the same old cracked tablets,
> though soul and we touch tongue,
>
> somehow it seems less sure;
> somehow it seems we've come
> too far to get us there.
>
> > (*RS* 45)

If the relation between self and body is that of a skilled rider and a con-
tented horse going together along an unfamiliar trail, then the poet is a
centauress following not unskeptically in the footsteps of Moses.

The centauress and the same locution occur also in the poem "Relearn-
ing the Language of April" (*Our Ground Time Here Will Be Brief*), which
testifies to a long-lasting marriage in which the pleasures of body and soul
are finally indistinguishable. Kumin's husband strides through the first four
stanzas, rather like Orpheus in a garland of charmed animals and plants,
the circuit of their fields. And in the concluding pair of stanzas, Kumin
seems to be writing from the farm's heart, the farmhouse perhaps, where
she stays on thinking of him.

> I lie in the fat lap of noon
> overhearing the doves' complaint.
> Far off, a stutter of geese raise alarms.
>
> Once more, Body, Old Paint,
> how could you trick me like this
> in spring's blowsy arms?
>
> > (*GT* 12)

The earthly paradise is satisfactory. Not merely satisfactory but produc-
tive of deep and abiding satisfactions like the company of animals, the
reliability of fertile and well-tended land, the allegiances of marriage, the
resources of the English language, the figures of poetry.

Conclusion

It is not easy to write a poem that expresses a deep attachment. The poet can choose either contraction or amplification. Concision may work well, for deep feeling can often be tacit and gestural, something that lies too deep for words, to which a few well-chosen words may point. Yet Kumin trusts the power and accuracy of words: deep feeling, including grief, demands expression, and that utterance is not in vain. I would say that, on the whole, Kumin's tendency is to amplify and that her metamorphoses serve this purpose.

A poet's description of a loved person in a poem by means of a decorative simile doesn't produce much intensification of understanding and feeling. The more inert or conventional or merely pretty the term of comparison, the more artificial and arbitrary the joining, the less the reader is moved and the loved one is called back into the poem. Clever similes can be compounded and extended *ad libitum* without any corresponding increase in the poem's emotional import and its purchase on reality.

By contrast, Kumin's metamorphoses of people into animals are especially effective means of conveying her attachments, quickening them, revealing their meanings, and enlivening the reader's feelings. Her terms of comparison are creatures to whom she is also bound by strong, sometimes overpowering affective ties. So her transformations create a compounding of distinct but analogous feelings, a redoubling that does not obscure but clarifies. And as I have argued earlier, the connection between animal and human being is not presented (at the level of either language or thought) as the poet's willful construction but as an identity encountered in its stubborn thereness—the boy in the bear, the father-eyed dog, the winged friend, the centauress-self. Thus, Kumin's poetry of transformation produces a record of devotion unexampled in the strangeness of its means and in the great power of its effects.

Poised in the Galloping Moment: Maxine Kumin's Poetry

Poetically, Maxine Kumin is descended from the family of Hardy and Whitman rather than that of Yeats and Eliot. In fact, she seems in some ways to be a hybrid of skeptical Thomas and exuberant Walt, their two views melded into one clear voice that questions as it celebrates life in all its manifestations. The reader in search of lines propped by symbols and hung with the starchy laundry of allusion will have to look elsewhere, because Kumin's poetry is as clear as a spring-fed well and as deceptively deep. Nothing has been more difficult for scholars in our age than dealing with work of this kind. Better for them to have Irish folklore or *The Golden Bough* for their own digressions than to address the undiluted utterance of a poet like Kumin. Resembling the natural world it powerfully evokes, Kumin's poetry is at once accessible and profound. The critic, deprived of the rabbits and mirrors he has grown dependent upon to distract his attention, is obliged to enter the poems and be changed. To accomplish this feat, the critic must be careful to avoid what Kumin has called "creeping exegesis," "dissecting the poor poem until it wriggles around and is eventually killed" (*To Make a Prairie* 38). Fair warning for the textual dissector, whose smock I am wearing in this essay.

To place Kumin in a more contemporary and local context, we may note that she is a resident of New England whose poems grow out of the region. Often called a pastoral poet, she has even been dubbed Roberta Frost by some academic wags. Although she doesn't object to the appellation, out of respect and affection for the man she remembers in his later years, the name makes her sound secondary and derivative. It also feminizes her work, implying that her male predecessor has done all the heavy lifting or that she has replaced Frost's homilies with feminist rhetoric. While it is true that her poems represent a distinctly female point of view, Kumin herself re-

This essay was originally presented as the Aiken Taylor Modern Poetry Award Lecture in 1995.

sists the feminist label, insisting that "the creative process is androgynous" and occasionally referring to her androgynous muse (*MP* 52). She eschews as well the confessional tag, even though her poems are often personal and her earliest and most immediate influences were among the principals in the confessional camp. Difficult to categorize, her poetry must be viewed in its active stage, accommodating and resisting or absorbing and transforming the forces around it.

However she may resemble her contemporaries, Kumin differs from them in one very unusual respect: she is probably the only poet in America who has regularly traveled with a saddle. Checking it as baggage in its odd-looking case, she has been known to explain to curious onlookers at the airport carousel, "It's a tuba." Constructed of fiberglass and foam and adaptable to horses of varying girths, her saddle has allowed her to ride whatever is offered at her destination (*Women, Animals, and Vegetables* 45). But for this splendid piece of equipment, travelers might have been treated over the years to the sight of a horse being off-loaded on runways across the country. Happily for Amanda and her equine friends left behind on their New Hampshire farm, Kumin has been willing to swing astride a borrowed mount, sometimes wishing, even so, for the familiar ribs and spines of her own animals. A bad fit of rider to horse can cause her arthritis to flare up, however adaptable the saddle may be. Philosophically regarding this problem after one such mismatch, Kumin reflected, "It is humbling to be mounted on something so broad and massive and to strive, for the sake of my reputation, to maintain a balanced seat thereupon. But it is good for poets to undertake prose from time to time, and it is good for the rider to adapt to a different way of going" (*WAV* 47).

The analogy of poet and rider is characteristic of Kumin, who claims, "I almost never have to admit I am a poet in public. When asked 'What do you do?', 'I raise horses' meets with interest, even approval. 'What do you do?' 'I'm a poet' invariably invites, 'That so? Ever published anything?'" (*WAV* 55) With her eleventh poetry collection scheduled for release next year, she has indeed published some things, but if she wants to hide out as a horse breeder, who are we to argue? Horses appear in her poems and look approvingly over her shoulder in the jacket photos of several of her recent books. In fact, it is instructive to think of her books as horses, each one bred and raised by her, curried and set forth on the public pastures.

Consider this scene: Kumin and her editor, Carol Houck Smith, kneeling by the bed in Kumin's hotel room, pages spread across the comforter, the two of them trying to establish a final order for the poems in Kumin's forthcoming book, *Connecting the Dots*. Smith, who by coincidence is also my editor, confided that someone observing them might have thought they were praying. I like this notion but can't help feeling they were really engaged in the occupation of midwifery, the two of them bringing another of Kumin's foals into the world. More than whimsical, this conflation of horse and poetry has its uses and admits us to the heart of Kumin's work. Each poem in each book is a mounted moment—Kumin taking her horse through its paces. To be well seated requires control and a simultaneous yielding to the motion beneath her. At full gallop, all four feet are off the ground in each stride—rider and animal bonded in midair—not Pegasus but a ponderous, fleshy spirit bound to and repeatedly touching the earth.

Such moments are everywhere in Kumin's work, opposites made luminous at their points of contact, not reconciled in a visionary aura but perceived in their dependent difference. Positioning herself at the dividing threshold, Kumin draws power from both animal and human, the two sometimes broadened in her poetry into nature and civilization or abstracted to belief and doubt. To view her poised on the seam between these opposed pairs is to observe a person keeping a difficult balance, not a static meditator but an active participant in the world's life. Her point of perception cannot be reached sitting cross-legged on an oriental rug; rather, she must ride the horse she is given from her muse's stable, however difficult the mount. Only then can she achieve the transient sensation that horse and rider are one animal, illuminated by their shared corporeality.

Kumin tells us whatever glories can be found must be sought in the world, and she gives us woodchucks sniped in the garden, green tomatoes picked at summer's end and wrapped in newspaper to ripen, a hibernating bear so deep in his winter slumber she can touch him in his cave, and everywhere the rich, rank earth full of worms and bones and wonders. Her poems are redolent of blackberry jam, the sweet bouquet of the haymow, and the stench of manure. Paying homage to excrement, she exclaims, "I honor shit for saying: We go on" (*The Retrieval System* 50), proving herself a true celebrant of life as we must live it at both ends of the alimentary canal.

For Kumin, the natural world is neither paradigm nor allegory; it is the realm where things mean themselves. Her exacting challenge, as she has observed, is to name and particularize, to give the world utterance through her poems, to serve as orifice rather than oracle. Consequently, a Maxine Kumin poem is as likely to praise Amos the butcher, who transforms the gamboling lambs into chops, as it is to look up in wonder at emerging maple leaves, "still wearing their dime-store lacquer, / still cramped and wet from the journey" (*The Privilege* 73). Death and life are abroad on the land, the compost of one made from and enabling the fecundity of the other. Beauty is not "an Odalisque / oiling her body for the artist" but a "great lumbering sow of a grizzly / two cubs hanging off her teats / . . . her coarse fur / alive with ticks, her snub snout / hooked claws, and so white teeth" (*CD* 45).

In Maxine Kumin's poetry, even the song of the cardinal is transcribed as "*fierce, fierce!*" (*CD* 30), its music an insistent reminder of the world's difficult loveliness. To represent such unsettling beauty, Kumin has bred a unique poetry, one with a regional American bloodline going back to Thoreau by way of Modernist formalism but adapted to her particular needs and circumstances. Her Walden is no temporary, ruminative retreat but a permanent way of life, with beans in the garden, yes, but also with spouse, children, horses, lambs, and the demanding chores of two hundred acres. Out of this place poetry grows, and Kumin considers herself "especially lucky because my daily life provides a metaphor for my work, allowing me instant access at all times, crosshatching reality with the snail tracks of the unconscious, enabling me to pull poems up out of the well of the commonplace" (*In Deep* 168).

Spontaneous though the process may be, the finished poem always reveals its formalist lineage, sometimes in strict metrics, often in a flexible adaptation shaped to the materials at hand. Speaking of the relationship between form and content in her poems, Kumin says,

> I generally choose something complex and difficult. The tougher the form the easier it is for me to handle the poem, because the form gives permission to be very gut-honest about feelings. The curious thing for me is that rhyme makes me a better poet. Invariably I feel it does. This is a mystic notion, and I'm not by any stretch a mystic, but it's almost as though I'm not capable of the level of language and metaphor that form enables me to achieve. It raises my language to heights that I wouldn't be up to on my own. (*MP* 25)

Beginning in an age when most of her contemporaries were going bareback or slapping their own haunches and shouting "Giddy-up!" Kumin's devotion to traditional metrics and rhyme set her apart from all but her elders and a handful of younger poets. Her Boston of the late 1950s and early 1960s was the breeding yard of confessionalism, with Robert Lowell presiding over the deepening self-interrogations. Poets who began in formalism eventually shifted to free verse, finding open-endedness better suited to their interior travels; and a few, like Lowell, shifted back. While Kumin's poetry, early and late, is often about her personal life, she has nevertheless remained true to her paradoxical concept of drawing near to difficult material through the distancing elements of form. One of the finest illustrations of her technique is "Letters," the crown of sonnets addressed to her mother that begins her forthcoming collection, *Connecting the Dots*.

Although usually read for its autobiographical elements, "Halfway," the title poem of Kumin's first book, also accounts for her metrics, as its opening stanza illustrates:

> As true as I was born into
> my mother's bed in Germantown
> the gambrel house in which I grew
> stood halfway up a hill, or down,
> between a convent and a madhouse.
> (*Halfway* 16)

The convent, of course, is a place of order, where ritual and tradition are observed. The madhouse is where some of Kumin's acquaintances, including her dearest friend, Anne Sexton, occasionally found themselves. One represents stability, the other a dangerous loss of control—the traditional restraints of form and the revelatory explosions of free verse. Positioned between these extremes, Kumin heard a strange music: "The plain song and the bedlam hung / on air and blew across / into the garden where I played" (*HW* 16-17). In her memory, the tunes jumbled together, leaving her uncertain which was which. Resonant in her inner ear the two songs merged, rising or falling from her as poetry.

The central brilliance of Maxine Kumin's work is its refusal to be boxed and labeled. She is pastoral, yes, but also confessional, though not in the usual way; formal, too, but not rigidly so. Her "halfway" stance has been achieved not through refusal to make a choice but through a monumental effort of receptivity. In regarding her house as "halfway up a hill, or down," she chooses to have both views simultaneously, symbolically pairing hope and despair, not as options but as mutual conditions. That she emerged intact from the milieu of Lowell, Schwartz, Berryman, Roethke, Jarrell, Sexton, and Plath has caused some, like Peter Davison, to wonder if she benefited from psychotherapy or perhaps "never felt the need to prop poetry upon [her] bleeding flesh."* Strange, indeed, when stability and long life must be accounted for as aberrant. Kumin settles the issue best in "Life's Work," when she says, "I didn't come to grief. / I came to words

---

*Peter Davison, "Country Matters: Maxine Kumin, Donald Hall, Philip Booth, 1955–1960," in *The Fading Smile: Poets in Boston, from Robert Frost to Robert Lowell to Sylvia Plath, 1955–1960* (New York: Alfred A. Knopf, 1994), 106.

instead" (*House, Bridge, Fountain, Gate* 18). And in a stunning final elegy to her friend Anne Sexton, she compares her life after Sexton's suicide to a landscape raked by wildfire, changed utterly but insistently blooming "with low growth, sturdier than before" (*CD* 49).

The opportunity to entertain disparity came early for Kumin, who was raised in a Jewish household but sent to convent school for her early education. Speaking of this unusual mixture of religions, she observes,

I did grow up next door to a convent and did go to convent school because it was so convenient. My parents sent me there to attend nursery school and kindergarten. I think I stayed through first or second grade. To a child who is looking for absolutes these two opposing views of the world are terribly confusing. You really come out of the womb looking for absolute simple truths to guide by, and you spend the rest of your life learning that just staying alive is a compliment. (*MP* 60)

Being a Jewish Catholic is more than improbable, but while Kumin recalls the nuns filling her with "anxiety about [her] immortal soul" (*MP* 12), she also feels they represented "a terribly safe, highly idealized, asexual, and direct route to the kingdom of heaven" (*MP* 97), even for a child "born wrong for the convent games." Recording her affectionate memories in "Mother Rosarine," she transforms the nuns into benign animals, "like rows of cows in their stanchions / softly mooing . . . making the sound of prayer." The child in the poem overhears them as she slips through the convent at sunset, having stolen a rosary: "The seeds grew wet in my palm. Going down, / clicking the blessings I made my own / and testing the treads for creaks, I could hear / Mother Rosarine's voice turn the churn downstairs" (*TP* 13).

The figurative representation of nuns as cows is significant because it places them wholly within Kumin's world, complimenting them in the best way she knows how. Speaking of animals in her work and life, Kumin refers to them as her "confederates" and explains, in terms reminiscent of Whitman, "They arrive, sometimes with speaking parts, in my dreams. They are rudimentary and untiring and changeless, where we are sophisticated, weary, fickle. They make me better than I am" (*ID* 168). By sharing in this bestial nobility, the nuns are elevated rather than denigrated. Moreover, their offices of prayer are transformed into something Kumin can more readily understand, just as the rosary is put to her own purposes when the child appropriates the blessings.

Perhaps because of her early exposure to two very different religions, Kumin often ponders the nature of religious faith and belief. Among the best of her poems on the subject is "To Swim, To Believe," offered here in its entirety:

The beautiful excess of Jesus on the waters
is with me now in the Boles Natatorium.
This bud of me exults, giving witness:

these flippers that rose up to be arms.
These strings drawn to be fingers.
Legs plumped to make my useful fork.

Each time I tear this seam to enter,
all that I carry is taken from me,
shucked in the dive.
Lovers, children, even words go under.
Matters of dogma spin off in the freestyle
earning that mid-pool spurt, like faith.

Where have I come from? Where am I going?
What do I translate, gliding back and forth
erasing my own stitch marks in this lane?

Christ on the lake was not thinking
where the next heel-toe went.
God did him a dangerous favor

whereas Peter, the thinker, sank.

The secret is in the relenting,
the partnership. I let my body work

accepting the dangerous favor
from this king-size pool of waters.
Together I am supplicant. I am bride.
                    (*HBFG* 31–32)

Built on Christian imagery, this poem discloses a secret—"the relenting,"
which is as good a definition of faith as one could hope for. Entering the
water becomes an entry into the womb where the speaker is only a bud with
flippers and strings instead of arms and fingers. To dive is to give up the
self and its burdens, to erase the individual identity and abandon existen-
tial questions by not thinking, as Christ must have done when he stepped
onto the surface of the water. To become entangled in the mechanics of
the process is to go under. Better to accept "the dangerous favor" of relin-
quishment and be sustained.

Of course, Kumin is not walking on water but swimming through it,
held in her characteristic poise between two elements. She is not an ortho-
dox believer but fashions her own blessing in the moment of effort that
upholds and releases her. Significantly, no mention is made of the spirit or
soul. Rather, it is the body working, without the intervention of too much
thought, that elevates her to the spiritual position of supplicant and bride.

An earlier poem, "Morning Swim," captures a similar experience in its concluding lines:

> My bones drank water; water fell
> Through all my doors. I was the well
>
> That fed the lake that met my sea
> In which I sang *Abide With Me*.
> (*TP* in *GT* 191)

The movement is circular, with the self as source and destination, a focus the hymn title also implies. Releasing the body from the mind's intervention permits an interior freedom, a liberty at once contained and unrestrained. The result is a moment of illumination seemingly attained by the body. Religious mystics have characteristically arrived at such perceptions of unity by abjuring the body and elevating the spirit, but Kumin believes foremost in the reality of the physical world. Sensing an immanence, an indwelling meaning in the world and in her own life, she fashions for herself the belief of a nonbeliever.

This paradox is played out even more fully in "Young Nun at Bread Loaf," which describes a mushrooming expedition with Sister Elizabeth Michael, characterized by Kumin as "the youngest nun I have ever known." After finding enough chanterelles to fill their basket, they return to the conference campus:

> Hiking back in an unction of our own sweat
> she brings up Christ. Christ, that canard!
> I grind out a butt and think of the waiting bourbon.
> The sun goes down in disappointment.
> You can say what you want, she says.
> You live as if you believe.
>
> Sister
> Sister Elizabeth Michael
> says we are doing Christ's work, we two.
> She, the rosy girl in a Renoir painting.
> I, an old Jew.
> (*HBFG* 68-69)

Smoking and wishing for her glass of bourbon, Kumin regards herself as anything but devout. Still, she doesn't seem dissatisfied with the young nun's assertion that she lives as if she believes. Because the context shared by the young believer and the older teacher is the double world of nature and writing, Sister Elizabeth Michael's remark must be seen as a reference to both. Kumin herself has said, "Without religious faith and without the sense of primal certitude that faith brings, I must take my only comfort from the natural order of things" (*ID* 162). Calling herself an agnostic, she remarks, "I do not really have any faith, any coherent religious faith, and yet the one thing in my life that I feel passionate and evangelical about is poetry" (*MP* 42).

Judging from Kumin's observations about the creative process, we may conclude that Sister Elizabeth Michael is right. Speaking of the "aura that overtakes you, that forces you to write," Kumin says, "I suppose, in a sense, it's in the nature of a religious experience. It must be the same kind of feeling of being shriven that you would have if you were a true believer and you took communion. You feel, to that degree, reborn. Well, ideally, that's what writing a poem does" (*MP* 23). The difference between the "as if" of belief and true belief becomes difficult to distinguish when Kumin refers to words as "holy," saying, "The only sanctity really, for me, is the sanctity of language" (*MP* 25), and proclaims, "Yes, I regard the act of writing in part as an act of worship" (*MP* 57). Clearly, the creation of poetry affords her perceptions unavailable through any means other than religious devotion.

Without question, we can find in Kumin's work a great longing to believe, expressed in poems such as "Body and Soul: A Meditation," wherein her pragmatic mind measures her desire and finds it wanting, in both senses of the word. Addressing her body, she ponders aloud the existence of the soul. Nothing in her literal experience, including a fifth-grade tour of "the Walk-Through Woman," has shown her evidence of its presence, although she speculates that she may have missed it in the lower extremities, as "[t]he Walk-Through Woman ceased / shortly below the waist. / Her genitals were off limits" (*RS* 44). The poem's whimsical tone betrays an uneasiness about the very speculation Kumin is undertaking, suggesting it is foolish to ponder the soul's existence. Concluding the poem, however, she drops her bravado and lets her true feelings show:

> Body, Old Paint, Old Partner
> in this sedate roundup we ride,
> going up the Mountain in
> the meander of our middle age
> after the same old cracked tablets,
> though soul and we touch tongue,
>
> somehow it seems less sure;
> somehow it seems we've come
> too far to get us there.
>
> (*RS* 45)

Speaking to her body as if it were a horse, Kumin identifies with the animal who elsewhere carries her beyond herself. Having turned inward, however, she is lost in her own version of the Walk-Through Woman, and the voice riding her is her conscious mind. Significantly, while this is a poem of doubt, the search is far from over, as the word "seems," ringing its keen bell twice in the last three lines, indicates. No surprise, then, that we find Kumin in a recent poem sounding more hopeful:

> We eulogize autumn, we long
> for a better world, we seek to deliver
> a purer hemidemisemiquaver,
> the one brief note that says we mean,
> roughshod and winged, to last forever.
> (*Looking for Luck* 58)

The plodding horse of a body has given way to one that is "roughshod and winged," better equipped for the mountainous climb. The "one brief note" refers to the mockingbirds in the poem, but it also represents the poet's effort to make an enduring song, to find, by singing, a passage beyond autumn. Speaking of her ongoing search, Kumin says, "I keep writing about the lowercase soul as though it were an actual organ in the body for which I'm looking. That tickles my imagination. It amuses me intellectually at the same time that it expresses a real driving need" (*MP* 62).

The curious effect of Kumin's avowed agnosticism is its invigorating power. When she grapples with matters of belief and the soul, even though she resolves none of her own doubts in any final way, she projects an odd assurance. Unbelief seems as impossible as belief, and when Kumin stands between these two impossibilities she sparks more light than a dozen ecstatic poets. Hers is the voice of doubtful hope or hopeful doubt, a human voice uttering its truest yearnings. Located at the point of greatest potential, she dissipates neither option by choosing but stands between them, conducting power.

Such liminal moments abound in Kumin's work, sometimes taking on the surreality of dreamscapes. Kumin professes "a lot of reverence for what goes on at the dream level in the unconscious—those symbolic events" (*MP* 22). Dreams, too, are midway places, from which poetry and her own peculiar vision arise. Among the most interesting are the dream poems including animals, as they often do, and one of the best is "Amanda Dreams She Has Died and Gone to the Elysian Fields":

> This morning Amanda
> lies down during breakfast.

The hay is hip high.
The sun sleeps on her back
as it did on the spine
of the dinosaur
the fossil bat
the first fish with feet
she was once.
A breeze fans
the deerflies from lighting.
Only a gaggle of gnats
housekeeps in her ears.
A hay plume sticks out of her mouth.

I come calling with a carrot
from which I have taken
the first bite.
She startles
she considers rising
but retracts the pistons
of her legs and accepts
as loose-lipped as a camel.

We sit together.
In this time and place
we are heart and bone.
For an hour
we are incorruptible.

(*HBFG* 88–89)

Hidden here is a variation of the story of Eden. This time, the fruit is a vegetable, bitten first by the human and then offered to the horse as an act of communion. Through this sharing, the human visitor is permitted for an hour a sense of union with Amanda, an incorruptible Edenic moment of wholeness. Characteristically for Kumin, however, the merging is one of "heart and bone" rather than spirit. Bound still to time and place, horse and human partake of a kindred knowledge—breathing the air, feeling the sunlight, the two of them beautifully mortal in a garden already fallen.

In her 1992 book, *Looking for Luck*, Kumin begins with a poem titled "Credo," in which she celebrates "the grace of animals / in my keeping, the thrust to go on." The physicality of the word *thrust* indicates how strenuous and demanding Kumin's vision and art must be for her, especially as she cannot found them on "trust," the word one might expect to find in such a statement made by almost anyone else. Because she does not place her faith in a transcendent power, her life and craft depend upon her sustained effort to maintain a poise between opposites. Walking the top of the dividing wall, she knows balance depends on forward momentum, on the "thrust" that carries and upholds her.

In a poem titled "The Rendezvous," Kumin shows how much thrust she still has, as she consolidates many of her old themes and reconstitutes them in the form of a fable borrowed partly from Native American legends of human/animal transformations:

> How narrow the bear trail
> through the forest,
> one paw print following
> the other in the manner
> of good King Wenceslas
> tagged by his faithful serf.
>
> How, according to the legend,
> a bear is able to feel shame
> and if a woman meets a male bear
> she should take off all her clothes,
> thereby causing him
> to run away.
>
> How I meet a male bear.
> How I am careful not
> to insult him. I unbutton
> my blouse. He takes out
> his teeth. I slip off
> my skirt. He turns
> his back and works his way
> out of his pelt,
> which he casts to the ground
> for a rug.
>
> He smells of honey
> and garlic. I am wet
> with human fear. How
> can he run away, unfurred?
> How can I, without my clothes?
>
> How we prepare a new legend.
> (*LL* 91–92)

Dreamlike in content, this poem discovers in legend and folklore another threshold between the human and animal worlds. Through their encounter, woman and bear move nearer to one another, one becoming more animal-like by shedding her human clothing, the other becoming more human by dispensing with his bestial teeth and fur. At poem's end, they stand in stalemate, unable to run away and yet not quite certain how to accommodate one another. Their mutual unclothing suggests a sexual consummation, and the poem's last line teases us with that possibility. Nonetheless, we are taken no farther than an awkward precoital stance, the woman wet with fear, the bear peeled down to a fragrance of honey and garlic. Everything is potential, and we turn from the poem as from a dream, with nothing finally consummated but with all the possibilities intact.

One of the things desired of such human/animal contact is communication, and Kumin has begun in recent poems to wish for a shared language. In "Nurture," the title poem of her 1989 collection, she admits to suffering what "the critic proclaims, / . . . an overabundance of maternal genes," a condition that leads her to take in the "fallen fledgling," the "bummer lamb," "the abused, the starvelings." Acknowledging her need to nurture, she imagines herself susceptible to "a wild child" of the kind described in nineteenth-century accounts—"*filthy and fierce as a ferret*." Taking him into her home, she would construct with him a language "from sign, / scratch, grimace, grunt, vowel: // Laughter our first noun, and our long verb, howl" (*Nurture* 3).

Similarly, in "The Word," a poem in her forthcoming collection, *Connecting the Dots*, Kumin longs for the language of the doe she and her horse flush from cover. Pleading with the animal to return, Kumin presents her credentials as one who has earned the trust of the birds she feeds and even of "the vixen in the bottom meadow," who permits her to overhear the command she gives her young to send them running for their burrow and then call them out again:

> Its sound is o-shaped and unencumbered,
> the see-through color of river,
> airy as the topmost evergreen fingers
> and soft as pine duff underfoot
> where the doe lies down out of sight;
> take me in, tell me the word.
>
> (*CD* 38)

No longer content with nonverbal moments of communion, like the one with drowsy Amanda, Kumin is actively seeking a mutual tongue. Should she find it, of course, the barrier would presumably fall, and human and animal would enter a new age—or perhaps an old age, as it is described in the fairy-tale narrative of "Déjà Vu," where the "bear-prince" waits in a blackberry patch to encounter his human lover, and "What will be already has been" (*CD* 42).

Perhaps without realizing it, Kumin has possessed the secret word all along. Formed of intent, it is heard as a scent understood by the fox, who does not fear her, by the birds who transform her into a tree, and by the horses bending to breathe in her human breath, knowing her for the person she is. The language she wants is the one she already has, informed by trust and mutual acceptance. Kumin's tongue utters only honest statements, things we sometimes might prefer not to hear, as when she advocates for the endangered manatee by suggesting we serve the last ones up as steak marinara and thereby "stop pretending we need them / more than they need us" (*N* 9). Modestly proposing that our best intentions sometimes produce devastating results, Kumin reminds us of the world's connectedness, how one thing depends upon another, how the world needs its opposites, arctic foxes and Aleutian geese, one preying upon the other but sharing a balance unperceived until it is disrupted by human intervention.

Kumin has clung to her own opposites when it might have been easier to sign on with the confessionalists or enlist in a polemic cause. Practicing her own version of formalism and advancing her personal concept of what it means to be a female poet, she has removed herself from the crowd and done her best to contribute to the well-being of poetry, as she once said she hoped to do. The reader turns to her work for its honest, striving human voice, which celebrates the living/dying moment in its fullest potential. Arising from her is a compassionate vision of the world she generously shares each time she climbs into her adaptable saddle and rides, not transcending life but revealing to us its immanent wonder in the revelatory instant of the now.

Making the Connection: The Nature Poetry of Maxine Kumin

I

> Our genes declare themselves.
> —"The Knot," *Our Ground Time Here Will Be Brief*

Which of her poetic peers does Maxine Kumin resemble? Unlike Sylvia Plath and Anne Sexton, she keeps her demons bridled. Unlike Elizabeth Bishop or May Swenson, who remained cautiously reticent in the work they published during their lifetimes, she can be intimately and even bawdily personal. Like Adrienne Rich, she makes us pay respectful attention to images of strong female identity, to issues of family life, and to questions about our relationship to the earth, yet she avoids the systematically ideological. The yoke of her tutorials is light, glinting with humor and rue.

Perhaps the gender wars should leave us all feeling like the walking wounded, but Kumin seems to be—dare one say it?—comfortably heterosexual. It may well be that Western civilization stands in crisis, shortly to be doomed. The animals are going under as well, species by species, occasionally with the help of well-meaning human intervention. But Kumin avoids the apocalyptic mode. True enough, as the title poem of her 1982 volume of new and selected poems reminds us in an extended conceit on airports and life spans, "our ground time here will be brief." But Kumin prefers to speak directly of our personal and common mortality and only obliquely of humanity's potential to destroy and self-destruct. So, for instance, in "Getting Through," after a lyric opening in which "the calendar of bad news" is covered over by "snow lucid, / snow surprising, snow bees . . . an elegiac snow of whitest jade" (*The Long Approach* 57–58):

> Even if the world is ending
> you can tell it's February
> by the architecture of the pastures.

Snow falls on the pregnant mares,
is followed by a thaw, and then
refreezes so that everywhere
their hill upheaves into a glass mountain.

Truth is being defeated, as it were, by beauty. Thanks to the blizzard, with
the phone dead and the mail and newspapers undelivered, "Bombs and gre-
nades, the newly disappeared . . . go unrecorded," while the foals

flutter inside
warm wet bags that carry them
eleven months in the dark
. . . .
If there's an April
in the last frail snow of April
they will knock hard to be born.

To be "in the dark" of prebirth parallels human ignorance about political
terror. The two conditions are equally temporary, but the poem chooses to
conclude with the probability of birth, an image of hope shadowed by the
conditional "if" and by the "frail snow" that obliquely signals the frailty of
all life. The close of "Getting Through" is like a pragmatic farm woman's
version of Shelley's Armageddon-like "trumpet of a prophecy . . . If win-
ter comes, can spring be far behind?" When you live with the weather of
New England, neither winter nor spring stands for finality, and the small
births can be allowed to balance the large deaths—though one must always
hedge one's bets. Again, in "The Green Well" (*Looking for Luck* 32–33), the
daily trip to

a kitchen midden
where the newly dead layer by layer
overtake the long and longer vanished

evokes memories of a dead mare ("After the lethal phenobarb, the vet / ex-
changed my check for his handkerchief") and a dead friend whose suicide
still burns like betrayal. From and through such losses, life continues:

The cats clean themselves after the kill.
A hapless swallow lays another clutch
of eggs in the accessible nest. It does
not end with us, not yet, though end it will.

"We go on" is a phrase Kumin has used more than once. Sanity, notwith-
standing tragedy, is her way. It is the way of someone rooted in a chosen
set of routines and responsibilities. Kumin differs from other feminists in
her capacity to locate strength in normality. And is there another feminist

poet who finds or invents such a sweet male alter ego, a bit like and a bit unlike herself, highlighting continuities and distinctions across gender and other boundaries?

Henry Manley, the country neighbor who is one of several recurring figures in Kumin's poems, could be the most endearing animus in the business. "Last fall he dug a hole and moved his privy / and a year ago in April reamed his well out," though in his dotage. Having had a phone installed, he tramps two New England miles, "shy as a girl," to ask the poet if she'd be so kind as to call him one day. Stricken with aphasia, Manley is "as loose in his skin as a puppy" and frightened after dark. But at dawn,

> he gets up, grateful once more
> for how coffee smells. Sits stiff
> at the bruised porcelain table
> saying them over, able
> to with only the slightest catch.
> Coffee. Coffee cup. Watch.
> (*RS* in *GT* 57)

Typical of Maxine Kumin's art are the sensory weight, the play of alliteration and assonance sliding into the closing couplets, the perfectly expressive halting and crystallizing rhythms. In another poem, Henry breaks his hip, is taken in by neighbors, enjoys his new role of story-telling sage. When he goes on crutches to see his old collapsing house, presently occupied by porcupines, he says, "You can't look back."

Mirroring his creator, Henry Manley is a capable countryperson of multiple skills. He will die before the poet does and is one of her many means of studying mortality. Like the unnamed "hermit" of *Up Country*, Henry is no macho type but a relatively feminized male whose old age makes him charmingly unthreatening. He is also, however, what the poet is not, or can be only through him: an *isolé*. He is alone, not looking back. In this respect his masculinity governs. For her, not looking back would be intolerable. What drives her poetry, slamming the accelerator to the floor, is attachment. If she had her way, no loved (or hated) human or animal would die unremembered. What Kumin calls her "tribal poems," poems on family, have always formed the core of her work. The longer she writes, the more inclusive her conception of family grows. Father, mother, brothers, husband, daughters and son, great-grandfather, uncles—they are only the beginning.

"Sperm," a tragicomic celebration of seventeen look-alike cousins,

> O Grandfather, look what your seed has done!
> Look what has come of those winter night gallops.

> You tucking the little wife up
> under the comforter that always leaked feathers.
> You coming perhaps just as the trolley
> derailed taking the corner at 15th Street
> in a shower of blue sparks.
>
> *(GT 96)*

typifies Kumin's insistence that family is both biological and social phenomenon. Biology may not be destiny, but it is reality, generating "chromosomes tight as a chain gang." A sequence of poems on a beloved dying brother offers that insistence another way. In "The Incest Dream," shortly before the expected death, a grieving hangman brings the brother's severed penis, "pressed as faithfully / as a wild flower" for the poet to keep "and lie back down in my lucky shame" (*GT* 27). When the brother has died, "Retrospect in the Kitchen" describes the forty pounds of plums harvested from his tree and brought three thousand miles to preserve. The making of preserves is a recurring metaphor, in these poems and in Kumin's essays, for what the poet wants to do with the world at large. Other tricks also work. People fade, but animals "retrieve" them, as the title poem of *The Retrieval System* explains. Ponies begging for apples equal two elderly aunts; a boy buried at sea reappears in a yearling's gallop; splitting logs at the woodpile simultaneously releases the soul of the beech and recalls the soul of the lost friend, Anne Sexton.

Children, especially daughters, keep cropping up, growing as they go, from Kumin's earliest work to her most recent. Though the poems commonly explore the delicate process of releasing the young ones into their own lives, "our genes declare themselves" (*GT* 109) in passionate attachment. Children have lately been joined by grandchildren, newborns with whom "[b]ody to body my monkey-wit soaks through" (*LA* 13). Notice how in both these quotes biology is metaphorically associated with intelligence and expression, in tacit defiance of nature-culture dualisms. The maternal voice, once virtually nonexistent in poetry, has become in the past few decades one of the most significant products of the women's literary renaissance, and no poet writes more intelligently of mother-child relations. Or for that matter, of animal-human relations, since her maternal attachment and attention extend to the forms and gestures, the detailed lives and deaths of mice, turtles, frogs, goats, beavers, cows and calves, sheep and lambs, bears, toads, dogs and kittens, interdependent sloths and moths, and—most powerfully—horses.

Creatures gravitate toward Kumin, or she does to them; she tells their tales like family anecdotes; she anticipates their doom. At times, as in

"Woodchucks," "How It Goes On," or "Taking the Lambs to Market," she is their doom's guilty agent. "The Vealers" invokes the single day when newborn calves may root and suckle, their ten weeks' mechanical feeding, "never enough to set them loose / from that birthday dividend / of touch," and their handing over to the knacker, whence they will emerge "wrapped and labelled in a plastic sheet, / their perfect flesh unstreaked with blood / or muscle, and we will eat" (*NF* in *GT* 163-64). At other times, as in "Thinking of Death and Dogfood" or "A Mortal Day with No Surprises," she contemplates the uses of horseflesh and her own potential "to sweeten the crop / when the clock-hands stop" (*HBFG* in *GT* 139) and wishes her mare and herself good endings. Yet again, she is midwife of foals, milker of cows, feeder of birds, mucker-out of barns, maker of hay, grower of vegetables.

Vegetables as well as animals, in Kumin's writing, receive affectionately graphic attention. Pea plants "saying castanets, saying dance with me, / saying do me, dangle their intricate / nuggety scrota" (*GT* 11). A final purple cabbage in the garden is "big as a baby's head, big as my grandson's brain" (*LA* 78). "Darlings, it's all a circle," she explains in "Family Reunion" (*GT* 18), and those she addresses might be plants, beasts, or human kin. Thoreau, whom Kumin often cites, would commend her honesty, the precision of her language, her adhesion to the rituals of farm life, and her occasional moral allegory. The practical thumb more than the theoretical hymn of American nature worship is what molds her writing, as it did his.

Whether Thoreau would approve the emotional and sexual attachments that for her are inseparable from her attachment to nature is another matter. An amusing swerve from Thoreau occurs in "Beans," a poem in *Up Country* not later reprinted. Recalling Henry David's boast of "making the earth say beans instead of grass," Kumin addresses a lover who keeps her weeds down and makes her say beans at his touch. The bachelor Henry David would likely not have been pleased by a woman claiming for herself the latent sexuality of that metaphor. And this brings me to the question of Kumin's uniqueness as a poet in her chosen field—her chosen landscape, I should say, of fields, woods, barn, farmhouse, pond, garden—in which nature by being semidomesticated becomes something new and interesting in the history of poetry.

II

> nor is it one thing to save animals
> and people another
> but seamless
> — "Caring: A Dream,"
>   *The Long Approach*

Suppose we place Kumin in the general category of "nature poets" or see her work as belonging to a long tradition of pastoral or bucolic poetry that began with Hesiod and Theocritus in Greek, Virgil and Horace perhaps in Latin. That tradition explodes in the English Renaissance with the tremendously influential poetry of Sir Philip Sidney and Edmund Spenser, includes lyricsts like Campion, Herrick, and Marvell, reaches a romantic climax with Wordsworth, Shelley, and Keats, and flickers on through the Victorians as a sort of remembrance of things past in Tennyson, Arnold, and Hardy. Nature in this richly accretive tradition at times is presented realistically; Hesiod's *Works and Days* offers a versified farmer's almanac-cum-agricultural manual, gritty with the sweat of experienced manual labor. Virgil's *Georgics* describe, albeit from a refined distance, actual practices of farming, fishing, horse rearing, and beekeeping in first-century Rome.

More often, the natural world represents an idealized innocence of amorous or tuneful shepherds and shepherdesses, simple villagers, inspiring landscapes, mythically charged sublimities, rural retreats. The wild, the free, the spontaneous, the untamable, the refreshingly uncorrupted: Shelley's liberating west wind and the "unpremeditated art" of his skylark. Keats's nightingales, his bowers, his zephyrs. Radiating through the sublime and the beautiful are death and decay, as nature's cycles provide the inevitable setting for elegy. Milton's "Lycidas," Shelley's "Adonais," Tennyson's "In Memoriam" are among the loftier monuments of English poetry; Hopkins's "To Margaret" and Dylan Thomas's "Refusal to Mourn the Death, by Fire, of a Child in London," among the most haunting.

In America there scarcely seems a nineteenth-century poet who *doesn't* write nature poetry. Thanks to the frontier, with a little help from Whitman, America *is* Nature, as opposed to the wicked Old World, which is Culture. And among twentieth-century poets, we have an extraordinary number who not only write about nature but live in/on it and in a variety of ways feel called upon to defend it. Think of Frost, Jeffers, Robert Penn Warren, Theodore Roethke, A. R. Ammons, Robert Bly, Gary Snyder, Donald Hall, W. S. Merwin, and Wendell Berry, to name a few.

The astute reader will have noticed that the above grouping includes no women. In fact, Kumin is among a handful of women poets for whom observation and advocacy of nature are primary activities—notably herself, May Swenson, Mary Oliver. Why is this? Women and nature, according to certain tenacious cultural habits, at least in the West, tend to be confused with one another. That is to say, in the languages of literature, philosophy, and psychology (and sometimes science), nature is construed as female and females construed as natural, therefore wild, therefore dangerous as well as desirable, requiring conquest and control. From the Greeks to the Enlightenment and beyond, the ooze of femaleness lurks and laps at the borders of male rationality, threatening rot and decay. A female chaos waits to devour a male order. "There's hell, there's darkness, there's the sulphurous pit," cries King Lear, thinking of women's nether parts, "burning, scalding, stench, consumption, fie, fie, fie"—just as T. S. Eliot in an excised passage of "The Waste Land" invokes "the hearty female stench."

Within Western religious discourse, from Eve to the Whore of Babylon, natural women mythically represent the aggressive and vile sexuality of an immanent Mother Nature requiring to be subdued by a transcendent Father God. The anthropologist Sherry Ortner observes that "Woman is to Nature as Man is to Culture" in numerous societies both primitive and advanced.[1] Susan Griffin's exhaustive and brilliant *Woman and Nature: The Roaring Inside Her* pursues the analogy's encoding of power and oppression according to which males, like deities, ought to act, think, judge, speak, stare, control, possess.[2] Females, and nature, had better be acted upon, judged, spoken about, stared at, controlled, owned—or, of course, all hell breaks loose. Languages of authority, from mathematics to poetics, are masculine, the theorists tell us, while maternal language remains a set of meaningless murmurs. Man declaims, Nature is silent.

Margaret Homans speculates that the identification of women with objectified nature in men's poems was a serious obstacle to the nineteenth-century woman poet.[3] If, for the purposes of poetic tradition, one *is* nature and ought to hold still (like a violet by a mossy stone) and be described, then how is it possible to write *about* nature? The problem defeated Dorothy Wordsworth and partly defeated Emily Brontë, according to Homans; Dickinson just barely conquered it through an art of intense paradox and doubleness in which nothing means what it says. Homans's theory, with its reliance on a Lacanian paradigm in which the "symbolic order" of language depends on rejection of nature and femaleness, has always seemed to me exaggerated; but how are we to explain the paucity of female nature poets? Is it not significant that Marianne Moore's elaborate fauna, for example, are so much more textual than actual?

Kumin's solution—which is not to say that she consciously thinks of Homans's problem as a problem for herself—is to accept the identification of herself and/as nature and run, or rather gallop, with it while steadfastly refusing to recognize any order "higher" than nature or "beyond" nature or "outside" nature. A firmly secular poet, she does not mythologize the natural world—it does not stand for something other than itself—and with one exception, to which I will return later, she does not personify earth as mother. Nor does she mythologize language or culture, as if they were separable from physical reality. Particularizing rather than generalizing, she employs metaphor not to *elevate* but to *articulate* phenomena—in the double sense of expressing them clearly and showing their connections and conjunctions. In doing so, it seems to me, she tacitly dismantles the philosophical and psychological scaffolding upholding much of what we recognize as nature poetry and simply builds on another plot.

Most nature poetry actually inscribes man's alienation from nature. Court poets write pastorals; shepherds do not. What used to be called poetic diction may have been invented precisely for the purpose of distinguishing countrified matter from dignified manner. As Joseph Addison explains in the preface to Dryden's translation of Virgil's *Georgics*, the poet must carefully avoid "letting his subject debase his style. . . . [N]othing, which is a phrase or saying in common talk, should be admitted into a serious poem." Rather, he must clothe his theme "in the pleasantest dress that poetry can bestow upon it," with "metaphors, Grecisms, and circumlocutions, to give his verse the greater pomp, and preserve it from sinking into a plebeian style."[4] To the classicist, writing nature poetry is a class act, dependent on the privileging distance of aristocracy. To the romantic, who wants to avoid class privilege (or more likely, isn't born to it), nature poetry offers access to a mode of lament, a form of rebellion, and an always doomed attempt to return to a sacralized maternal unity that language and consciousness forbid.

When a disaffected Wordsworth complains that the world is too much with us—"little we see in nature that is ours"—nature's wildness is feminized as (among other images) "[t]his Sea that bares her bosom to the moon," and his longed-for self is appropriately infantilized in "Great God! I'd rather be / A Pagan suckled in a creed outworn." Wordsworth's most famous evocations of a nature that nurtures man's inner self—"Tintern Abbey," the Immortality Ode, the Lucy poems, *The Prelude*—recount the same fable of loss and resignation. Shelley's impassioned cries for union with the tumultuous natural energies of skylark, cloud, wind—"Be thou, Spirit fierce, / My spirit! Be thou me, impetuous one!"—apostrophize precisely what is beyond the reach of the feeble self. Keats pursues his death-defying nightingale to an imaginary eroticized landscape from which he inevitably and forlornly wakes.

Like their English cousins, the poets of the American Renaissance often seem peculiarly remote from the nature they contemplate. Emerson's transparent eyeball sees yet does not touch, and his natural world (commonly figured as maternal) is usually generalized to a transparency through which the Unitarian Oversoul manifests its disembodied glory. Emerson's postlapsarian New Englanders have already forfeited a proper relation to earth: "Hamatreya" mocks landlords who falsely claim to own the land; Earth laughs "at her boastful boys" and buries them. "Blight" complains that we invade nature "impiously for gain" and are "shut out" from it.[5]

Thoreau boasts that he makes the earth say beans, and he is surely as acute an observer of New England's physiognomy as God ever made. Yet one feels ever the shade of distinction between the naturalist's gaze and the object gazed at. "I am no more lonely than a single mullein or dandelion in a pasture, or a bean leaf, or sorrel, or a horse-fly, or a humble-bee," he claims. Nonetheless, to a crucial question Thoreau asks shortly thereafter in *Walden*, "Shall I not have intelligence with the earth? Am I not partly leaves and vegetable mould myself?" the answer is mysteriously negative: "Nature puts no question and answers none which we mortals ask." In the chapter "Higher Laws," Thoreau argues for outgrowing one's "slimy beastly life" of "animal" appetites; "Nature is hard to be overcome but she must be overcome."[6] Toward the close of *Walden*, Thoreau invokes a feminized nature of another sort, an elusive beloved whose attractiveness is somehow one with her cruelty:

At the same time that we are in earnest to explore and learn all things, we require that all things be mysterious and unexplorable, that land and sea be infinitely wild, unsurveyed and unfathomed by us because unfathomable. . . . I love to see that Nature is so rife with life that myriads can be afforded to be sacrificed and suffered to prey on one another; that tender organizations can be so serenely squashed out of existence like pulp,—tadpoles which herons gobble up, and tortoises and toads run over in the road; and that sometimes it has rained flesh and blood! (P. 318)

Nature as femme fatale appeals to Thoreau as Other, however, not as Self. Even Whitman views nature from without, as much as he participates in it. "I think I could turn and live with animals," he says, but the device is the familiar one of pastoral satire; the poet uses the appeal of animals ("they are so placid and so self-contained") to mock the folly of humans. Whitman finds he incorporates gneiss, considers the grass to be the flag of his disposition, and would far rather be outdoors than in a stuffy drawing room, but he does not say he is himself an animal. In the magnificent "Out of the Cradle Endlessly Rocking," the mourning bird and the maternal death-whispering sea are of an alien order from the boy who will be initiated by them into poetry. "When Lilacs Last in the Dooryard Bloomed" uses its natural images almost exactly as Milton and Shelley use theirs.

Among the twentieth-century poets, disinclined as they usually are to mythologize nature, Robert Frost can treat "putting in the seed" as something both agriculturally and humanly erotic and can represent himself as an active participant within a natural world in poems like "Mowing" and "After Apple-Picking." Yet most of the time one feels in Frost the tacit remoteness of the observer or controller of nature—a remoteness regretted, for example, in poems like "The Most of It," where nothing in the natural world returns a man's need for "counter-love, original response," or in "Never Again Would Birds' Song Be the Same," where an Adam attributes to Eve's voice the capacity to "influence" the birds—"And to do that to birds was why she came"—or "Neither Out Far Nor In Deep," where people "look at the sea" despite their inability to penetrate its essence. Similarly with poets like Ammons, Merwin, and Berry: however tenderly they love and mean to protect the world of nature, the habit of assuming that man is essentially differentiable from nature lingers.[7] Insofar as mythopoetic versions of nature haunt American poetry today, they are likely to perform the old gender functions. Williams goes from "Spring and All" (dazed virgin) to *Paterson* (blowsy female Park). We see Stevens's "Madame la Fleurie," at the close of a lifelong dichotomizing of Reality and the Imagination, swallowing her dead poet whose "crisp knowledge is devoured by her, beneath a dew":

> The black fugatos are strumming the blacknesses of black . . .
> The thick strings stutter the final gutturals.
> He does not lie there remembering the blue-jay, says the jay.
> His grief is that his mother should feed on him, himself and what he saw,
> In that distant chamber, a bearded queen, wicked in her dead light.[8]

Robert Bly's "The Teeth Mother Naked at Last" reaches as far back as Babylonian myth for an image of violence as quintessentially female. An important exception is Gary Snyder, whose adaptations of Native American and Buddhist perspectives enable him largely to shake the vertical standard whereby mind is superior to matter and spirit to nature. Not accidentally, I think Snyder shares with Kumin a penchant for particulars in his poems—how many Snyder poems there are with the exact place marked, the activity—and a mistrust of dualism in his philosophy. We need, Snyder says, "to look clearly into the eyes of the wild and see our self-hood, our family, there. . . . At the root of the problem where our civilization goes wrong," he continues, "is the mistaken belief that nature is something less than authentic, that nature is not as alive as man is, or as intelligent, that in a sense it is dead, and that animals are of so low an order of intelligence and feeling, we need not take their feelings into account."[9]

Even more than Snyder, Kumin does say she is an animal—or like one. She says it again and again. She says animals are like people too, using a colloquial and anecdotal mode that is the precise antithesis of the language recommended by John Dryden, avoiding the aura of myth and sacrament cultivated by the Romantics and some of the Moderns and avoiding as well their separation anxiety. When Kumin says these things, it feels perfectly normal and obvious, so one is a little startled to remember how rarely one finds parallel moments in other poets.

"June 15" is one of the entries in "Joppa Diary," Kumin's first sequence of poems based on her New Hampshire farm experience. It is typically anecdotal, but the unpretentious diction disguises a radical poetic agenda. I quote the poem in its entirety:

> On this day of errors
> a field mouse brings forth her young
> in my desk drawer.
>
> Come for a pencil,
> I see each one,
> a wet steel thimble pulled out of its case,
> begin to worm its way uphill
> to a pinhead teat.
>
> As if I were an enlarged owl
> made both gross and cruel,
> I lean closer.
>
> The mother rears and kills.
> Her forelegs loop like paper clips
> as she tears at her belly fur,
> shredding it fine as onion skin,
> biting the blind and voiceless nubbles off.
> Later, she runs past me.
> I see her mouth
> is stuffed full of a dead baby.
>
> (*GT* 207)

Technically, I think it is important to notice, in this apparently casual poem, the veiled internal and end rhymes (errors/drawer, pencil/steel thimble/uphill/owl/cruel/kills, loop/clips, me/see/baby), alliterations like "wet . . . worm," "biting the blind," the assonance of "mouse" at the opening with "mouth" at the close, and the startling effect of saving the human term "baby" for the very end. More interesting and less obvious is the poem's defining balance of literal and metaphoric—"realistic" and "literary" language—and the way it effectively balances the scales between viewer and viewed. The mouse begins as an actual mouse, although "brings forth her young" has a comfortably literary sound. Then the desk drawer images (wet steel thimble, pinhead, paper clips, onion skin) make semicomic play with the invasion of desk space by outdoor creature, while the parallel grotesque figure of poet as owl—standing for wisdom and also predation—traverses the boundary in the opposite direction. The last stanza drops metaphor completely. One remembers the Dickinson who observed that "Nature, like us, is sometimes seen / Without her diadem" and watched as a bird "bit an Angleworm in halves / And ate the fellow raw." The refusal of sentiment in the depiction of motherhood is central for Kumin, as is the unstated lesson that our own behavior may parallel that of other mammals; but notice too the refusal of weighty symbolism. The devouring mother is not glamorized enough to be a Devouring Mother.

I have already mentioned some of the "retrieval" poems in which animals wear the visages of lost kinfolk. The following is a representative sample of passages that make clear Kumin's crossing of species boundaries in a variety of moods. In a love poem, "we" are "two lukewarm frogs . . . our tongues at work in their tunnels / our shut eyes unimportant as freckles" (GT 157). In "Eyes," a woman's "grand / comedy of anguish" in front of a highball glass is like a sparrow in a hawk's hands, a monarch butterfly flailing in a gauze net (GT 134). In "The Summer of the Watergate Hearings," worms in Amanda's droppings are like the parasites falling out of the government on TV (GT 136). When the poet is tired, her arms "hang down simian style" (GT 110). Anger, in one of many poems limning the independence of children, "turns the son into a crow, / the daughter a porcupine" (GT 59). The poet off to teach a class on prosody, a colleague recording mockingbird imitations of cardinals, crows, and semis' airbrakes—and the birds themselves—are all working on "our single-minded imperfect song" (LL 58). Wild turkeys in a blizzard approach the farmhouse "like swimmers daring the deep end." April lambs keep the poet awake with "their separate baaings . . . all of us missing our mothers" (LA 67).

In a dream poem, "Making the Connection," the poet, falling asleep, hears an old dog's ghost arrive "on metal toenails," whimpering, soon to "howl in the prison of his deafness," reminding the dreamer of the dog's grim death.

> I sit up, breaking the connection,
> like hanging up on my brother.
>
> I am ten. I go down terrified
> past a houseful of bubbling breathers,
> unlatch the cellar door, go further
> down in darkness to lie on old carpet
> next to the incontinent puppy.
> His heartbeat, my heartbeat, comfort us . . .
>
> (GT 50)

This descent to the remembered "Brother Dog" parallels the descent in Adrienne Rich's "Diving into the Wreck" and concludes similarly with a dissolving of self into other. Women poets in quest of "the thing itself and not the myth" typically "go down" rather than surmount. The antiheroic gesture of memory and reunion subverts the male commandment to transcend. The connection is many connections: waking and dreaming, living and dying, adult and child selves, as well as human and animal siblings.

The specificity of Kumin's attachments so rarely gives way to any alternative poetic dimension of symbolism that it is worth noting one poem that comes close to personifying earth as mother—even as dangerous mother—if only to show how the poem deflects and perhaps even mocks its own Freudian paradigm. "Mud" begins by evoking a chthonic female whose simultaneous sucking and pouring threatens to overwhelm and uncreate her own cosmos:

> You would think that the little birches
> would die of that brown mouth sucking
> and sucking their root ends.
> The rain runs yellow.
> The mother pumps in, pumps in
> more than she can swallow.
> All of her pockmarks spill over.
> The least footfall
> brings up rich swill.
>
> The streams grow sick with their tidbits.
> The trout turn up their long bellies.
>
> (GT 154)

All sensuousness, no mind, heavily contrasted with the human world (which "would think"), this excessively mucky maternal mouth and surface closely resembles Thoreau's "slimy beastly" appetites and the happily destructive Nature who "must be overcome," or Stevens's "bearded queen." A long array of formless maternal monsters in English literature, including Spenser's Error and Milton's Sin, similarly gorge and spew their own substance.[10] But by the end of Kumin's "Mud," after the evocation of slugs, of "an army of lips . . . in its own ocean" and of boulders giving birth to rocks, something different happens:

> Meanwhile the mother is sucking.
> Pods will startle apart,
> pellets be seized with a fever
> and as the dark gruel thickens,
> life will stick up a finger.

The surprise is that the blind, formless maternal soup, thickening like a plot, yields form, consciousness and differentiation. The "finger" is admonitory, mocking, and wicked all at once. As with all Kumin's representations of offspring, the newborn does and does not belong to its source. Is earth here a phallic mom? If so, it is but to amuse and not to frighten. Like many another irrational fantasy, facing it dispels the fear.

III

> My job is metaphor.
> —"Lines Written in the Library of Congress,"
> *Our Ground Time Here Will Be Brief*

   Disinclined to the egoistic posturing we expect of the artist, Kumin has published few poems about art. One of those few, "*Ars Poetica*: A Found Poem," does not mention poetry but describes the retraining of a problem horse:

> I'd go in on my hands
> and knees and crawl over to him so that
> I wouldn't appear so threatening. It took
> six or eight months before I could simply walk in
> and sit with him, but I needed that kind of trust.
>
> I kept him on a long rein to encourage him
> to stretch out his neck and back. I danced with him
> over ten or fifteen acres of fields with a lot
> of flowing from one transition to another.
>
> (*LL* 24)

By implication, the poem is itself a wild creature whom loving patience makes orderly without loss of spirit and energy. As one need not "break" a horse to tame him—and I gather this is the current theory, which is making headway even among cowboys—so one can get a poem to cooperate and show its best stuff by putting it on a long lead (not the same as no lead at all). It is an interesting view of poetry that I haven't seen elsewhere. In another, the poet gently rebukes Georgia O'Keeffe for writing "*I have no theories to offer*" and then withdrawing to

> the disembodied
> third-person singular: *One works,*
> *I suppose, because it is the most*
> *interesting thing one knows to do.*
> (*Nurture* 49)

"Syntax," claims Kumin, "like sex, is intimate," so she urges the shy artist to "come out, stand up, be heard!" (*N* 49) Called "A Calling," this poem combines and enacts a view of poetry as vocation and one of forthright communication.

Both these poems are remarkable for absence of pretension, as are "Marianne, My Mother, and Me" (*N* 41-46) and "A Brief History of Passion" (*LL* 71-73), in which the poet's attachment to artists like Marianne Moore, Katherine Mansfield and Middleton Murray, D. H. Lawrence and Frieda, Rilke and his mistress is paired with the attachment to her unexceptional parents—especially the mother who gave up the piano for bourgeois family life. It is as if the poet refuses, against the rules, to honor art above family.

Having written this last sentence, I catch myself. What are these rules, who makes them, and who profits by them? Why should we continue to support the assumption of art's transcendent superiority to our biological affiliations? If what family means is permanent, lifelong, inescapable entanglement in the most ancient and intractable emotions we possess, it also means an inescapable simultaneity of presence and absence, likeness and difference. The fact is, it requires artistry to convey what family signifies in our lives.

Three characteristics of Kumin's style especially promote its familial content. One is a line that moves inconspicuously between three and five feet, rhyming some portion of the time, somewhere between heavy and light. Supporting this is the voice's slightly jocular, conversational tone, a few shades more informal than Frost's. It would be difficult to play dominance games using this voice, and part of Kumin's intention is to dismantle the old hierarchical models of family, as well as the old hieratic model of the poet. Most important is the device of the metaphor, especially as it attaches to her otherwise literalizing bent.

A number of postmodern critics have suggested that metaphor is dead. Like the death of the author, the death of "the unified subject," the death of the novel, the death of the lyric (and so on), metaphor's supposed demise speaks to a conviction that the shared literary culture of the past is irretrievably oppressive and that unless one ruptures its habitual forms, one is invariably trapped. "Language" poets operating on that assumption seem to replace metaphor with metonymy as a means of leveling, as it were, the verbal playing field. Making sure that no term swallows another or blurs another's integrity is a sort of linguistic enforcement of democracy. One word, one vote. An unlimited potential set of words, none superior to another (and no subordinate clauses either), is one mark of avant-garde poetics today.[11] Suspicion of metaphor's power to "distort" rational discourse has been a recurrent feature of rationalist philosophies from Bacon and Locke to Wittgenstein, but only recently have poets themselves rejected the defining feature of poetic language.

Such cleaning up of slates could make sense if metaphors were always binary objects composed of clear-cut tenors and vehicles, or if metaphors were always ornamental. They are not, and it seems to me that a poetics that denies metaphor must also deny (and commonly does) the facts of relationship. Aristotle argues in the *Poetics* (1458B) that "the greatest thing by far is to be a master of metaphor. It is the one thing that cannot be learnt from others; and it is also a sign of genius, since a good metaphor implies an intuitive perception of the similarity in dissimilars." A literature that hopes to discourage such perception would disparage metaphor as well.

Kumin's profusely metaphoric style is her primary means of conveying relation and the ambiguity of relation. Desire is the topic here. In her tribal poems an ethos of combined sameness/difference, attachment/release governs personal relationships. The same principles govern her treatment of nature; that is, she represents human beings (chiefly herself) as both alike and different from, attached to and detached from, the richly depicted world of animals and plants. In each specific case, life is cyclic, necessarily loved, necessarily lost. Metaphor tacitly underlines this sense of human connection and separation—what Kumin in a tribute to a long marriage calls "our working distance." (*N* 61) As a figure of speech, metaphor depends precisely on the assertion of likeness in difference. Further, the implication of identity in metaphor, which we as readers must simultaneously accept and reject if any metaphor is to "work," is a figure of desire and of the recognition that desire both succeeds and fails. We (the poet, the readers) want a sense of connection to each other and the world. Metaphor helps us understand that we can and cannot have it. Metaphor bridges gaps of categorical difference while drawing our attention to them. What it carries is a density of information, along with pleasure and pain—pleasure, I would say, overriding pain.

The reader of this essay may look back over its quotations, or look anywhere in Kumin's poetry, to observe metaphor's multiple functions. For a final example, consider these lines about horses from the opening poem in *Looking for Luck*, "Credo:"

> I trust them to run from me, necks arched in a full
> swan's S, tails cocked up over their backs
> like plumes on a Cavalier's hat. I trust them
> to gallop back, skid to a stop, their nostrils
>
> level with my mouth, asking for my human breath
> that they may test its intent, taste the smell of it.
> (P. 15)

Without the association of the horses' beauty with nobility and artifice, without the linking of involuntary physicality (breath, taste, smell) with the "higher" faculty of intention, without the quiet assumption that horses can "ask" with their nostrils as normally as we do with our voices, we would have less information and less of a poem. Certainly we would have less pleasure.

At the end of "Credo," Kumin says she believes in herself as the animals' sanctuary and the earth as hers. A sanctuary is a safe but also an archaically and metaphorically holy location. Etymology here links with an only partially ironic title. The poet's credo, overtly having to do with the connections between humans and animals, covertly is a belief in trope. Secular though she is, Kumin can let metaphor express the belief, which is simultaneously true and false, that things are on earth as they are in heaven.

Notes

1. "Is Female to Male as Native is to Culture?" in *Women, Culture and Society*, M. Zimbalist-Rosaldo and L. Lamphert, eds. (Stanford: Stanford University Press, 1974).

2. (New York: Harper & Row, 1978).

3. Margaret Homans, *Women Writers and Poetic Identity* (Princeton, N.J.: Princeton University Press, 1980). Homans's *Bearing the Word: Language and Female Experience in Nineteenth-Century Women's Writing* (Chicago and London: University of Chicago Press, 1986) proposes a tradition of literary language that depends on the repression of the mother and concentrates on Victorian women novelists' response to the dilemma of being defined by the very literature they wish to enter, as "either a speaker or a mother but not both" (p. 38). Homans distinguishes between masculine postoedipal "symbolic" and feminine preoedipal "literal" orders

of language—the one depending on an absent referent, the other on a present one, which will always lack cultural authority. I will argue in this essay that Kumin claims both literal uses of language (in her insistence on biological reality, and in her habitual anecdotal framing and rejection of generalization) and symbolic uses (in the form of profuse metaphor).

4. John Dryden, *Works*, vol. 14 (London: James Ballantyne, 1808), 20.

5. "Hamatreya," in *The American Tradition in Literature* (New York: W. W. Norton and Co., 1974), 682–84.

6. Henry David Thoreau, *Walden* (Princeton, N.J.: Princeton University Press, 1989), 137–38, 218, 221.

7. In *Stealing the Language: The Emergence of Women's Poetry in America* (Boston: Beacon Press, 1986), 114–19, I discuss the hypothesis that women poets are generating alternative myths for the relationship between nature and consciousness, involving neither subservience nor special status for the human, or for the relationship between nature and femaleness, in which nature is not virginal, seductive, nor maternally bounteous but functions as an ally or equivalent to the female self. Passages by Susan Griffin, May Swenson, and Elizabeth Bishop, as well as Kumin, are cited to illustrate this thesis.

8. Wallace Stevens, *Collected Poems* (New York: Vintage, 1990), 507.

9. Gary Snyder, *Turtle Island* (New York: New Directions, 1975), 102, 107.

10. Sandra Gilbert and Susan Gubar, *The Madwoman in the Attic: The Woman Writer and the Nineteenth Century Literary Imagination* (New Haven and London: Yale University Press, 1979), 29–34, comment on this recurrent figure in men's writing as one that projects onto women man's "horror of his own carnal contingence," in Simone de Beauvoir's words, and illustrates "infantile dread of maternal autonomy." A nice example is Swift's "Goddess Criticism" in *The Battle of the Books* (cited by Gilbert and Gubar, p. 33):

> Her Eyes turned inward, as if she lookt only upon Herself; Her diet was the overflowing of her own Gall; Her Spleen was so large, as to stand prominent like a Dug of the first Rate, nor wanted Excrescencies in forms of Teats, at which a crew of ungly Monsters were greedily sucking; and what is wonderful to conceive, the bulk of spleen increased faster than the Sucking could diminish it.

11. For instance, Rachel Blau DuPlessis, commenting on Beverly Dahlen in *The Pink Guitar: Writing as Feminist Practice* (New York: Routledge, 1990), 112, says: "To write metonymy is to write all margins, no page. Is to make some critique of the center such that the binary distinction between text and space disappears. . . . And the once-compelling binaries like full, empty; frame, presence; absence, mark, become pluralized into voided markings, marked void."

The Retrieval System

There is a kind of poet who turns many poems into a payment on some public account, taking on a large theme, nuclear war or ecological disaster, and making it his or her personal, odd, unique, and essential expression. The successful public poet is rare. And even though Americans reproach themselves with their complacency, no amount of self-laceration can make a poet's idiosyncratic voice, as W. S. di Piero has recently observed, into a successful or convincing public one.

Maxine Kumin seems to be the kind of poet who feels compelled by the large themes and has written compellingly about them. Yet her essential poems, with their personal, odd uniqueness, look elsewhere, into surprising conjunctions, while the urgencies of the late twentieth century, with which many of her poems are fraught, become dated.

This is a hard thing to say in a garland for Maxine Kumin, and many will not agree with me. But a perfect example of Kumin at her best, "The Retrieval System" (*RS* in *GT* 45), follows, in *Our Ground Time Here Will Be Brief*, Kumin at her most earnest, "Lines Written in the Library of Congress After the Cleanth Brooks Lecture" (*GT* 36–42). These poems demonstrate that there is a Kumin who is pressed to say the right thing and another who, when she is not so pressed, says things right.

"Lines Written in the Library of Congress After the Cleanth Brooks Lecture" is a fast-moving, longish poem in very short lines that, like its journalistic title, describes a day in the life of Kumin as Consultant in Poetry to the Library of Congress (today the post is that of Poet Laureate). Much of the poem includes quick takes of the suburban Maryland morning, keen juxtapositions of imperialism then and now, worries about nuclear arms proliferation, and reflections on her farm in New Hampshire. It is one of those poems that, because it is like a journal entry, anything can enter. Anything like this:

> This week Pakistan
> has reinstituted public floggings
> with an electronic refinement:

victims wear
microphones around their necks
to amplify their screams.
In an inspired flair
one cut above reading entrails
our government rewards that regime
with military hardware.

A few stanzas later she remembers herself as a young student.

When I was eighteen and believed
in infinite perfectibility
I marched at Fore River
organizing the shipyard for the CIO.
Equal pay for equal work
we Cliffies chanted
meaning blacks and women
then took the subway back
to Jolly-Ups and dinners in the dorms
waited on by Irish biddies
in pale green uniforms.
Now I believe in infinite depravity.

At certain points the poem addresses the critic Cleanth Brooks and attempts to compare the poet's sense of history with his. But the issues introduced, including the survival of poetry in "the valley of its saying," as W. H. Auden called it, have about them the air of a fraternal sign that initiates will recognize and return. If you are not repelled by our government's selling military hardware to the government of Pakistan, then you are not part of the inner circle. Many political poems are like this, and Maxine Kumin's are no exception. If we agree with her politics, then we know the handshake and the shake of the head.

Her best poems, like "The Retrieval System," are disturbing, surprising, and do not expect us to return a secret sign. I find "The Retrieval System" utterly foreign, utterly fascinating, and profoundly moving. When in the second to last of its five stanzas the poet says, "Fact: it is people who fade, / it is animals that retrieve them," I know I am hearing from the same poet who assumes that I am as outraged at the world's depravity as she is, but in this case I am convinced, even though I have never had any experience like the one she describes in her poem.

I suppose one of the interesting things about "The Retrieval System" is that it reads as if the poet were flying blind, finding a way to associate images within the realm of a mysterious, even dubious, idea announced in the very first line as "It."

> It begins with my dog, now dead, who all his long life
> carried about in his head the brown eyes of my father. . . .

Many people have mnemonic devices, ways of remembering the exigencies of life, like tying a piece of string around the finger, and some enter the larger realms of memory through aids like Proust's cup of tea or Schiller's rotting apples. But Kumin's "system" is the strangest one I have ever heard of. And yet as a system of resemblances, it has a great deal in common with the making of poetry itself.

Kumin calls it uncanny and sets it squarely in the realm of her daily life, on her farm in New Hampshire.

> Uncannily when I'm alone these features
> come up to link my lost people
> with the patient domestic beasts of my life. For example. . . .

And what follows is a Noah's ark of examples. There is the goat who "blats in the tiny voice of my former piano teacher," the ponies who remind her of her elderly aunts, the cat with the same "faint chin" of a sister who "died at three . . . and cried catlike in pain." At her funeral they recited, "The Lord is my shepherd." A boy the speaker loved and who was killed in war and buried at sea "keeps coming back as my yearling colt." Finally, the weatherman resembles "my resident owl"; and her dentist, whom the speaker has outlived, is owlish, too.

But the poem is more than a clever list of similitudes, someone's amazing way of finding likenesses among the animals to whom she is closest. There is that "It" hovering back at the beginning. "What is this all about anyway?" we might ask, as we ponder what "It" really means.

The poem is a kind of elegy; otherwise, no one would have to be retrieved. It is about Kumin's lost people, as she says: her daddy, her piano teacher, her aunts, her sister, a boyfriend, her dentist. The list is totally authentic because it is as arbitrary and sentimental as memory itself. The trivial—a weatherman—is included along with the most serious, her father. Part of the uncanniness is in her reference to "these features." What are they? They are not always the eyes. She sounds as if she were talking to herself. We are allowed to overhear; the poem's gaps occur because we cannot overhear everything. Yet this is another aspect of the poem's oddness, part of its appeal. It is almost totally devoid of a sense of an audience or a public.

The additional gracenotes for each remembered dead human being are also elegiac. Daddy's eyes, "keen, loving, accepting, sorrowful, whatever" have been "handed on" to the dog, who is also dead. Their "phosphorescent gleam tunneling the night" was, the speaker concedes, a "separate gift." When the goat's voice captures the piano teacher's, what also comes back are her bones, which "beat time in my dreams and [her] terrible breath" that "soured" the music the poet had to learn. The aunts are "willful, intelligent ponies" begging for apples. The cat that the sister resembled is more vivid than the sister herself. Yet to brood about the issue that these resemblances raise—the persistence of our animal nature—might sink the poem into bathos.

A poem of the profoundest grief, "The Retrieval System" skirts the lip of that profundity where the sentimental toys and embroiders and tinkers. The poet herself tinkers with form, as if to commit herself wholeheartedly, which Kumin is perfectly capable of doing, might also disturb the poem's delicate balance. Throughout the first three stanzas, each of them six lines long, there are hints at rhyme, but not until the end of the fourth stanza is there the click that rhyme can provide, as closure or interruption. After the memory of the dead infant sister, there comes the boy in the body of the colt:

> . . . racing his shadow
> for the hell of it. He runs merely to be.
> A boy who was lost in the war thirty years ago
> and buried at sea.

With that rhyme of "be" and "sea," which includes the shortest line in a poem that is mostly tetrameter and pentameter, the emotional charm is set, or wound up. "He runs merely to be." In a way, so does the poem.

The rhyme introduces time and place, two things that do not seem at all relevant in the preceding parts. In the final stanza the poet winds the charm tighter.

> Here, it's forty degrees and raining. The weatherman
> who looks like my resident owl, the one who goes out and in
> by the open haymow, appears on the TV screen.
> With his heart-shaped face, he is also my late dentist's double,
> donnish, bifocaled, kind. Going a little gray,
> advising this wisdom tooth will have to come out someday,
> meanwhile filling it as a favor. Another save.
> It outlasted him. The forecast is nothing but trouble.
> It will snow fiercely enough to fill all these open graves.

The forecast is trouble because of the weather, because death looms, but what are the other reasons? Again, "it" becomes pivotal—"it outlasted him" and "it will snow." And "these open graves" stare, yawn at us, asking to be understood as more than the embodiments of animals, but as a whole family vault. We see the mind leave its system, leave its logic and make other associations, acknowledging the snow of forgetfulness that obliterates the dead and recognizing the need to have some way to honor them.

In Kumin's retrieval system the dead have the immortality Keats imagined for his nightingale:

> Thou wast not born for death, immortal bird.
> No hungry generations tread thee down. . . .

The ever procreant animal world, which seems to reduplicate itself so faithfully (simply because we never look that closely), makes the humans in the poet's life immortal by resembling them. Like the nightingale's song, which is heard down through the ages by emperor and clown, the retrieval system is the heaven that unites and holds the dead. And the revery among invisible flowers that Keats charms us with at the end of his great ode, becomes at the end of Kumin's the forecast of bad weather. Instead of suspending us in a midsummer night's dream, the poet spellbinds us in front of the television set on a winter night. The snow outside and the snow of the screen as the station signs off hold us in limbo.

In the penultimate stanza of "Lines Written," after the poet has ruminated about the indifference of the middle class and the race hatred of the cities, the assassination attempts on President Reagan and Pope John Paul II, she strikes an apocalyptic note:

> Early in May in
> suburban Maryland
> a new bird is singing
> something oracular and bright:
> *history history*
> *time*
> *running out*
> the bomb Mr. Brooks
> in the furious grip
> of the Libyans
> the Iraqis Israelis Argentinians
> the bomb written large
> in the Domesday Book.

The poem ends with a vision of poets, "making nothing happen," as history is "inching toward Armageddon." It is hard to feel the urgency here except as a vestige of history. And yet pressing political matters, as in Yeats's poetry about civil war in Ireland, can endure with all their urgency and passion, even when their currency is long gone. It may be that in Yeats's political poetry one does not sense an obligation to write.

Emergent here and there in "The Retrieval System" is a praise of freedom. The goat who reminds the poet of her piano teacher "runs free in pasture and stable," the colt who brings back her boyfriend is "cocksure at the gallop, racing his shadow / for the hell of it." The "resident owl," whose face reflects the TV weatherman's and the former dentist's, "goes out and in / by the open haymow." However the poem may have arisen, by whatever struggle and act of will, it expresses a freedom from obligation, from seriousness and relevance and solemnity and urgency and all sorts of things that might otherwise make a poet write what she feels she must, instead of what she might. There is also a certain cruelty, a certain coldheartedness, a certain lack of courtesy here as the poet reveals inadvertently but movingly that she might very well prefer animals to people. Certainly, when she is not expressing concern for their extinction or her bad conscience about eating them, as she does in other poems, Kumin's writing about animals equals any we have. "The Retrieval System" implies that the human features she remembers from her dead already suggested animals when the people were alive. Her love for both her animals and her people is deepened by their resemblances.

In a political poem like "Lines Written in the Library of Congress After the Cleanth Brooks Lecture," Kumin's stance is clear. If we reread it, it is simply to check on the currency of the issues. The complicated feelings of "The Retrieval System" give it a freshness and durability that repay rereading in another way altogether. With each return to the poem, the reader will find something new, surprising, even disturbing, but always worth retrieving.

Maxine Kumin's Sense of Place in Nature

[A] Swedish doctor . . . weighed the deathbeds of his terminal patients just before and after they lost their vital signs. There was a twenty-one gram difference.
—MAXINE KUMIN, *The Designated Heir*, 1973

On the outside all the life of the earth is expressed in the animal or vegetable, but make a deep cut in it and you find it vital. . . . The earth is pregnant with law.
—HENRY DAVID THOREAU, *Journal: March 1854*

What Thoreau noticed in 1854, the steady replication of forms throughout nature, contemporary New England writer Maxine Kumin describes in language wrought to its uttermost. Her nature essays, from their most serviceable accounts of life on the farm—how to find and keep a horse, tell a mule from an ass, or identify a puffball ("Mushrooms are not a fast food," she reminds foragers)—through their lyrical catalog of seeds for her sustenance garden: "the little cobbles of beet seeds that separate when rolled between your fingers, the flat, feathery parsnip ones that want to drift on air enroute to the furrow, the round black dots that will be Kelsae onions, fat and sweet by September, the exasperatingly tiny lettuce flecks that descend in a cluster and the even harder-to-channel carrot seeds" ("Jicama, without Expectation" in *Women, Animals, and Vegetables* 95) or speculative fabrications: "[c]onsider the lotus seeds found under an ancient lake bed in Manchuria. Carbon-dated at 800 years old, they grew into lotus plants of a sort that had never been seen in that particular area. Such extravagant longevity makes me hopeful that we humans too will ever so gradually advance into new forms, a higher level of lotus, as it were" (*WAV* 95)—demonstrate that the human mind in its intricate workings is both animal and vegetable and everywhere governed in its perceptions by the possibilities of language. Her work invites literary and cultural analysis as a part of a gathering international concern with the preservation of the earth and the methods to be used. What she brings to the discourse is art made from a woman's life.

This essay was originally prepared for *American Nature Writers* (2 vols.), edited by John Elder. © 1996 Charles Scribner's Sons, an imprint of Simon and Schuster Macmillan. Used by permission of the publisher.

Maxine Kumin is best known in the literary world as a formal poet. From her first book of poems, *Halfway* (1961), through her most recent collection of essays and stories, *Women, Animals, and Vegetables* (1994), Kumin has written in almost every genre, twenty-seven books in all, excluding limited editions and broadsheets. A sense of place in nature, underwritten by private and public history, has been her ground for three decades and more. Coming to maturity during the years of the Holocaust, the Korean and Vietnam wars, the civil rights and women's movements, the Kennedy and King assassinations, the factionalizing of the geopolitical world, and the increasingly dire ecology news, she has made her reputation in a profession that little honored and rarely noticed the work of women.

In 1952, critic Edmund Wilson wrote of his friend the poet Edna St. Vincent Millay:

There is always a certain incommensurability between men and women writers. But . . . she was able to identify herself with more general human experience and stand forth as a spokesman for the human spirit . . . putting herself beyond common embarrassments, common oppressions and panics. This is man who surveys himself and the world in which he moves, not the beast that scurries and suffers; and the name of the poet comes no longer to indicate a mere individual with a birthplace and a legal residence, but to figure as one of the pseudonyms assumed by the spirit itself. . . . [which] made itself felt, in all one's relations with Edna, that it towered above the clever college girl, the Greenwich Village gamine and, later, the neurotic invalid. ("Epilogue, 1952," in *The Shores of Light* [New York: Farrar, Straus and Young, 1952], 752)

Wilson's assumptions that men and women writers have no common attributes to compare, that spirit and body are gendered, one male and the other here female, and that a successful woman writer must divide herself from her body and her life are representative of the time in which Maxine Kumin began to write.

Although Kumin has won the Pulitzer Prize and fellowships from the Academy of American Poets and the Mary Bunting Institute at Harvard, was consultant to the Library of Congress, is Poet Laureate for New Hampshire, received the Poetry Society of America's William Marion Reedy and Lowell Mason Palmer awards and *Poetry* magazine's Eunice Tietjens Memorial Prize, some critics say her nature essays "dote" on "minute particulars" and are "charming." Her poems are said to be "pastoral," suggesting simplicity and charm to avoid a more provocative analysis. In fact, Kumin called her own country poems pastorals, acknowledging by the conventions of that form a critique of the dominant society. Sixteenth-century English poets had used Virgil's Latin eclogues as models for tales of happy shepherds and shepherdesses in an idealized country- side. They evoked the prelapsarian garden where urban materialism, moral expediency, and favoritism at court were absent. These representations of "natural" and virtuous human lives in the peaceable kingdom, where the lion lay down with the lamb, criticized by contrast the corruptions of gov- ernment and society. Edmund Spenser's *The Shepheardes Calendar* (1579) considered the moral nature of poetry as well as the responsibilities of the poet in the life of the state. Kumin's contemporary pastorals mention ear- wigs, weasels, acid rain, and thrip, as well as reasons for the failure of the small farm and the role of the writer in an international community. Her local standards require successful competition as well as creature empathy. Material consumption depends on chopping firewood and harvesting the garden. Her moral vision is implacable. She meets critical dismissal with a wire of irony in her voice: "although I [am] . . . concerned with the smallest particulars in the natural world, I too have a thesis to advance" (*To Make a Prairie* 107). Later, she elaborates: "Now I must face the issues of survival, of hunger and genocide, of natural (or unnatural) human depravity" (*In Deep* 178).

The 1992 *Bloomsbury Guide to Women's Literature* notes that Kumin has been increasingly concerned with "humanity's troubled relationship with the natural world, and nature's domination and exploitation by humans." Susan Ludvigson, in the *Dictionary of Literary Biography* (1980), agrees: Since Kumin won the 1973 Pulitzer Prize, she "shows man now asserting his sometimes irresponsible dominance over the natural world."

Her story "Other Nations" introduces Martha Carpenter, "with a de- gree in veterinary medicine" who prefers to be called an "ethologist." She lectures and writes books on "conservation, behavioral adaptation, and the ethics of man/animal relationships" but "does not begrudge the current spate of folksy tales by veterinarians . . . they promote empathy. . . . She flies from conference to symposium raising the issue the Judeo-Christian tradition dismissed when it separated man from the natural world. She illustrates her thesis with colored slides" of animal atrocities. "In a world that divides out between the tortured and the torturers, Martha Carpenter knows it is difficult to sustain that sense of outrage necessary for change." She also knows "that animals are neither our spiritual brothers nor our slaves. As Henry Beston has said, *they are other nations, caught with ourselves in the net of life and time*" (*Why Can't We Live Together like Civilized Human Beings* 59).

Maxine Kumin is a writer who teaches, an expert rider, trainer, and breeder of horses, and a farmer. She is a poet, not "an ethologist." She reminds us in interviews that poets write because they must, out of "an inner need to sing." But the distance between the created Martha Carpenter and her complex creator marks the field of Kumin's work. Kumin is a Jewish woman writer who claims the natural and literary landscape of the Puritan fathers. The wild and non- or prelingual sides of existence draw her attention, which she expresses with the tools of culture and language. She writes to honor and preserve the continuum of a small and particular tribe of family, friends, and other poets, yet she attempts to breach large boundaries of culture, gender, and species. Empathetic blurring is her most powerful literary prop, but she sees herself at work as solitary, androgynous, and alert. She is a critic who writes in many genres, mixing stories with essays, poems with journal entries, and children's books with her most characteristic metaphors. Yet when she refers to herself in the third person, she is always "the poet." Although she is committed to the radical formulations of women, she often cites male authority. She honors androgynous values yet writes of women's experience and elaborates new conceptions of the maternal. A champion of wilderness, she has a consuming passion for cultivation. The woman poet with semipermeable boundaries is balanced by the separate and solitary, nongendered worker. Her survival depends both on the resonant sounding of the Bangkok gong, made from industrial castoffs in Thailand, and on the fact that, though it is the gift of a loved but absent daughter, "some days I barely touch it."

Born in 1925 in the predominately Protestant suburb of Germantown Philadelphia, Maxine Winokur was the youngest and only daughter in a Jewish family of four children, whose father, Peter, a stern patriarch, owned one of the largest pawnshops in the city. Her mother, Doll Simon Winokur, referred to him as "a broker." Kumin grew up in a Victorian house next door to the Convent of the Sisters of Saint Joseph, where she attended nursery school and the first years of elementary school. The tension between her background and the lessons of the nuns, as well as the stories that Fräulein, the children's nurse, read aloud — original stories from the Brothers Grimm, with their vivid details of mayhem, and Heinrich Hoffmann's moral tales for children, *Der Struwelpeter*, which promise that the dog will eat you up if you don't eat your dinner, the tailor will snip off your thumbs if you suck them, so "mind me, says Fräulein. God stands up in Heaven. / See how He watches? He snatches the bad ones" ("Fräulein Reads Instructive Rhymes," *HW* in *GT* 213)—provided material for her early poems. When Kumin was eight, Hitler came to power in Germany, and soon thereafter the European Holocaust began. "The terrible unexpungeable fate of the six million sat like an iceberg" (*The Abduction*) in Jewish consciousness. The title poem of her third collection of poetry, *The Nightmare Factory* (1970), introduces images of blight, "blind sockets / of subways and mine pits" where "nazis and cossacks ride / klansmen and judases / . . . and for east asians / battalions of giants / dressed in g i fatigues." These heavy oppressions of nature and peoples weigh upon all of her work. Her early memories include the tradesmen's skinny horses laboring uphill, to which she responded with compassionate gifts of her brothers' camp blankets. Kumin wrote in "How It Goes On," "animals in general and horses in particular represent [for me] a kind of lost innocence in our technological society and they often stand as a symbol for mute suffering" (*MP* 100). Horses join images of water as redemptive, first in her life, then in her work.

Kumin began to write as a child to work out feelings of "isolation and solitude" (*HBFG* in *GT* 102–103). Her poem, "Life's Work," blends the story of her mother's training as a concert pianist with hers, as a distance swimmer. Both women thrived under the rigors of practice. Her mother married when she was not allowed by her parents to go on tour. Kumin, who thought she would be an Olympic swimmer, was not allowed to join Billy Rose's Aquacade when the job was offered for the summer she was eighteen. The family thought it "was just not a decent" occupation for a young woman. Still, the strong body—"I was all muscle and seven doors"— is a measure of health in her work and the site of the "little ball-bearing soul" ("Body and Soul: A Meditation," in *RS* 43–45). Nor did her family encourage or discourage her writing. "A Hundred Nights," an early poem reprinted in *Our Ground Time Here Will Be Brief*, evokes her father chasing bats with a carpetbeater: "my father had his principles. / He smacked to stun them, not to kill." Nevertheless the girl, "frozen underneath the sheets, . . . heard the bats mew when he hit. / I heard them drop like squashing fruit. I heard him test them with his foot." The family says the bats came only twice, but Kumin says, "before my father died, / I meant to ask him why he chose / to loose those furies at my bed" (*GT* 217–18). Her mother, whose reserved presence in Kumin's work is most vivid in stories of barnyard and kitchen, girls' and women's work from her southwest Virginia childhood at the turn of the century, especially was pleased by her daughter's later success. She set a standard for Kumin, who reminds us that her mother couldn't escape housekeeping chores for the "dramas of field and barn" that she imagined ("Enough Jam for a Lifetime," *WAV* 65).

In 1942, Kumin entered Radcliffe College. She never during her undergraduate years found "a female instructor, assistant, associate, or, heaven forfend, full professor in any discipline" ("Breaking the Mold," 101). In 1946 she received her A.B. degree and married Victor Kumin, an engineer to whom she is still married. In 1948 she received the A.M. from Radcliffe and gave birth to their first child: "I was housebound, dutiful, and diligent . . . pacifying and feeding three youngsters born between October of 1948 and June of 1953." She began ghostwriting articles for medical journals and writing rhymed fillers for magazines, earning money at home. "Luckily, we were poor and the money I earned was significant, which gave my work some stature" ("The Care-Givers," 62).

In the late 1950s, Kumin joined a writing workshop taught by poet and Tufts University English professor John Holmes at the Boston Center for Adult Education. There she met Anne Sexton, and their much documented friendship began. They were suburban neighbors, "two shy housewives, a pair of closet poets," with two husbands and five children between them. Together they heard George Starbuck read at the New England Poetry Club in 1958, and he and Sam Albert, Kumin, Sexton, and Holmes met as a biweekly workshop for three years, writing and revising the poems that went into their books. Kumin's and Sexton's first books were an initiating part of the watershed of women's poetry that overflowed in the 1960s; each was to win a Pulitzer Prize in their years of intense collaboration, and each was to write prose as well as poetry. As "intimate friends and professional allies" they worked together every day, wrote children's books to make money, provided company and instruction for one another's children, and critical response, titles, lines, dialogue, and ideas for each other's work. "As one another's most immediate and sympathetic audience, I suppose it was inevitable that we take on some of the same subjects. But I like to think that our voices are distinctively separate, even as critics shuffle our poems today in search of overlapping images" ("A Sense of Place," *ID* 176). "My focus was always more in the natural world, Anne's focus was always more on human relationships" (George, "Kumin on Kumin and Sexton," 5).

Kumin's own speculations on human relationships appear most convincingly and perhaps most despairingly in her short stories about mostly middle-class white parents and children, heterosexual lovers and friends.

The formal restraints of the poems give way to narratives more broadly placed in the world. The nature explored in these stories is human and political, and the news isn't good. Only friendship and memory endure, often because of a survivor's determination. *Why Can't We Live Together Like Human Beings?*, the title of her collection of stories (1982), suggests the answer in the question: human behavior is supposed to be the measure of civility; in fact, human behavior is the problem to be addressed.

John Holmes supported Kumin for a teaching job at Tufts, "where I was a part-time English instructor, equipped, in the eyes of the university, only to teach freshman composition to physical education majors and dental technicians" (*MP* 30). From 1961 to 1963 she and Sexton were Radcliffe Institute for Independent Study scholars in an experiment for married, educated women not expected to publish or produce much but carefully selected for their promise and/or achievements. Although most of the women were privileged by their middle-class status, Tillie Olsen, also a Scholar, brought socialist, working-class perceptions, as well as the makings of her important book *Silences*, to the mix. With stipends, rooms, and some Harvard University resources, they were encouraged to make up time spent raising children instead of pursuing careers.

When Kumin and Sexton were raising small children, white middle-class women in America were valued as homemakers, mothers, and lovers. "We were second-class citizens, the repository of all goodness and truth in the home and seldom welcome outside it" ("Breaking the Mold," 104). Closed off from the world of economic power and isolated by the demands of family and household, some made protest in writing. "[W]omen's poetry was to provide a very important form of resistance during the next decades and much of the most influential was to be written by Sexton, . . . Kumin, Denise Levertov, Sylvia Plath, and Adrienne Rich," who were Boston friends (Middlebrook 39–40).

Maxine Kumin's first book, *Halfway* (1961), was published when she was thirty-six (she remembers she was forty: "I never had any early publications") in an edition of one thousand copies, seven hundred of which were remaindered or destroyed. Her work was marked by skill with the traditional prosody favored by male poets of her generation, but her poems took on then radical subjects. With what Alicia Ostriker calls "tender bawdiness," Kumin presented examples of female discourse and culture in and outside the family as well as talk of the female body and women's sexuality. While "it was not popular . . . to speak of the uterus or the birth canal," her work made aspects of women's experience a primary subject. Sexton's work developed more flamboyantly under Kumin's tutelage, but both writers, with the support of their seventeen years of daily collaboration that continued until Sexton's suicide in 1974, provided a keenly interested audience with, in Ezra Pound's definition of art, news that stayed news. They were poets, each said, whose business is words. Sexton, using synecdoche, called her work "Language." Kumin's work disclosed a conviction that words are only part of the equipment of human beings, whose presence in nature is not remarkable and whose ways of communicating are not superior. A poem in *Halfway* addressed to Thoreau, "My Quotable Friend," shows the speaker's disappointment because Thoreau stays in his rowboat on Walden "as if that pond were meant for oars / and plumb-line measurements" (39–40). Thoreau's desire to observe and measure, to separate himself from the natural world of the pond, she eschews. She would prefer he swamp the boat to drift and lose himself "until the lake soaked you in two and only / your head was real or dry." Thoreau chooses to measure; Kumin goes for melt. The better use of mind is to describe the body's reunion with water.

In 1963 the Kumins bought a neglected 200-plus-acre dairy farm in New Hampshire. The previous year, Rachel Carson had brought ecology to the attention of the general public with her book *Silent Spring*, which Kumin remembered twenty-six years later in a book review for the *New York Times*: Carson "warned us . . . nature does not operate in isolation, and that pollution of ground water is total pollution." *Ecology*, from the Greek for house (*oikos*) and word (*logos*), must have engaged Kumin's desire for an expanded domestic environment where words are commodities. The Kumins moved their family and her increasingly successful "cottage industry" of writing from the suburbs to rural New Hampshire each summer while Sylvia Plath moved from Boston to London, Adrienne Rich to New York, and Anne Sexton to a larger suburban house near Boston. These writers took refuge in urban centers. Kumin's removal was another kind of resistance to the sexism of the fifties. "I . . . have settled into a hillside farm out of sight or sound of neighbors. All this chaos is of my own devising" (*ID* 53). She chose this site as her necessary home: "If I am to write . . . words arranged in their natural word order in the conversational tone of voice used between consenting adults, I need the centrality of the natural world to draw on."

The move to Joppa Road in the Mink Hills signaled a change in her books, which now began to document life in a particular place, where all creatures are esteemed and work—physical and intellectual—is done for the renewal of life. *The Privilege* (1965), her second book of poems, took its title from Joseph Conrad's letter to his aunt: "One must drag the ball and chain of one's selfhood to the end. It is the price one pays for the devilish and divine privilege of thought." The first mention of the farm appears in "Joppa Diary," a group of daily poems about the rigors, death, and especially the seasonal resurrections of country life, which follows "Despair," the final conceit in a series. Despair "is a mildewed tent" the city camper must kneel to enter "blind end first." After introducing a woolen blanket roll, the brown moth, weasel, and toadstools, the poet asks, "what makes you think that rattling your ribs here will / save you?" The poem ends, "Yank up the pegs and come back! Come back in the house" (*GT* 204). The city camper, come for a holiday out of doors, brings along despair. Better the disappointments of a life in the house. In "Joppa Diary," Kumin finds an alternative life in nature, where the human self is no longer the thinking center of the world and the house of the body takes up a wider residence. "Joppa Diary" was reprinted in *Up Country*, which won the 1973 Pulitzer Prize.

To praise Kumin on the back cover of *The Privilege*, Babette Deutsch echoed Montaigne's comment on his own essays: "Elsewhere you can commend or condemn a work independently of its author; but not here: touch one and you touch the other." Deutsch wrote, "Who touches this book touches a woman, as candid as she is compassionate, and deeply aware of what her forebears gave her to pass on to her children. . . . There is a person behind the poems." The endorsement's tone suggests that touch invites intimacy even as it lists the requirements for female inscription: candor, compassion, motherhood, the burden of memory and the responsibility for passing it on.

Up Country: Poems of New England (1972) begins with poems of retreat from urban society into country solitude, poems Kumin said were "written in a male persona" because "when I was writing them I did not think that anyone could take a female hermit seriously, so I invented the hermit who, of course, is me." *Through Dooms of Love*, her first novel, about her father, was published in 1966, followed by a second, *The Passions of Uxport*, called *Keeper of His Beasts* in paperback (1968). *Publisher's Weekly* in an openly antifemale and antisemitic review said, "Sex-in-the-suburbs fans will find this episodic novel just their cup of tea, as well as those who relish Freudian psychology, family sagas and novels dealing with the problems of American Jews." In 1966, Kumin won a National Council on the Arts fellowship; in 1968, the year she won the Poetry Society of America's William Marion Reedy Award, she was invited to teach at the Bread Loaf Writers' Conference in Vermont, which she continued to do for seven seasons. There she was called the witch of fungi for her mushroom hunts, her acerbic wit, and the power of her writing and her presence. *The Nightmare Factory* (1970), poems, was followed by a novel about the depredations of life in the inner city, *The Abduction* (1971). In 1972 she won *Poetry* magazine's Eunice Tietjens Memorial Prize.

Present in this early work are signs of a familiar attachment to creatures as relief: Consider "Quarry, Pigeon Cove" from *The Privilege* (*TP* in *GT* 192–200), where, in a mined out stone pit filled with water, "The dead city waited, / hung upside down in the quarry / . . . / Badlands the color of doeskin / lay open like ancient Egypt." Into this water—whose images yoke the destruction of nature with culture—Kumin dives, in danger: "I might have swum down looking / soundlessly into nothing, / down stairways and alleys of nothing / until the city took notice / and made me its citizen." But she is saved by a vision of life: "A dog was swimming and splashing. / Air eggs nested in his fur. / The hairless parts of him bobbled like toys / and the silk of his tail blew past like milkweed / The licorice pads of his paws / sucked in and out, / making the shapes of kisses." Saved, the swimmer surfaces. "Coming up, my own face seemed beautiful. / The sun broke on my back." The poem recalls Muriel Rukeyser's "Sand Quarry with Moving Figures," published in 1935, and anticipates Adrienne Rich's "Diving into the Wreck," published a decade later.

The Designated Heir (1974) shows Kumin establishing a careful distinction between the healing properties of nature and an anthropomorphic appropriation. Her protagonist, Robin, becomes a vegetarian after adopting a vealer, a baby calf raised for the table, whom she can't stand to see sent to the knacker. Warned off by the farmer, she nonetheless raises the calf as a pet. Grown into a bull, he gores and kills the farmer's puppy. And is sent to the knacker. This novel about family, town and country, and continuance, dedicated to her daughter Jane, was published the year of Anne Sexton's suicide. Now Kumin begins the labor of mourning Sexton's daily absence in poems of great range and power: "I open a tree. / In stupefying cold / —ice on bare flesh a scald— " ("Splitting Wood at Six Above," *The Retrieval System* 47), begins one of the first elegies. "How It Goes On" (*RS* 65–66), another in the series for Sexton, was "initiated by a fact: I had a pair of lambs (Southdown ewes, named Gertrude Stein and Alice B. Toklas)." One of the lambs strangled by accident; the survivor was traded for hardwood for the stove. Naming the ewes, those two devoted partners, in her essay about the poem's genesis, suggests the magnitude of her loss (*MP* 101). But the lamb's death is not privileged in the poem; she is not named who goes to be slaughtered in trade for "two cords of stove-length oak" (*RS* 65). The loss is catastrophic but must be transmuted for the sake of survival. The most recent of the series, "On Being Asked to Write a Poem in Memory of Anne Sexton" (*N* 36), conflates and transforms Sexton and her reputation into an elk burdened by antlers "destined to ossify," destined to be sloughed off. "What a heavy candelabrum to be borne / forth, each year more elaborately turned: // the special issues, the prizes in her name. / Above the mantel the late elk's antlers gleam." To the figure of the trophy elk add Cernunnos—his iconography, *the figure with elk antlers* in Celtic and other mythologies—guardian of wild creatures, who presides over sacrifice to insure continuance; his companion gives birth to human and other animals and plants and is guardian of the dwelling places of the dead. Myth begins to resonate in Kumin's poetry.

What began as the hard labor of exorcism, ghosts laid out and examined, informs the poems in Kumin's next book. "History Lesson," published in *House, Bridge, Fountain, Gate* (1975), shows her empathic connection to her foster son, Steven Burgess, "a bi-racial product of the Korean War who lived with us from age 14 thru high school, followed by 2 years at the U of Chicago" (letter to Raz, 7 November 1994): "That a man may be free of his ghosts / he must return to them like a garden. / He must put his hands in the sweet rot / uprooting the turnips, washing them / tying them into bundles / and shouldering the whole load to market" (*GT* 92). Images of the natural world evoke, then fix, then bleed off particular loss—of the familial, tribal, and gendered—in order to address the subject of continuance, how it goes on. The price of human thought—an egocentric world— invoked in the epigraph to *The Privilege* is refunded: "Christ on the lake was not thinking / where the next heel-toe went. / God did him a dangerous favor // whereas Peter, the thinker, sank" ("To Swim, to Believe," in *GT* 112). Both a sense of the self as mortal, sentient, and individual, as well as generic and anonymous—an immortal part of the life force—are essential for survival. The book's title comes from the German poet Rilke, who gives language the moral charge to witness: the poems name and recall parents, uncles and aunts, cousins, grandparents, lovers, children—all departed—and their stories. Her own stories are of travel, for teaching, "changing houses like sneakers and socks." After winning the Pulitzer Prize and much in demand, she began to teach at an accelerated pace, to convey her particular gloss on traditional texts and introduce new ones. Reading and teaching trips—to Washington University, Brandeis, Columbia, Princeton, among others—helped support the animals and the growing expenses of the farm's renovation. In the Amanda poems, written about her horse, we see the bud of the nature essays and poems that blur boundaries between human and animal, woman and nature.

By 1975 she had "let go of the large children." Jane, the eldest, graduated from Radcliffe in 1970; Judith in 1971; Daniel followed, from Bennington. In 1976, in what may have begun for Kumin a "pervading desire to be totally self-sufficient" to "be really outside the mainstream," she and Victor made a permanent move to the farm. "[E]quine compensations" for the empty nest along with the pleasures of raising Scotch Highland heifers, sheep, and goats appear in the essays and stories: "As if in search of sainthood . . . [they] anointed themselves daily hauling water, mucking stalls, paring hoof abscesses till they bled, poulticing sore ligaments and keeping up a soothing banter with their herd of home raised [horses]" ("Jack," *WAV* 186). One hundred taps a year ran from their sugar bush, leading to this ecstatic description in "Journal—Later Winter-Spring 1978" (*MP* 182): "Putting in the spiles I lean on the brace and bit, having to use all my weight to keep the metal spiral angling upward into the tough tree. How astonishing, after the hole is bored, that the sap glistens, quivers, begins to run freely. To think that I have never seen or done this before. I am as captivated as the city child finding out where milk comes from." In "Menial Labor and the Muse" (*WAV* 18), published fifteen years later, we learn they "probably won't be setting any taps this March. Acid rain and the depredations of the pear thrip that followed have weakened the trees to a possibly fatal point."

The poems in *The Retrieval System* (1978) link explicitly the eulogizing power of language with the evocative power of the daily round. Life on the farm with its repetitive and labor-intensive service to animal and land invites her "androgynous, pagan muse." In Kumin's poems, memory is stimulated by resemblance. "For Kumin there is no hierarchy: humans, animals, and plants uncannily resemble each other, are often metaphorically interchangeable, enjoy the same energies, and suffer the same downfalls" (Ostriker, *Stealing the Language* 116). This pattern of free association with the resulting poems seems final to the poet: "I just don't see where I can go after *The Retrieval System*," she says in a 1980 interview (Armitage). But she is learning a new culture and language of care, for the horses. In the barn, where men traditionally have held sway, Kumin is taking up residence.

To Make a Prairie: Essays on Poets, Poetry, and Country Living (1979) names Henry David Thoreau, the nineteenth-century nature writer and inveterate New Englander pioneer, her progenitor; she continues to express her growing concern about human damage to the environment. "Where there are questions of survival, the poet belongs on the battlements," Kumin says.

She may well have chosen Thoreau because her choices were limited; the work of Susan Fenimore Cooper, his contemporary and the first woman nature writer in America, had long been out of print. Cooper, whose journal of the seasons, *Rural Hours*, was published in 1850, four years before *Walden*, grew up when many northeastern, middle-class, Euro-American women were confined to the home and domesticity. Cooper's work, widely read during her lifetime, was lost to us along with the work of Mary Treat, Olive Thorne Miller, and Florence Merriam, all contemporaries of Thoreau. Their writings about home and garden became less popular as the public turned to stories of wilderness written by Edgar Rice Burroughs, Teddy Roosevelt, and Jack London. Certainly both men and women wrote about nature, but accounts of exploration by men were more popular than the home-based accounts of women. Even Thoreau was praised for his work as a pioneer rather than for meditations on his garden.

Thoreau's graceful prose was available to Kumin and appealed to her knowledge of herself as a serious writer, but she chose from his work the materials necessary for her own. "All of us who write, however tangentially, about the human place in nature hold a legacy from Thoreau. His language of specificity, from its soaring allusions to mythology to its startling metaphors, goes beyond the clinical measurements of the laboratory biologist, with whom he shares a passion for accuracy. Thoreau makes us see ourselves as part of the picture, looking in both directions, to the mountains, and into the moss at our feet" (*ID* 156). Cooper counseled ignorance of the Latin taxonomies, to make more readily available to interested observers the names of things. Kumin loves the Latin names. Kumin's language of specificity includes, most importantly, *heterosis*, or hybrid vigor, a geneticist's term she applies particularly to the bloodline of her horse, who had been so badly abused she was unrestrainable; her feisty nature, her refusal to surrender, gave strength and tenacity to her descendants. We also encounter "anthelmintic" (having deworming properties), "decurrent, adnexed, and adnate" (mushroom gills), "cryptobiosis" (suspended animation), "snowball poppers" (winter pads for horses hooves), "defalcated" (embezzling, more or less), bummer lamb (rejected by the ewe, so bottle-fed), and "slickensides" (the slick sides of granite).

Thoreau's nonhierarchical respect for difference in the natural world also appealed to Kumin. His description of weeds—"Roman wormwood, —that's pigweed,—that's sorrel,—that's piper-grass" in "The Beanfield" essay are as rich in detail about the "small white bush bean" as about the actions of woodchucks. "Shall I not rejoice also at the abundance of the weeds whose seeds are the granary of the birds?" asks Thoreau, who seems to take equal delight in the workings of the mind as in the workings of nature. Culture (Greek) and nature (beans or broccoli) were one to him (at least in these passages), which Kumin notes in a passage cut from "Jicama without Expectations": "His daily record is delightfully discursive, ranging from 'I put in a little Greek now and then, partly because it sounds so much like the ocean,' a good example of naturalizing culture, to noting that he found some broccoli growing in a Wellfleet garden [which] . . . is possibly the earliest reference to broccoli in North America."

In the same essay, Kumin points out his gendered attitudes toward the wild forest and the civil garden. "Even Thoreau, who wanted to break with the past, start over as a sort of new Adam, an innocent in Paradise on the shores of Walden Pond, was susceptible to the blandishments of growing things. He narrowly escaped enslavement by hoe when he 'made the earth say beans instead of grass.' In *A Week on the Concord and Merrimack*, he pronounced gardening 'civil and social, but it wants [lacks] the vigor and freedom of the forest and the outlaw'" (*WAV* 95). The new Adam wants the vigorous, free, and uncivilized forest but the seductive powers of the domestic garden are apparent in Kumin's trope.

Thoreau's nonhierarchical respect for difference, along with his ability to naturalize culture served, if not mirrored, Kumin's literary ambitions, one of which was to blur and breach boundaries. The mixed genres of *To Make a Prairie*, for example, defy traditional arrangements: interviews and essays on poetry and nature mingle with journal entries and poems. Kumin's ability to effect merging with language shows in essays about her mare, Taboo, rescued from the slaughterer. Taboo's foal is Boomerang. The *o* sounds repeat. In early poems, *o* rises as the sleep sounds of an infant and later as a protest against the single howl of chaos, the boundless forces of dissolution. Most movingly, the *o* is apostrophe. "O to turn away," she says at the end of "Journal—Late Winter-Spring, 1978," one of her most eloquent essays, when all the forces of burgeoning spring in human, animal and vegetative life come to climax not in birth as expected but in an eleven-month, full term, stillborn foal she buries in hard soil "behind the old chicken coop." "I got down beside . . . [the foal] and folded the long legs in, tucking them back into fetal position, and then we shoveled the earth back over it and finally packed the top with stones so that nothing will disturb the grave" (*MP* 145). At the time of burying, woman and foal enter the grave together. The maternal horse already has turned away. But human imperatives demand a recapitulation before boundaries between child and mother will stand again. What is taboo, forbidden, is inscribed as news of the body giving birth, and dying, and in empathic merging of species.

With equally charged detail, Kumin writes about attending the birth of a grandchild: the grandmother empathizes with the laboring woman to experience simultaneously both labors, the woman's and her own years before. Only when the new child crowns does she return to herself, in time to deliver him to his mother, her grown child ("Beginning with Gussie," *WAV*). Kumin's poem "After Love" begins: "Afterwards, the compromise. / Bodies resume their boundaries" (*NF* in *GT* 182), giving voice to a strongly female sexuality. She extends that understanding of the female body to childbirth, where maternal empathy works its magic blur.

Blurred boundaries between species show in her story "The Match" (*WAV*), where the slogan of a radical environmentalist group called Animals All is "A rat is a cat is a dog is a pig is a boy." The embodiment of the slogan is a tapestry whose border is interlocking animals—"an oversized mouse . . . linked to a cat, in turn hanging onto a dog that seemed to be chasing a pig. At the front of the little parade, a child. The pattern repeated all the way around" (*WAV* 262). Genre boundaries and perspectives may mix and blur, but Kumin also measures the mark where blurring leads to collapse—of an image, a narrative, a life. In the poems, rhyme and rhythm govern emotionally chaotic subjects; in her novels, in a detail taken from life, obsessive rhyming signals emotional breakdown, and too regular rhythm a heartbeat-like insistence on unavailable infant comforts. Kumin has marked Thoreau's careful observations of difference in the natural world. She is careful to define "a working distance" in her own work.

Referring both to women's writing in a white, male culture and the contemporary loss of faith, Joyce Carol Oates, reviewing *Up Country*, had said,

Maxine Kumin's book acknowledges its debt to Thoreau, though in my opinion Kumin's poetry gives us a sharp-edged, unflinching and occasionally nightmarish subjectivity exasperatingly absent in Thoreau. The most valuable, because most powerful, statements of the transcendental experience are those rooted firmly in existence, however private or eccentric. We are ready to believe Miss Kumin's energetic praises of nature, her insistence upon her own place in it—"we teem, we overgrow . . . we are making a run for it"—because we have suffered along with her the contraction of the universe . . . , her occasional despair, her speculations upon forms of mortality in an old burying ground."

In 1981, Maxine Kumin was named Consultant to the Library of Congress. She presented her lecture at the library on 5 May 1981. "Rather than bring it out as a separate pamphlet—the usual custom—the L[ibrary] of C[ongress] sequestered it in their quarterly bulletin" (letter to Raz, 7 November 1994). It appeared in the winter issue of the *Quarterly Journal of the Library of Congress*. "Stamping a Tiny Foot against God: Some American Women Poets Writing between the Two Wars" discusses the poetry of seven women poets whose work had attracted a broad audience but little serious critical attention: Amy Lowell, Hilda Doolittle, Sara Teasdale, Edna Millay, Marianne Moore, Muriel Rukeyser, and Louise Bogan. Kumin takes her title from poet Theodore Roethke, one item in his list of the "aesthetic and moral shortcomings" of women poets. In a review of his friend and once lover Louise Bogan's work, he lists others, which include "a concern with the mere surfaces of life . . . hiding from the real agonies of the spirit . . . running between the boudoir and the altar; caterwauling; writing the same poem about fifty times." Kumin praises Millay's use of images from nature to comment on public events, since she acknowledged in her work the power of human beings to subvert nature for destruction. Muriel Rukeyser's *Wake Island* by "linking the struggle in Spain with the war in the Pacific connects all antifascist struggles into a whole." Kumin reveals the powerful Louise Bogan's enmity for Rukeyser to suggest one reason for public neglect during her most productive years, and she notes the difference in voice between lifelong friends Marianne Moore and H.D., who were classmates at Bryn Mawr. She introduces evidence of difference to challenge the idea that women writers are essentially bonded by mutuality, sisterhood, and nurturance. At the same time she uses her own visibility to discuss both the critical neglect and misreading of the work of some uncanonized women poets. Kumin's history includes literary gossip: the influential critic and poet Ezra Pound put "an old-fashioned tin washtub on his head like a helmet" during one of Amy Lowell's dinner parties, a disrespectful gesture Horace Gregory reports as one indication of Pound's "coolness" toward the lesbian poet. Acknowledging the difficulties inherent in a single category for the range of difference in their work, Kumin nevertheless constitutes women's poetry as worthy of sustained inquiry.

Our Ground Time Here Will Be Brief: New and Selected Poems was published in 1982. In the diction of the recycling citizen, Kumin had said that art should "create something natural out of all the used-up sticks and bureaus of our lives, the detritus of our lives" (*MP 25*). Recycler and artist meet in an elegy for her brother: "After the funeral, I pick / forty pounds of plums from your tree / . . ./ and carry them by DC 10 / three thousand miles to my kitchen // and stand at midnight—nine o'clock / your time— on the fourth day of your death / putting some raveled things / unsaid between us into the boiling pot / of cloves, cinnamon, sugar" ("Retrospect in the Kitchen," *GT* 29).

In 1985, Kumin won an Academy of American Poets Fellowship. In 1988 she published two books, *The Long Approach* (poems) and *In Deep: Country Essays*, which closes on "A Sense of Place," an *ars poetica* with a central tenet: "Without religious faith and without the sense of primal certitude that faith brings, I must take my only comfort from the natural order of things" (p. 162). Kumin had echoed and revised Thomas Hobbes, the seventeenth-century British political philosopher, when she said, "I don't put terribly much store by human nature. . . . I think we're infinitely depraved, and brutish, and nasty" (*MP* 20). Hobbes's much quoted observation on nature, "No arts; no letters; no society; and which is worst of all, continual fear and danger of violent death; and the life of man, solitary, poor, nasty, brutish, and short," places humanity in the center of the natural morass. Human beings, as part of nature, need the lessons of the prevailing culture, he thought, as well as a king, for taming and survival. Kumin invokes not culture but "the saving nature" of family and friends, the tribe. In time, the tribe comes to include not only creatures of her ilk and in her care but nature itself. And her vision increasingly incorporates myths from other cultures to account for what is not patterned but is unpredictable and chaotic. *In Deep* gathers vision in service to traditional ways of working the land. Her longtime commitment to a "tribe" of family, poets, and a few friends loosens to admit others—horse people and farmers and a family of species. What she has called "the tribal notion of succession" modulates to admit the place where succession happens. Sentience is redefined, as is nurture. In more recent collections, *Looking for Luck* (poems, 1992) and *Women, Animals, and Vegetables* (essays and stories, 1994), she considers nonhuman systems of communication to better understand nonverbal systems that operate between genders and generations and among nationalities. "Sleeping with Animals" (*N* 20) explicates the effort: "Nightly I choose to keep this covenant / with a wheezing broodmare who, ten days past due, / grunts in her sleep in the vocables / of the vastly pregnant. She lies down / on sawdust of white pine, its turp smell blending / with the rich scent of ammonia and manure. / I in my mummy bag just outside her stall / observe the silence . . . What we say to each other in the cold black / of April, conveyed in a wordless yet perfect / language of touch and tremor, connects / us most surely to the wet cave we all / once burst from gasping, naked or furred, / into our separate species."

While the same sensibility informs Kumin's poems and essays, the essays show Kumin as a moralist; her outrage can be palpable and contagious. What she calls "the extra long taproot of the transplant" holds her fast to the farm, fourteen acres of which are now pasture because of annual applications of manure and the ashes from the wood stoves, as well as "lime annually, and as little commercial fertilizer as possible (every few years). Acid rain is not helping the situation" (letter to Raz). She speaks of "the old Hebraic Puritan inside me, equating tranquillity with hard physical labor" (*ID* 170). Her sense of freedom only within rigorous discipline carries over to her poems, where the most deeply personal narratives are expressed within a strict formal prosody, and the "rigors of form" are "a forcing agent" (*MP* 85). She expresses reservations about "any kind of didacticism" in poetry, which is "too fragile a vessel to bear the weight of polemic." Yet she notes that some of her poems are angry. The nature essays take up battle. Speaking of the treatment of animals raised for slaughter, she asks, "Does it matter how they live, since they are all going to die to feed us? I think it matters mightily . . . because how we treat the animals in our keeping defines us as human beings" ("Jicama without Expectation," *WAV* 106).

Kumin has said that in poetry everything is metaphor, perhaps in disguise. Yet as an essayist she refuses to claim the poet's trick of seeing the natural world with a "master eye . . . in a double or multiple sense"—that is, with an eye for metaphor. She says, "It's true that minutiae fascinate me [but] . . . I don't think I see objects in a multiple way at all." She wants "the Latin names of things after I find out what they properly are" (*MP* 5). As an amateur naturalist, she is true to the task of recording information, true to the task of naming and particularizing. "Since, as a writer, my business is words, I tend to put my faith in the printed page. Much of what I have learned about the natural world came to me from handbooks" (*WAV* 76). Her large collection provides a continuity of women's perceptions of nature. She admires Nina Marshall's 1904 study of mushrooms, for example: "published as Volume 10 of a very ambitious Nature Library, this text is rich in hand-colored or -tinted photographic illustrations . . . and represents what must have been an enormous undertaking at that time" (*WAV* 83). At the turn of the century, women's nature writing had been eclipsed by a public taste for heroic undertakings in the conquest of wilderness. But at the same time, women with artistic ability were being employed as scientific illustrators by the government (Norwood 54). Their precise and often beautiful drawings brought knowledge about the natural world to the public. While women artists were encouraged to avoid "heroic landscape painting," their observations and artful reproduction of *minute particulars* did not detract from the wider apprehension of their modesty and their role as keepers of garden and home. Kumin uses these images and conveys her pleasure in the knowledge they bring, which she can affirm or alter. This generous urgency to extend knowledge informs the essays. Where the poems invite empathic deciphering, the essays bring information and suggest action. The formal poems cinch up at the end. The essays sprawl, held together by the urgencies of observation and their particular vision.

A superb collection of poems, *Nurture*, was published in 1989. Its title begs for a weighing of the old dualities, nature/nurture: which is more important as to the absolute influence on a human being? The motive for "Nurture" in the book's title poem "seems less a compulsion to exercise an ethic of care than a deep yearning for the embrace of all things wild. The [feral] child imagined in the last moments of the poem comes from and brings access to a pre-linguistic, pre-social realm, where 'laughter [is] our first noun, and our long verb, howl'" (Constance Merritt, unpublished essay). "Nurture" comes from the Latin word for "nurse." Language is the milk exchanged here, not English or even human, but a language reciprocal and constructed, not created. "Think of the language we two, same and not-same, / might have constructed from sign, / scratch, grimace, grunt, vowel." In Kumin's work, dualities obfuscate.

Another old duality, nature/culture, however, is important to ecofeminism, a recent international discourse that unites ecology with feminism. Any discussion of women writing about nature must take it into account. According to Karen J. Warren, the term "ecological feminism" appeared first in 1974 in the work of Françoise d'Eaubonne, who showed the theoretical and practical connections between "the oppression of women and the domination of nature, . . . conceptual frameworks and practices which sanction the subordination of both women and nature . . . by feminizing nature and then assuming that both women and nature are inferior to men and men's culture" ("Toward an Ecofeminist Ethic," *Studies in the Humanities* 15 [December 1988]: 140–56). American poet Susan Griffin's mixed genre *Woman and Nature: The Roaring inside Her* (New York: Harper & Row, 1978) found in Western thought the distinction between teeming nature, of which woman is a part, and a taming masculine culture. By quoting texts as authority she presents assumptions held in common about nature and women. Some contemporary ecofeminists turn to popularizers of quantum physics for a more flexible model, "a complicated web of relations between the various parts of a unified whole" (Fritjof Capra, *The Tao of Physics*, quoted in Norwood, p. 269) and "use the shifting boundaries between matter and energy to argue with any sort of duality, particularly the assertion that nature is merely the passive subject of objective scrutiny" (Norwood 20). Ariel Salleh, an Australian ecofeminist writer and activist, says in "Second Thoughts on Rethinking Ecofeminist Politics: A Dialectical Critique" (*Isle: Interdisciplinary Studies in Literature and Environment* 1 [fall 1993]: 93–106) that ecofeminism "is concerned about the oppression of all life forms . . . [and posits] that the same patriarchal attitudes which degrade nature are responsible for the exploitation and abuse of women." But, she notes, "a *real* political shift means letting go of the culture versus nature polarity all together." The changing issues of ecofeminism are apparent in Kumin's work. She repeats that nature is neither moral nor immoral—"Nature pays me no attention, but announces the autonomy of everything. Here nothing is good or bad, but *is*, in spite of" (*MP* 162).

Euro-American women in nature are rarely depicted as working. The gardens in which they rest seem to flower because of the work of others. Kumin's work on the farm is never hidden; she is never a passive recipient of scrutiny, rather has described herself as a jock (*MP* 64), has always been athletic. As a child, she found escape from the restrictins of family and gender in long-distance competitive swimming; as an adult, she is an expert and competitive long-distance rider, at home in the breeding barn or working the two- and three-year-old horses on the longe line. The work of the body is a central subject of the essays. She and Victor carve fourteen hard-won acres of pasture for the horses from granite outcroppings, raise five hundred pounds of produce from the garden for the kitchen, split twelve cords of wood for the winter stoves, and make productive order from "rampant growth." She assigns value to diligence and productivity, not gendered roles. While Kumin's life honors androgynous values of performance and training, in her work the farm seems an extension of a sensual subjectivity, part of what she calls "the moi."

James Galvin's much praised *The Meadow* (New York: Henry Holt, 1993) sexualizes landscape from a familiar male perspective: "all summer long flotillas of sheepish clouds sailed in and tried to look like rain. They turned dark and sexual. They let down their hair, like brushstrokes on the air, like feathers of water, like the principle [*Virga*] it was named for, sublime indifference its gesture, its lovely signature over us." In 1968, Edward

Abbey wrote of Arches National Park: "I want to know it all, possess it all, embrace the entire scene intimately, deeply, totally, as a man desires a beautiful woman."

Kumin says plowed fields "release a sweet rancidness / warm as sperm" ("Relearning the Language of April," *GT* 12) and that "Peeling Fence Posts" is finding "hard as it is, / ash splits its skin clean, / . . . / comes away like a glove. / I finger the torso under, / pale, wet alive" (*GT* 8). Or she discovers "In the Pea Patch" plants "saying dance with me, / saying do me, dangle their intricate / nuggety scrota" (*GT* 11) and in the final stanza, "under the polishing thumb / in the interior / sweet for the taking, nine little fetuses / nod their cloned heads." In the green world of the vegetable garden every sexuality bends to her trope. In a more recent poem, "Surprises", the older poet/farmer finds red peppers in her garden for the first time in fifteen years, which "hang / in clustered pairs like newly hatched sex organs / . . . Doubtless this means I am approaching the victory of poetry over death / where art wins, chaos retreats, and beauty / . . . / rises again, shiny with roses, no thorns. / No earwigs, cutworms, leaf miners either" (*N* 47). The pastoral tradition's idealization of nature is linked here with sexual generation in a wry reunion of culture and nature.

Kumin valorizes sexual and empathic merging in her work but she also calls for the careful preservation of a respectful "working distance"—in this case ("Distance," *N* 60) between herself, driving a huge mowing machine, and two bear cubs and their mother seen on the poet's birthday. She notes that old age is androgynous, as is the skill necessary to drive this heavy machine, itself androgynous in detail, "with two forward speeds and a wheel clutch, nippled hand grips, / a lever to engage the cutting blade." She salutes in her mind (both hands are occupied in the driving) the wild mother and cubs, a vision of sexual continuance she no longer identifies as her own, with the poet's trick of rhyming: "Androgyny. Another birthday. And all the while / the muted roar of satisfactory machinery. / May we flourish and keep our working distance."

Kumin's writing has both noted and honored the boundaries between and among living things as well as their histories and taxonomies. She also has brought to her nature essays one among many feminist visions: where knowledge builds and commitment enters, boundaries blur and may dissolve and fall. In *Looking for Luck* (1992), poems about travel, hard boundaries and insoluble differences rise again: between "paid-up overfed" Americans and "[p]eople who / cannot come in from place of origin / and steadfastly refuse to go back to"; the poet and her careless and impoverished neighbors, the Scutzes; women in Kansas, where "[l]ike wind in the wheat, the boundary blurs but keeps"; Japanese immigrants and Southern Californians; in the local jail, representatives of Alaska's native peoples and their colonizers; the local butcher, "a decent man who blurs the line of sight / between our conscience and our appetite"; strange animals like the sloth; or the barn cats whom she ironically thanks for "doing God's work—fledglings, field mice, shrews / moles, baby rabbits—else why would He / have made so many? I bury what I deplore"; even Anne Sexton, her "suicided long-term friend . . . / All these years I've fought somehow to bless / her drinking in of the killer car exhaust / but a coal of anger sat and winked its live / orange eye undimmed in my chest / while the world buzzed gossiping in the hive" ("The Green Well," *LL* 32). This book is filled with anger and the jingle, jangle of tight form to keep it cinched. No spring resurrection can justify time's harsh separations. How to reconcile these compelling differences with a sense of common identity? The artist's answer here is an athletic leap into faith by remaking Kiowa legend so that blurring between species is made real and eternal—at least in the text. The epilogue of *Looking for Luck* remakes the Tlingit legend of encounter between bear and woman. In the legend, the woman is counseled to undress. A male bear feels shame before a naked woman, so he will run away. The woman in "The Rendezvous," undresses. The bear takes out his teeth, shucks his skin and drops it for a pallet. "He smells of honey / and garlic. I am wet / with human fear. How / can he run away, unfurred? / How can I, without my clothes? // How we prepare a new legend." The legend Kumin uses in "The Rendezvous" (p. 91) and others about bears—the Navaho, for example, where Bear Woman transforms herself from woman into bear by thrusting her weaving spindles, one of which surely pricked Sleeping Beauty's finger, into her gums for teeth—reveal the bear as one of the great symbols of transformation. Potentially destructive power is channeled into less malevolent forms. Kumin is shaping myth to her liking.

The addition of "women" to Thoreau's catalog—"the life of the earth is expressed in the animal or vegetable"—for the title of *Women, Animals, and Vegetables* (1994), essays and stories, emphasizes difference as well as gender in the continuum. "I carry the ghost of my mother under my navel . . . / a miracle / folded in lotus position" ("The Envelope," *RS* 40). "A transformation has taken place in the childbearing process. Now it is our mothers, as well as our children, whom we carry about with us, internalized lares and penates" (*MP* 123). Her mother, who lived to be an old woman and died easily in her sleep, reappears in dreams, poems, essays, and in the kitchen, helping with the jam making, as her absent daughter had, performing the essential chores. Both daughters live far from Joppa Road: Jane is a lawyer in San Francisco; Judith, who attended the Fletcher School of Law and Diplomacy at Tufts, lives with her son Yann in Bonn, Germany, where she runs an agency of the United Nations for Eastern Europe. Daniel, whose name appears in *Books in Print* as the author of articles in *Stereo Review* and other journals, lives twenty minutes away from his parents with his wife, a lawyer, and their son Noah. The dedication to *Looking for Luck* (1992) is "For Yann and Noah, lucky cousins." Kumin's passionate sense of family/tribe is informed by necessary separation, as Ostriker says, "the need to possess and the need to release" all living things in our care. Listening to her visiting daughter play the cello, "fierce now in the half light / at her harmonics," the poet is also telling another mother about her daughter's permanent move to Germany where "[n]ow she will raise her children / in a language that rusts in my mouth, / in a language that locks up my jaw" (*LL* 74). Her companion here is a swallow—like Athenian Procne and her sister Philomela changed in the myth to escape their violator, Tereus—as her companion in another poem, "We Stood There Singing," is a Swiss stranger who takes in the touring family of mother, daughter, and grandson, and sings and rocks the cranky child: "We stood there singing. / I remember / that moment of civility among women" (*N* 59).

In the essays in *Women, Animals, and Vegetables*, Kumin is still mucking out the stalls, tapping the sugar bush, planting and sowing and preserving earth's plenty. Now when she travels on "po-biz," her saddle goes, too. Riding in different landscapes, she sounds a less distanced, more crotchety voice. Her connection with animal presence appears in complaints about absentee animal owners, who ought to be licensed as drivers are. Time now has a full measure: the last of the dalmatians, puppy Gus who appeared as one of a lively pair (Gus, short for Augustus, and Claude [Claudius], since dogs should be named for royalty) turns into an arthritic old denizen unable to climb the stairs. A new puppy, Josh, surrenders his hard-won place at the foot of the bed to sleep in company with the old geezer by the stove. These creature stories, as much exempla as *Der Struwelpeter* of her youth, are replete with compassionate examples. They evoke not nostalgia but an appropriate introspection.

Kumin's vegetable garden is the locus of one of her best essays, "Jicama without Expectation." It leans on the cultural ironies of using the *New York Times*, America's most admired popular newspaper, for mulch. If civilization poisons, then news of civilization not only doesn't stay news but can best be used to keep the weeds at bay. Nineteenth-century images of white women placed them at home in their flower gardens as symbols of female nature tamed; Arnold Genthe's familiar photo of a static Edna Millay framed by a blooming magnolia appears in the publication of Kumin's Library of Congress address. In the late twentieth century, Maxine Kumin mixes the garden with the farm and extends domestic space for the making of art. Her pleasure is not identified so much with fecundity as with the usefulness and beauty of provender. She views landscape with the farmer's eye, preferring, as she says, pasture to forest. Aware that her domestic economy depends on money earned from "po-biz," Kumin laments because "[t]here is not one full-time farmer left in my community." Po-biz—teaching, readings, writer-in-residence semesters in academie, the royalties and payments for published work, and the prizes—pays for the horse business, but it's all one business, "a very expensive one." She looks now, in the spring of 1994, "for the right stallion for Boomer" because she wants to have another foal coming.

In Kumin's work the sounds of life carry in echoing vowels, slant rhymes, the rhythms—the *feel* of the English language on the tongue. When the poet is least guarded, her essays address the question asked in Heidegger's *Poetry, Language, Thought*: "What is it to dwell?" (*The Designated Heir*). The answer, "Dwelling is the manner in which mortals are on earth," invites Maxine Kumin's complicated response. With an accretion of living detail, she works to inscribe the contract we make with death: she connects, as Heidegger did, life with text. "I think there wouldn't be any art whatsoever if we were immortal."

Although her subject is making blackberry jam, we might now understand something slant in this passage: "There is no quality control in my method. Every batch is a kind of revisionism. It makes its own laws. But the result is pure, deeply colored, uncomplicated, and unadulterated blackberry jam, veritably seedless, suitable for every occasion" (*WAV* 66).

In her catalog of women, animals, and vegetables, where *human* takes up but one entry, language and memory are used in service to all. Few better writers than Kumin take up residency in the world, to record similarities and celebrate differences in the rich sensory imagery of flesh. And who but Maxine Kumin can conjure "blue and dainty, the souls. / They are thin as an eyelash. / They flap once, going up" (*GT* 69)—and then, in another context, remind us of the exact weight of each one.

WESLEY MCNAIR

Kumin's Animal Confederates

At the heart of Maxine Kumin's poetry about nature is her relationship with animals. In her poem "Credo," the fullest statement we have in verse of her feelings about the natural world, she speaks extensively of the harmony she has found with the creatures of both pasture and forest. In "A Sense of Place," her credo about nature in prose, she asserts that her connection with animals is essential to her work as a poet, and later implies that through her association with them she has discovered a creatural self that is deeper and better than her human self: "The animals are my confederates. . . . They are rudimentary and untiring and changeless, where we are sophisticated, weary, fickle. They make me better than I am. . . . Also, they rescue the past. They are the Golliwogs, the Would-be-goods of my childhood. Guileless, predictable, they help define who I am" (p. 168).

A description of contemporary American poetry written by David Perkins in *A History of Modern Poetry* suggests how unusual Maxine Kumin is in her sense of the possibilities of the creatural life. According to Perkins, today's American poetry is based on what he terms a "creatural realism" that tends to emphasize man's physical and psychological "vulnerability and weakness." For Kumin, creatural reality is what humans have the good fortune to find, since it may lead to personal renewal as well as a spiritual connection with the natural world. Thus, her poems about animals are important both in defining her nature poetry and in the uniqueness of her poetic vision.

Kumin's themes about animals and their value to humans are given full play in her fourth book, *Up Country: Poems of New England*, containing new and selected poems derived from her experiences on a rural property she and her husband acquired in Warner, New Hampshire. The book also firmly establishes Kumin's relationship with place. In the volume she lays claim to her property and, by implication, rural New England as a poet. So *Up Country* opens with the well-known "hermit" poems, in which Kumin plays the role of a recluse in retreat from society—a role paralleling her own departure from the Boston suburbs (not to mention the flight from Concord, Massachusetts, undertaken a century earlier by her long-standing model, Henry David Thoreau). In the guise of her character, Kumin explores and discovers the true life of the territory she has chosen for her new residence.

The animals of the hermit poems include, among others, raccoons, birds, frogs, squirrels, and skunks. Though one of the latter group sprays the hermit's dog with a deadly stench and though the hermit is plagued by mosquitoes, he finds the creatures around him mostly mean no harm. In "The Hermit Picks Berries," we are shown how Kumin's character, a gentle spirit himself, coexists with them.

> At midday the birds doze.
> So does he.
>
> The frogs cover themselves.
> So does he . . .
>
> The snake uncoils its clay self
> in the sun on a rock in the pasture.
> It is the hermit's pasture.
> He encourages the snake.
>
> (GT 147)

In addition to being more or less peaceable, some creatures of Kumin's opening sequence, along with others elsewhere in the book, are female and linked with procreation or nurture. In the most spiritual poem of the opening sequence, "The Hermit Prays," the hermit offers a prayer to the "god" of the bird, holding a nest in his hand as he does so:

> I hold in my hand this cup
> this ritual, this slice of womb
> woven of birchbark strips
> and the woolly part of a burst cocoon
> all mortared with mud and chinked
> with papers of snakeskin.
>
> (GT 146)

The resonant image of the nest suggests the significance of the female principle in the nature of *Up Country* as a whole, initiating a theme that is repeated often in later books. Moreover, the hermit's appreciative coexistence with birds and other creatures introduces an ideal that is essential to Kumin's understanding of the human role in nature.

Two later poems in *Up Country* show what results when the ideal is violated. In one of them, "The Vealers," the female is under attack. The poem explains how calves raised for veal are taken from their mothers after birth and placed in individual pens where milk "comes on schedule in a nippled pail." The result is torment for calves and cows alike:

> . . . Bleating racks the jail.

> Across the barn the freshened cows
> answer until they forget who is there.
> Morning and night, machinery
> empties their udders, Grazing allows
> them to refill. The hungry
> calves bawl and doze sucking air.
> (*GT* 163)

"Woodchucks" reveals a narrator who becomes so obsessed by the wood-chucks entering her garden that she gasses their underground homes, and when that method fails, turns to her .22, "righteously thrilling / to the feel" of bullets. Given the value of femaleness and nurture in *Up Country*, it is significant that the first animals she kills are two babies and their mother. Yet the speaker is unfazed; she hunts the last of the woodchucks to the very end of the poem:

> . . . Old wily fellow, he keeps
> me cocked and ready day after day after day.
> All night I hunt his humped up form. I dream
> I sight along the barrel in my sleep.
> If only they'd consented to die unseen
> gassed underground the quiet Nazi way.
> (*GT* 155)

The poem's last two lines are telling, for by linking the woodchuck hunt to the murders of Nazis, Kumin shows us how dark the narrator's obsession really is and how far from the hermit's ideal of coexistence the speaker has taken us.

Despite human lapses, however, Kumin's poetry strongly affirms our relationship with animals. That affirmation is summarized and extended in "Watering Trough," a poem whose apparent modesty of subject might at first obscure its importance. The narrator of the poem opens by praising the Yankee practice of placing old bathtubs outdoors as watering troughs for livestock.

> Let the end of all bathtubs
> be this putting out to pasture
> of four Victorian bowlegs
> anchored in grasses.
> (*GT* 165)

It does not matter, she implies here and in later lines, that the tubs will never again be used indoors for the civilized ritual of bathing; for now, they have entered a truer existence as vessels for the animals, who come to them carrying burdock and thistle, to "slaver the scum of / timothy and clover / on the castiron lip that / our grandsires climbed over." No verse in *Up Country* is more amusing than this one, yet "Watering Trough" has a serious side as well. By making her bowlegged tub a comic symbol of the civilized order and by inviting both the animals of the field to drink from the tub and us to join in her celebration of its new function, Kumin allows us to think beyond the barriers civilization has placed between us and animals and to appreciate our connection with the creatural life.

The humor of "Watering Trough" is mixed with an inspirational tone Kumin returns to and amplifies in several later poems. Often, the subject of these poems is horses. Consider "The Grace of Geldings in Ripe Pastures" from her sixth book, *The Retrieval System*. It is hard to say just how this poem manages its uplifting praise of three horses grazing as a rain commences. Partly, the effect comes from their great size and their elemental quality; partly, it comes from the innocence of the metaphors used to describe them as they browse half-asleep in the shower (they "soak up drops / like laundry waiting to be ironed" and their sides "drip like the ribs of very broad / umbrellas"); and certainly part of the effect results from the oneness they have with the natural world, releasing their own restorative water as they stand in the restorative rain of nature:

> . . . And still they graze
> and grazing, one by one let down
>
> their immense, indolent penises
> to drench the everlasting grass
> with the rich nitrogen
>
> that repeats them.
> (*RS* 67)

In "Amanda Dreams She Has Died and Gone to the Elysian Fields," from the Amanda poems of *House, Bridge, Fountain, Gate*, the human observer draws much closer, participating in the elemental and changeless reality the horse represents. The narrator of the poem may encounter Amanda in a particular moment in a hayfield, but she also finds her in a timelessness that includes all creatural life, going back to prehistory:

> This morning Amanda
> lies down during breakfast.
> The hay is hip high.
> The sun sleeps on her back
> as it did on the spine
> of the dinosaur

> the fossil bat
> the first fish with feet
> she was once.
>   (*HBFG* in *GT* 133)

Identifying with Amanda's timelessness on this radiant morning, the speaker experiences a purity even though, given her human limitations, she must at last reenter the world of time. As the speaker puts it, "For an hour / we are incorruptible."

Given the possibilities of such connections—given simply the need for a coexistence with animals, as initially presented in *Up Country*—Kumin is continually troubled in her later volumes by the ways humans exploit other creatures. "The Selling of the Slaves," also from *House, Bridge, Fountain, Gate*, shows how racehorses are auctioned off, their value determined by the status and wealth they may bring to the humans who own them. From the same book, "Heaven as Anus" tells us:

> In the Defense Department there is a shop
> where scientists sew the eyelids of rabbits open
> lest they blink in the scorch of a nuclear drop
>
> and elsewhere dolphins are being taught to defuse
> bombs in the mock-up of a harbor and monkeys
> learn to perform the simple tasks of draftees.
>
> It is done with electric shocks.
>   (*HBFG* in *GT* 127)

Nor is it only *others* who have failed in their dealings with animals. The speaker in "Territory," from *The Retrieval System*, suggests that Kumin knows failure, too: "Mistaking him for a leaf, I cut a toad / in two with the power mower." The poem concludes with an irony directed at all twentieth-century humans, including herself.

> . . . We are
> in it willynilly with our machinery
> and measurements, and all for the good.
>
> One rarely sees the blood of a toad.
>   (*RS* 64)

Several of Kumin's poems indicate her guilt about exploiting animals for food. In "Diary," from *The Long Approach*, the creatures so exploited are two sheep, whom her narrator prepares with grain as though they are "Hansel and Gretel." The poem's final, ironic lines, addressed to the sheep, show an ambivalence about the animals' slaughter: "We meant you no harm / but this. Forgive our full plates" (*LA* 68). The theme of eating animal flesh also surfaces in *Nurture*, where "The Accolade of the Animals" recalls George Bernard Shaw's vision of all the creatures he never ate appearing "single file in his funeral / procession." Speaking of herself and all others who are not, as Shaw was, vegetarian, Kumin comments

> . . . How we omnivores
> suffer by comparison
> in the jail of our desires
> salivating at the smell of char. . . .
>   (*N* 17–18)

The suggestion that Kumin is not blameless in the harm done to other creatures is the more significant when one considers the section from which this poem comes. Called "Catchment," the section deals with the ways in which our civilization, whose advancement we are all "willynilly" part of, has betrayed other creatures, particularly those in danger of extinction. Using the pronoun *we* in many of these poems, Kumin accepts that her membership in modern society implicates her in the harm brought to animals; at the same time, the pronoun allows her to speak to her fellow humans about how serious that harm is. There is no American poet in her generation who has written a comparable series of poems about species both menaced and endangered by our civilization, and no poet for whom the subject is more appropriate. The series demonstrates how, in her later career, Maxine Kumin has enlarged upon her theme of the relationship between humans and animals, moving from the local to the global.

The menaced animals of "Catchment" cover a wide range, from caribou to aquatic mammals to trumpeter swans. The menaces are technological expansion, land development, littering the seas, wholesale hunting, and other offenses, including even bungled attempts to forestall animal extinction. Recalling Kumin's old themes of procreation and nurture, the creatures under attack are often females with eggs or young—an approach that makes us the more aware of their vulnerability. For instance, in "Thoughts on Saving the Manatee," the manatees, "mostly cows and their calves" ingest "snarls of fishing line or / the plastic ribbons that tie / beer cans together" as well as "metal pop tops that razor // their insides." And in "Homage to Binsey Poplars," the Norway rat, introduced by the Allies during their tenure on the poem's island, have "stayed to suck / the yolks from the eggs" of the rare Aleutian goose.

Near the end of "Catchment" are two poems—"Sleeping with Animals" and "Encounter in August"—that imply more appropriate behavior and attitudes toward animals. The narrator in the first keeps a "covenant" with a "vastly pregnant" brood mare, attending her during the night in case the horse should give birth. In the poem, Kumin returns once more to the communication that is possible with animals and the connection all creatures share:

> What we say to each other in the cold black
> of April, conveyed in a wordless yet perfect
> language of touch and tremor, connects
> us most surely to the wet cave we all
> once burst from gasping, naked or furred,
> into our separate species.
>
> (*N* 21)

The speaker in the second poem discovers a bear eating Kentucky Wonders in her green bean patch. At last the bear goes, she tells us,

> supreme egoist, ambling
> into the woodlot on all fours
> leaving my trellis flat and beanless
> and yet I find the trade-off fair:
> beans and more beans for this hour of bear.
>
> (*N* 22)

This verse's exemplum of mutual benefit through coexistence has early precedents, of course, in Maxine Kumin's poetry. Another familiar aspect of "Encounter in August" appears at the margins of its action, where Kumin comments that the natural world in which the charmed meeting of human and bear takes place is "not Eden." Whatever guidance she may have found in the work of her fellow New Englander, Thoreau (she has written that she rereads *Walden* every one or two years), Kumin's nature is hardly a benevolent source of "higher laws," as his is, even though hers is often collaborative. So in this poem, she refers to killing frosts; in others, to an assortment of natural hardships: high winds and oppressive heat, fatal lightning storms, winter blizzards. Sometimes the darknesses of Kumin's nature are associated with human darknesses, as in "Getting Through," from *The Long Approach*, where the continuous falling of snow brings on thoughts of "[b]ombs and grenades, the newly disappeared" and the ending of the world (*LA* 58). One more example, from the same volume, is "In the Upper Pasture," which likens an evergreen grove whose closely grown trunks could trap an unsuspecting foal to a painful woods all creatures must travel. "Each of us," Kumin says, "whimpers his way through the forest alone" (*LA* 64).

Yet the couple in this poem carry on with their work in the grove, limbing low branches and fencing off dangerous trees to create a shelter for mares and their foals. "Let the babies be safe here," Kumin concludes,

> let them lie down on pine duff
> away from the merciless blackflies, out of the weather.
> Under the latticework of old trees let me stand
> pitch-streaked and pleasured by this small thing we have done.
>
> (*LA* 64)

Celebrating her small ritual of protecting horses against natural adversity, the speaker also affirms the relationship between humans and animals found in Kumin's verse, early and late—a relationship that sustains the speaker in spite of the troubles nature disposes and may, she implies here as elsewhere, also sustain us.

All of which brings us to Maxine Kumin's 1992 collection, *Looking for Luck*. In this volume, one of the most integrated and moving of her impressive career, there are few verses without animals, and in many poems animals are essential. Recapitulating and broadening themes from her earlier volumes, *Looking for Luck* gives us Kumin's fullest statement about the relationship between humans and nature's other creatures; therefore, it deserves particular attention.

"Looking for Luck in Bangkok" (*LL* 19), the thesis poem that appears at the outset of Kumin's book, introduces the volume's central themes. In the poem the narrator joins a small congregation of Asians seeking miraculous relief from the misfortunes of "grief, unruly children, and certain / liver complaints." Significantly, the line these human seekers form leads to an animal—one of the East's most venerable: an elephant. Squatting in the shade of this "honest structure," she recalls the comforting smells of her mother's pantry; yet she is unable to keep thoughts of drought, parasites, and ivory poachers out of her mind, coming to the conclusion that the animal from whom she seeks relief needs relief also—that, as the poem puts it, her good luck is "running in / as his runs out." Following the hints of the story in "Looking for Luck in Bangkok," the later poems of Kumin's book explore misfortunes faced by both animals and humans in our time, and suggest the spiritual well-being we humans may find through a connection with other creatural life.

The warning of environmental dangers for the elephant in "Looking for Luck in Bangkok" deepens in a later poem, "Subduing the Dream in Alaska," where prisoners participating in a poetry workshop relate their dreams of conquering their first seals in the Inuit villages of their childhood. Kumin contrasts the surprising innocence of their dreams with the dark image of the true "conquerer," corporate and governmental development, whose wholesale corruption of the environment continues unchecked outside prison walls:

> At a gallop he rides them, building our highway,
> scratching up earthworks, laying our pipeline,
> uncorking the bottle and smiling betrayal.
>
> (*LL* 44)

Going a step beyond "Looking for Luck in Bangkok," this poem makes clear that violations of the natural world threaten their human perpetrators as well as animals.

Some of the other threats to humans in *Looking for Luck* parallel the afflictions of the Bangkok citizens in Kumin's introductory poem. So there are verses that deal with grief, sickness, and in a lovely lyric called "Telling the Barn Swallow" (about the departure of a daughter), trouble posed by a child (*LL* 74-75). The misfortunes of still other poems mirror the social distress of a difficult century. "The Chambermaids in the Marriot in Mid-Morning," for instance, is not only about the cleaning women whose mates "drink, run around . . . total their cars and are maimed" but about the forgotten women of the underclass (*LL* 79). "The Geographic Center" describes the long-term relationship between the narrator and her husband; and in the process, the struggles of their American generation, faced with World War II, race riots, and political assassinations (*LL* 65-67). In the verse "Fat Pets On" we learn of refugees from Abu Dhabi who may be sent home again to "death squads / or twenty years of hardship prison" (*LL* 51-53); in "The Poets' Garden," of the forced labor of poets in China (*LL* 63-64).

Yet *Looking for Luck* is nothing if not a hopeful book. In "The Geographic Center" the speaker declares herself, her mate, and her generation "prisoners of hope," even though "[w]e shoulder what this life has lots / of" (*LL* 67). Hope's image in the book is often the winged creatures of the natural world. The couple of "The Geographic Center" are uplifted by the daily arrival of a pair of pileated woodpeckers. And the mother of "Telling the Barn Swallow" relieves anxiety about her daughter's leaving by conversation with a bird mother feeding her young. In "The Poets' Garden," the wings belong to egg-laden cabbage moths in the fields where the poets are forced by their government to labor. Kumin's description of what will hatch from the eggs of the moths suggests a revolution to come:

> . . . it is still raining
> in the poets' garden. But they are planting

and busy white moths flutter
at random along the orderly rows,
a trillion eggs in their ovipositors
waiting to hatch into green loopers
with fearsome jaws.

(*LL* 64)

If winged creatures provide signs of hope in *Looking for Luck*, animals often make affirmation possible. The speaker of "Credo," the prologue poem of the book, states her belief in the importance of animals to her—and our—spiritual health, celebrating the wild she-bear and cub whom she offers "as much yardage / as they desire," and the bear to whom she "cedes a swale of chokecherries in August." Moreover, citing Kiowa legend, she praises the animal selves that are inside us waiting to be released and reveals the bond that is possible with animals through her "magic" horses.

I trust them to run from me . . . I trust them
to gallop back, skid to a stop, their nostrils
Level with my mouth, asking for my human breath
that they may test its intent, taste the smell of it.
I believe in myself as their sanctuary
and the earth with its summer plumes of carrots,

its clamber of peas, beans, masses of tendrils
as mine . . .

(*LL* 16)

As this passage implies, it is by experiencing our connection with other creatures that we may better know our connection with the natural world in general. Such knowledge may be increasingly hard to come by, Kumin suggests, given our historical period of threats to the environment and sociopolitical distraction and distress. Nonetheless, it is knowledge Kumin claims in *Looking for Luck* as essential. The theme of our link with animals and the natural world has, of course, been part of Kumin's work from the beginning. The difference in this book is that, building on her global approach in *The Long Approach* and *Nurture*, she has managed to place that theme even more fully in the context of social and historical realities, allowing us to better understand both what it means to her and what it might mean to us.

Horses, which populate a number of books preceding *Looking for Luck*, are at the center of this volume, clarifying the relationship she consecrates in "Credo." Two vivid portrayals of Kumin and horses show how early her bond with them was made. She encounters her first horse, recalled in "The Confidantes," at not quite four:

When he clops into sight the trees take fire,
the sun claps hands, dust motes are becalmed.
They boost me up to his shifting throne—
Whoa, Ebony!—and I put my palms
flat on the twitching satin skin
that smells like old fruit, and memory begins.

(*LL* 84)

"Hay," a long and moving tribute to the rural life, remembers Kumin at eleven riding a pony on a dairy farm in Pennsylvania.

Mornings we rode the ponies bareback
up through the eiderdown of ground fog,
up through the strong-armed apple orchard
that snatched at us no matter how we ducked,
up to the cows' vasty pasture, hooting and calling.

(*LL* 27)

In "*Ars Poetica*: A Found Poem," about retraining a deeply unhappy and terrified horse to accept cues from its human rider, Maxine Kumin returns to the issue of trust, first raised in "Credo." In the earlier poem, trust was given to the horse by the speaker; in this one, the speaker aspires to receive it from the horse. Webster's abridged dictionary calls *trust* "something committed to the care of another," something associated with "hope" and "belief." The commitment Kumin has in mind in both poems is just this delicate and interior. How the speaker manages to gain it in "*Ars Poetica*: A Found Poem" is through a patient and loving identification, becoming one with the horse in ways only the verse itself can say. I quote the poem here in full.

Whenever I caught him down in the stall, I'd approach.
At first he jumped up the instant he heard me slide
the bolt. Then I could get the door open while
he stayed lying down, and I'd go in on my hands
and knees and crawl over to him so that
I wouldn't appear so threatening. It took
six or eight months before I could simply walk in
and sit with him, but I needed that kind of trust.

I kept him on a long rein to encourage him
to stretch out his neck and back. I danced with him
over ten or fifteen acres of fields with a lot
of flowing from one transition to another.
What I've learned is how to take the indirect route.
That final day I felt I could have cut
the bridle off, he went so well on his own.

(*LL* 24)

Kumin's poem is not only about horse training but about the emotional and even spiritual exchange that is possible between creature and human. That the verse also hints at the process of bringing a poem into being shows how deeply the relationship with horses has informed the life of this poet.

If luck in Kumin's book is to be found in a special encounter with animals, as the thesis verse "Looking for Luck in Bangkok" implies, clearly she has found some in this poem. She discovers more in "Praise Be," whose narrator assists in the birth of a foal. "Praise Be" concludes with an invocation that combines reverence and ecstasy:

> Let them prosper, the dams and sucklings.
> Let nothing inhibit their heedless growing.
> Let them raise up on sturdy pasterns
> and trot out in light summer rain
> onto the long lazy unfenced fields
> of heaven.
>
> (*LL* 23)

The "let" of Kumin's moving invocation recalls the same verb in several previous poems that call upon readers to recognize the significance of animals and their significance to us.

The epilogue of *Looking for Luck* is a fanciful and startling verse about the relationship between humans and animals. Called "The Rendezvous," the poem features an encounter between a female speaker and a male bear. Mindful of the legend that a woman can cause a bear to retreat in shame by taking off her clothes, the speaker unbuttons her blouse and slips off her skirt. Surprisingly, the bear does not retreat, but instead, follows her example:

> . . . He takes out
> his teeth . . .
> He turns
> his back and works his way
> out of his pelt,
> which he casts to the ground
> for a rug.
>
> (*LL* 91)

"How," the narrator asks, "can he run away unfurred? / How can I, without my clothes?" She concludes her poem and the book itself with the one-line stanza that follows: "How we prepare a new legend."

Yet for anyone familiar with Maxine Kumin's poetry about humans and animals, the legend of "The Rendezvous" is really not new, however unusual the narrator's situation may be. The fact is, Kumin has been preparing that legend for a long time, in poems that challenge us to acknowledge and honor the bonds we share with other animals and to recover our creatural selves in the process. It is perhaps now up to us, the readers of those remarkable and wise poems, to make the legend an old one.

🐾 R O B I N   B E C K E R

Out of Our Skins:
Transformation and the Body in
the Poems of Maxine Kumin

As a formal poet, Maxine Kumin has an *a priori* commitment to metrical possibility and the rhetorical and prosodic strategies that have, historically, grounded English verse. As a poet who has written extensively in the first person, who has made the female subject the "subject" of much of her work, she is a pioneer in the realm of female subjectivity. How does a poet trained in traditional English meters and forms engage with the politically aware feminist survivor of the late twentieth century? Appropriated by men, the female body in poetry has often served as a site for male desire, as an unavailable object, as the muse, and in religious verse, as the vessel that contains the child-savior. It is only in the past century that women writers (with exceptions of course) in great numbers have produced their own images, offered alternative narratives and identities, and critiqued the masculinist vision of the body that overwhelmed (and to some extent continues to overwhelm) contemporary American poetry.

How does a lover of the "meter-making argument" step outside the received notions of where and how the female body belongs? I am interested in exploring Maxine Kumin's images and language for the body. How and where do the lines between bodies blur? And what of bodies of water? The bodies of other animals? The physical body is the starting point for this examination of the poet's "body-identity." However, a metaphysical "body of knowledge"—belief in the rebirth of the soul in another body, Native myth, magic—informs these poems. Practical horsewoman and bemused magician, Maxine Kumin gives her readers the singular human body bursting free from its isolation into communion with other animals, landscapes, elements. This identity with the "world's body" takes many forms. Examining poems from several books, I will investigate the prosody, politics, and particular metaphysics that undergird poems of physical transcendence and transformation.

I came to Maxine Kumin's poetry in the early 1970s, at a time when I was searching for women writers who wrote about women's experiences from an "embodied" position. Like many poets who articulated the anger they felt at misogynist culture, I identified and learned how to use personal rage. Others wrote of the war in Vietnam. Some wrote of their own impossible female circumstances as lesbians or straight women. Kumin offered images of women struggling to connect with life through the body, through activity: gardening, horseback riding, caring for farm animals, befriending other women. I needed all of those poets to put together a mosaic floor on which to stand. And I valued each for her particular insights into her own life.

One aspect of Maxine Kumin's work that continues to enrich my life is the sheer abundance and richness of poems that celebrate the body's struggle, survival, and joy in the world. While there are certainly grim poems (on family, personal loss, species extinction, the "nuclear night") in every book, Kumin often enough praises our human capacity to bear hardship and grief, to sustain ourselves despite forces of destruction that may seem unendurable. She finds much to love.

In "Morning Swim," an early poem from Kumin's 1965 book *The Privilege* (*GT* 191) the poet envisions a female athlete who, swimming and humming a Protestant hymn, embodies the "natural" and the "spiritual." Composed in strict iambic tetrameter, the poem consists of twelve rhymed couplets, nine of which are end-stopped. In the third and fourth stanzas, Kumin eliminates the known markers that orient us in space and time: "There was no line, no roof or floor / to tell the water from the air. // Night fog thick as terry cloth / closed me in its fuzzy growth." Of the seven syllables in the third line quoted above, all but two are stressed, creating a dense line and replicating in metrical terms Kumin's visual image. The onomatopoetic quality of "fuzzy" helps in the transition from the known to the unknown world of the lake.

I find few couplets as self-conscious and erotically charged as the fifth couplet in this poem: "I hung my bathrobe on two pegs. / I took the lake between my legs." Here the speaker claims the whole of the lake as her lover, with the anaphora emphasizing the declarative subject-verb construction ("I hung" and "I took") of the two sentences. Once the speaker is in the water, she assumes a new identity: "Invaded and invader, I / went overhand on that flat sky. // Fish twitched beneath me, quick and tame. /

In their green zone they sang my name." In these two couplets, ringing changes on the verb *invade*, Kumin gives us an "invader" who enters not to attack or damage but to join and thus set in motion her own transformation. Declaring herself both "invaded and invader," she finds a way to eroticize the lake swim without sacrificing female autonomy or agency.

In the last five couplets, Kumin names, describes, and transforms the parts of the body. She celebrates her communion with the fish, the lake, and her own internal music, inscribed in the hymn, referenced twice: "I hummed 'Abide With Me.' The beat / rose in the fine thrash of my feet." The caesura, occasioned by the period midline, reinforces the steady movement of the swimmer's body by sustaining a momentary pause. When the line turns, we're caught off course, opening with a trochee, getting back on course with an iamb, impelled forward again with a second ("thrash of") trochee.

By the end of the poem the speaker has become an altogether new creature. "My bones drank water; water fell / through all my doors. I was the well // that fed the lake that met my sea / in which I sang 'Abide With Me.'" In her new state, the bones "drink" and water flows through the body's "doors." The expressive substitution of a spondee for an iamb in "drank water" emphasizes the bones' sudden magical properties; and the repetition of the word *water* evokes a continuous fountain, a shifting sieve through which water restlessly moves. Beginning in "chilly solitude," the swimmer takes the lake as her lover; couplets facilitate this pairing. The final statement of identity begins with the declaration "I was the well," suggesting the speaker is a "source" or repository of emotion, information, wisdom. Through the rhythm of the iambic tetrameter, the swimmer achieves a spiritual connection with the natural world, and her body ("the well"), feeding the lake, becomes a living body of water. For the Jewish agnostic, the hymn by Henry Lyte (1793-1847) provides paradoxical accompaniment: though hymnal scholars believe the hymn is a call to Christ or God at the close of the day or at the close of life, Kumin uses it to summon all of nature ("beach," "air," "sky," "lake," and "sea") at the beginning of the day, at a time of health and vigorous activity.

To give a new bodily form to the human spirit is Kumin's project in many poems, and animals and birds frequently serve as these new "embodiments." In "The Retrieval System" (*RS* 1-2), from the book of the same name, reincarnation allows the animals in the poem to refract and reinvigorate the poet's beloved dead. "It is people who fade, / it is animals that retrieve them," the speaker says, and the poet goes on to offer explicit pairings, linking dog and Dad, goat and piano teacher, adored young man and yearling colt. When the poem opens, both dog and father are dead, though the dog, throughout his long life "carried about in his head the brown eyes of my father." By opening with this "double loss," Kumin immediately deepens the poem, complicating the grief by "having" the person (in animal form) and then losing him again. In the penultimate line, the poet tells us, "The forecast is nothing but trouble," a statement that honors the inevitable, upcoming losses and prepares us for the final image of the "open graves."

The lines in "The Retrieval System" lengthen out from Kumin's familiar four- and five-stressed line to include six and seven strong stresses per line. This feeling—of lines building and spilling over—is consistent with the poem's focus on "reappearance" and transformation. Kumin's word choice and diction are sometimes comic, such as her language for the goat who "blats in the tiny voice of my former piano teacher / whose bones beat time in my dreams and whose terrible breath / soured 'Country Gardens,' 'Humoresque,' and unplayable Bach." Recalling the funeral of her sister, the speaker quotes the first line from Psalm 23. In the context of this poem, "The Lord is my shepherd" imputes a divine presence to the family dog, consistent with the poem's purposes. She follows with "I don't want to brood," playing with the expected phrase ("I shall not want") by refusing to meditate on loss and choosing, instead, her cherished reincarnations.

Kumin manipulates stanza length strategically in this poem, as she does in others. Beginning with three stanzas of six lines, she adds two lines to the fourth and three lines to the fifth stanzas. These additions convey the emotional "weight" of the accumulating dead. Certain people "return" repeatedly: "A boy / I loved once keeps coming back as my yearling colt." This boy's repeated appearances justify the stanza's additional two lines.

While an iambic undercurrent runs throughout the poem, many substitutions create variety and surprise. Assonance, consonance, and internal rhyme give this poem its pleasurable music and help create unity. Consider two lines from the third stanza: "The sister who died at three has my cat's faint chin, / my cat's inscrutable squint, and cried catlike in pain." The word *cat* makes three appearances, but more subtle and more Kuminesque is the repetition of the short *i* sound in "sister," "chin," "in," "inscrutable," and "squint." In combination with the internal rhymes of "died" and "cried," "pain" and "faint," this music communicates Kumin's intent: to find beloved human beings in "the patient domestic beasts" of her life.

Imagining *herself* reincarnated is the task of the speaker in "Reviewing the Summer and Winter Calendar of the Next Life" from *Nurture* (pp. 52–53). Mediating sky and ground, birds activate the air with their "scolding," "bombing," and "sweeping," and they suit the poet's need to return in an acceptable (and graceful) form. Beginning in a jaunty tone, the poet makes us laugh at the barn swallows:

> If death comes in July, they'll put me down
> for barn swallow, consigned to an 18-hour
> day of swoopings and regurgitations.
> No sooner the first set of fledglings lined up
> five perfect clones on the telephone wire
> than another quartet of eggs erupts in the slap-
> dab nest. *Is there no rest in this life?*

The first and second stanzas open with if/then constructions, setting up, with dispatch, the hypothetical reincarnations in July and January. Kumin does not linger on the details of her own imagined death; she invokes the birds instead. Composed in twelve lines, the first stanza contains four complete sentences and a rhetorical question. Verbs such as *erupt, scold,* and *flap* evoke the activities of the barn swallow family and create a stop-and-start feeling in the stanza. The second, eleven-line stanza is one long, sinewy sentence composed, like the others, in loose blank verse. Here, Kumin considers life as a grosbeak, wild turkey, or junco, evoking each and implying, with her comic tone, that every life form has difficulties, like the junco "whose job description involves / sweeping up after everybody else."

Appealing to the "assigner" of bodies and souls, Kumin begins the third and final stanza: "I only ask not ever to come back as / weasel, present but seldom seen." Linked to treachery and evasiveness, the weasel embodies our least gracious qualities, and the speaker clearly wants no part of him. However, she can't help making a comparison to her own species: "Rat-toothed egg-sucker, making do / like any desperate one of us." Reincarnation prompts Kumin to think of formal structures — "systems" and "calendars" — that organize our lives and our time, much like the stately stanzas that comprise these two poems. Images of reincarnation allow Kumin to elide the distance and difference between human beings and our fellow creatures. Communication across species permits the poet to illustrate the "porous" nature of the body, the ability to "feel" for other bodies.

In Kumin's elegies for her friend Anne Sexton, she achieves an intimacy that bridges the distance between the dead and the living and provides readers with another way of thinking about the individuated female body and the ties of female friendship. (See "Splitting Wood at Six Above," "Progress Report," "Apostrophe to a Dead Friend," "On Being Asked to Write a Poem in Memory of Anne Sexton," and "The Green Well.") In "How It Is" from *The Retrieval System* (p. 46), Kumin blurs distinctions between the two women friends by metaphorically "taking on" Sexton's outward aspect.

In the opening line from "How It Is," Kumin addresses her friend with a rhetorical question that establishes the poet's (and poem's) claim: "Shall I say how it is in your clothes?" The three anapests create a ponderous feeling, the lightness of the first two syllables giving way to the final stress. The second line, four iambic feet and two trochaic feet, doubles the length of the previous line and introduces the poem's key image: "A month after your death I wear your blue jacket." In the first two lines of the poem, Kumin uses the word *your* three times, highlighting the separation between the two women. (In the course of the poem, she uses the words *you* and *your* eleven times.) However, she immediately undercuts that separation with the third and fourth lines. "The dog at the center of my life recognizes / you've come to visit, he's ecstatic." The dog's confusion aids in the blurring of distinctions here, as now the friends even smell alike, conflating them into a single, totemic being. In the tenth line of the eleven-line stanza, Kumin continues to bring the two women closer and closer together: "My skin presses your old outline." Here the word *presses* divides the line in half, putting one woman on either "side" of the word. At the same time, the speaker's "skin" touches the ghostly "outline" of her friend.

Kumin's canny use of sentence structure marks this poem. Eight complete sentences (including the opening rhetorical question) fill the eleven lines of the first stanza, in contrast to the single, lyrical sentence that comprises the second. Reconstructing the "last day" of her friend's life, the poet runs "the home movie backward," imagines Sexton rising from the "death car" and returning to "a kitchen place." End-rhyme yokes the lines together ("collage/garage," "paste/unlaced," "space/place"), and syntactical repetitions of prepositional phrases create steady, incremental movements. In the last line of the second stanza, we find the first mention of "our words," the personal pronoun shifting (from "your" or "my") and linking the two women beyond death. The emphasis on writirg as connection comes clear when "words" reappears in the final stanza.

Composed of three sentences in seven lines, the third stanza opens with the direct address, "Dear friend," echoing "old friend" from the second stanza. Here, Kumin contrasts the "excited crowds" who come to hear Sexton's work with herself: "I will be years gathering up our words, / fishing out letters, snapshots, stains, / leaning my ribs against this durable cloth / to put on the dumb blue blazer of your death." The daily life suggested by "letters, snapshots, stains" brings the poem into the plain, domestic sphere, far from the crowds "straining at your seams." The speaker's loss has been an intimate rather than a public loss, and Kumin's return to the image of the "dumb blue blazer" makes her point. The alliterated *b*'s and *d*'s, the force of the three strong stresses ("dumb blue blazer"), and the end-rhyme ("cloth . . . death") reveal Kumin's prosodic strategies. And the very personal act of putting on her friend's clothes transforms the speaker, visually and psychologically. From now on, she will "always already" be both herself and her friend.

Twenty-five years after the publication of "How It Is," Kumin is still experimenting with form while writing about the body. In her 1989 collection, *Nurture*, the poet employs couplets, rhymed tercets, blank verse, and variations on rime royale and ottava rima to shape her arguments. While her stanzas show a looser adherence to strict end-rhyme, she continues to work each line with subtle slant/internal rhyme, alliteration, and carefully crafted sentence constructions. Her ongoing investigation into "the body" now reflects her knowledge and concern about animal rights activism, the environment, globalization, public health, and media access. Kumin focuses on the interdependence between animals and people, posing questions about biodiversity, the utility of science and technology, and stewardship. In poems from the section called "Catchment," Kumin speaks in a public voice. She has not abandoned her concern for the spiritual realm; she has simply refused to see our earthly existence as "provisional." She refuses to postpone her vision of a "sustainable" world for some promised eternity, knowing that we have no recourse to a "private" realm once we have degraded our water or air. As the poet in "Morning Swim" celebrates her communion with the "body" of the lake, so the poet in "With the Caribou" (*N 5*) celebrates her identification with the (bodies of) animals losing habitat and facing possible starvation.

The poem begins in a "timeless" fantasy of sleigh-riding behind three reindeer. Kumin's iambic pentameter establishes a regular rhythm for her twenty-five lines, arranged into two eight-line and one nine-line stanzas. Four repetitions of the phrase "I want" create a recurring, self-absorbed narrative of individual desire in which the poet contrasts the luxury of human wishes ("I want to go for a drive"; "I want to sled over the alpine tundra"; "I want to leap up"; "I want to advise the species") with urgent ecological problems and the possibility of species extinction.

After creating the fantasy world of the first stanza, the speaker takes an admonishing tone in the second, warning the caribou parley about "radio-nuclides / absorbed from the lichen" and "crossings flooded / out by hydro-electric stations." Kumin uses her knowledge of geography and land forms to portray with vividness a landscape threatened by ignorance and greed.

In the third stanza, the speaker abandons the scientific language of an informed wildlife biologist; the distant, well-intentioned voice gives way to one who longs to "be caught up in the streaming southward, / the harsh crowding of antlers uplifted like thousands / of stump-fingered arms." The fantasy of participation jolts the reader as the image turns horrific. Thalidomide? The deformity in this simile suggests a vast chemical maiming, or Hiroshima, or perhaps an evolutionary foresightedness that ought to forewarn.

The poem that began, in the first line, at "the top of the world" slides "backward in time." Only by entering—through fantasy—an earlier historical time and evolutionary form may the poet reclaim her original longing. Transformation into a four-footed creature shows that a characteristic, Kuminesque identity swap has taken place, and the speaker, now one of the caribou herd, circles the South Pole according to the "laws of migration."

In her most recent collection of poems, *Looking for Luck*, Kumin shows her affinity for Native American myth by framing the collection with two poems that make use of bear legends to enact magical transformations. For the poet who sees her beloved dead reincarnated in domestic and farm animals, it is a simple leap into the magic she embraces in "Credo" (pp. 15–16) and "The Rendezvous" (pp. 91–92).

"Credo" is Kumin's statement of faith: in responsible stewardship of the earth, in mutually respectful relationships between human beings and other animals, in the power of myths, legends, magic. Repeating the opening phrase "I believe" eight times, Kumin establishes a quasi-religious tone that unifies the poem; each declaration of belief, however, becomes a sensuous description of the physical world and the poet's engagement with it. In fact, the poem is a prayer or meditation on the speaker's faith in the "embodied" world as it is known through "trillium," "bear," "earthworm," and "horse." Through word choice, Kumin emphasizes the religious/magical aspect of the poem, as when she refers to trillium as "resurrected wake-robin" or to herself as a "sanctuary" for her horses.

For her "manifesto," Kumin selects a simple form: nine four-line stanzas of four and five strong stresses per line. Slant rhyme and internal rhyme, phrasal repetition, and irregular end-rhyme give the poem balance and music. The imagery surprises with its exactness: "wet strings of earthworms" appear out of season; encountering a bear, the poet says, "I cede him a swale of chokecherries in August"; she calls her horses' romp in the pasture "the ballet of nip and jostle, plunge and crow hop." Vivid, tactile, Kumin's imagery invites the reader to experience the world as a "believer" in its mysteries and revelations. The marvelous movements of the horse take on a formal aspect, even as Kumin contrasts a "ballet" with the somewhat chaotic cavorting. In the opening stanza, Kumin introduces the Kiowa legend in which a boy turns into a bear. She returns, in the last stanza, to the legend and reverses the transformation: "I believe in the acrobatics of boy / into bear, the grace of animals / in my keeping, / the thrust to go on." By paralleling "acrobatics," "grace," and "thrust," Kumin weaves together story telling, the world of animals, and human perseverance.

In "The Rendezvous," a twenty-eight-line poem composed in five unequal stanzas, Kumin borrows from Tlingit legend to show a complex and potentially transformative intimacy between bears and human beings. From "The Rendezvous":

> . . . I unbutton
> my blouse. He takes out
> his teeth. I slip off
> my skirt. He turns
> his back and works his way
> out of his pelt,
> which he casts to the ground
> for a rug.
>
> (*LL* 91–92)

Basing her poem on the legend that says that bears may feel shame, that a woman should disrobe before a bear to make him run away, Kumin takes her poem in a more provocative and unsettling direction. She asks her readers to imagine an erotic connection between the species, a loving possibility that precludes the violence we usually associate with a bear rug on the floor. Walking upright some of the time, bears, like primates, return us to our evolutionary history. Kumin turns us away from images of human beings appropriating parts of the bear's body, eating the meat, clothing ourselves in the bear's skin for protection. But with her use of the monosyllabic "blouse," "teeth," "skirt," and "pelt," Kumin disarms bear and woman until they stand, as peers, before one another.

In the opening line of the poem, the poet exclaims "How narrow the bear trail / through the forest," evoking the "narrowness" of our vision for sharing the earth with other creatures. King Wenceslas and his "faithful serf" people this stanza, a relationship of inequality and subservience. Subsequently, each stanza in the poem begins with the word *how*, a strategy that creates an exclamatory as well as a directive tone and indicates that the order of things may be changing. Blended with the straightforward narrative, this repetition of *how* makes the final coupling of bear and woman feel inevitable, the "natural" outcome of the poem's encounter.

For Maxine Kumin, poetry is a place to "prepare a new legend" and transform the beloved—alive and dead. By living fully in the bodies we are given and by loving those creatures we may befriend (distantly or intimately), we transcend the physical limitations of species, gender, age, size, and social importance. Kumin addresses the political circumstances that shape our relationship to other animals and invites us to question our assumptions about what must be. From her I've learned that poetry, while a fine vehicle for sorrow, is also a place to celebrate the "embodied" world.

🐘 MICHAEL BURNS

A Satisfactory Machinery

"It is only by a miracle that poetry is written at all. It is not recoverable thought, but a hue caught from a vaster receding thought," Henry David Thoreau tells us in *A Week on the Concord and Merrimack Rivers*.[1] Referring to Thoreau at the beginning of an essay on Kumin might seem predictable to some readers—anyone who has read both of them knows that they share a geography, a literary vocation, and a life-style that celebrates physical labor—so let me get right to my point.

Although she would probably find *miracle* a dramatic choice of words, I think Maxine Kumin would agree that the art of poetry survives because it allows us a glimpse inside the collective human consciousness. She has discovered how, in her own life, to prepare herself for that "hue caught from a vaster receding thought" when it appears. One of her methods is the focus of my discussion.

First, let me detour. A long look back at the origins of humankind shows us the earlier, evolutionary miracles that have led us to this potential miracle of poetry that Kumin practices and Thoreau describes.

When (and because) we rose from our quadrupedal posture, we found ourselves with our hands freed to fashion tools. And when we had stood for long enough, we discovered in our faces and on our tongues the beginnings of language. So we have learned to make and to say, phenomena that, for the poet, are one and the same. Howard Nemerov, in a famous poem by the same title, calls the first poets "The Makers."

I say all that to say this: when I look at the collected poems of Maxine Kumin, I am drawn to the unique ways her poetry brings together the most defining acts of human existence: our use of tools and of language. One of the ways Kumin finds to share with us the captured "hue" is to write poems that focus on a speaker who is herself a maker, who owns a knowledge of tools, and respects that knowledge. The craft of her poems becomes a tool

---

1. Henry David Thoreau, *A Week on the Concord and Merrimack Rivers*, The American Tradition in Literature, ed. George Perkins et al., 7th ed., vol. 1 (New York: McGraw-Hill, 1990), 1259.

that enables her to cross the border between what she knows and what she may discover.

Consider, for example, these lines from Kumin's poem "Distance":

> Whoever mows with a big machine like this,
> with two forward speeds and a wheel clutch, nippled hand grips,
> a lever to engage the cutting blade, is androgynous
> as is old age. . . .
>
> Androgyny. Another birthday. And all the while
> the muted roar of satisfactory machinery.
> May we flourish and keep our working distance.
>
> (N 60–61)

It's this "working distance" that helps her maintain one of the most important qualities of her poetry—its persistent optimism. Facing the varieties of human loss, her poems show her romantic faith in the possibilities for redemption. And recognizing the aesthetic rewards of manual labor, she uses its rituals to create poetic habits of mind. In *Women, Animals, and Vegetables*, she describes her routine. Only the weather, she tells us, relieves her of the "Jewish-Calvinist urgency to do something useful with one or another of the young stock, to longe or drive or ride the current two-, three-, or four-year-old. Or, in season, to cut around the perimeters of the pastures, work that's known as brushing out. Or clean out and re-bed the run-in sheds and the central area under the barn." She goes on to describe the value of these activities: "Writing and well-being. In the most direct, overt, and uncomplicated way, my writing depends on the well-being that devolves from this abbreviated list of chores undertaken and completed" (*WAV* 17–18). Kumin's attention to chores, along with the necessary tools to get them done, makes it clear that hers is not a faith without works.

Reviewing *Looking for Luck* for the *New York Times Book Review* ("Empty Beds, Nests and Cities," 21 March 1993), Lisa Zeidner points out that Kumin's poems "often begin with a simple observation about the natural world, then fan out to include humans, so that the people seem *part* [italics Zeidner's] of nature rather than its point or apex." A closer look at many of the meditative poems will illustrate another component of the author's strategy. Kumin's narrator is often linked to nature through a specific physical activity that connects person and nature, creating a context for the poem to evolve into a larger philosophical discussion. The tool becomes the bridge.

Of course, Kumin wasn't the first to make such a connection. Here's an early example, from Thoreau at Walden:

One day, when my axe had come off and I had cut a green hickory for a wedge, driving it with a stone, and had placed the whole to soak in a pond hole in order to swell the wood, I saw a striped snake run into the water, and he lay on the bottom, apparently without inconvenience . . . perhaps because he had not yet fairly come out of the torpid state. It appeared to me that for a like reason men remain in their present and low condition, but if they should feel the influence of the spring of springs arousing them, they would of necessity rise to a higher and more ethereal life.[2]

Robert Frost was the modern master of the nature/tool connection, and "Mowing" is one of the most famous examples. He tells us in that poem that "[a]nything more than the truth would have seemed too weak." Kumin borrows that aesthetic from him in "Distance," her contemporary mowing poem:

> Around me old friends (and enemies) are beleaguered
> with cancer or clogged arteries. I ought to be
> melancholy inching upward through my sixties
> surrounded by the ragged edges of so many acres,
> parlaying the future with this aerobic mowing,
> but I take courage from a big wind staving off the deerflies,
>
> ruffling and parting the grasses like a cougar if there
> were still cougars. I am thankful for what's left that's wild.
>
> (N 60–61)

Without ignoring or sentimentalizing the "truth," Kumin presents us here with an almost comic description of the mowing itself, letting the meditation it induces serve as a natural vehicle for her personal statement of ecology.

Scattered throughout Kumin's books, we find a catalog of tools. Some, like Frost's scythe, serve simple, practical purposes, such as her hatchet or the fence posts and the barrel in "Peeling Fence Posts" from *Our Ground Time Here Will Be Brief*. Having used the hatchet to peel the bark from the posts, the speaker describes their transformation at the end of the poem:

> Turning brown as a tribe
> all stand leaning
> together in a barrel
> of oil deepened with creosote
> where, in rainbow blobs
> released from pith and cortex,
> their tree souls float.
>
> (GT 8)

2. Henry David Thoreau, *Walden*, The American Tradition in Literature, ed. George Perkins et al., 7th ed., vol. 1 (New York: McGraw-Hill, 1990), 1281.

In other poems, the tools are the intimate though somewhat more complicated examples of the personal machinery we use to get the job done, like the hay baler and three-quarter-ton truck in "Hay," from her newest book, *Looking for Luck*:

> . . . The old baler cobbled from
> other parts, repaired last winter
> cussed at in the shed in finger-
> splitting cold when rusted bolts
> resisted naval jelly, Coca-Cola, and
> had to be drilled out in gritty bits,
> now thunking like a good eggbeater
> kicks the four-foot cubes off
> onto the stubble for the pickups
> and aggie trucks—that's our three-quarter ton
> Dodge '67, slant-six engine
> on its third clutch, with a new tie rod,
> absent one door handle and an
> intermittent taillight. . . .
>
> (*LL* 26)

We are also given poems that present us with such sophisticated inventions as the implied jet plane and its accompanying vocabulary in "Our Ground Time Here Will Be Brief":

> Blue landing lights make
> nail holes in the dark.
> A fine snow falls. We sit
> on the tarmac taking on
> the mail, quick freight. . . .
>
> (*GT* 3)

The richness of these poems that name and describe and employ such a variety of tools lies in the way the tools lead us to a consideration, if not always an understanding, of the complexities of human experience, especially its losses. The poems themselves become tools for our ontological inquiries. Those blue landing lights, for example, on the strip where we must come down, nail us to a figurative, though mortal, cross. If our ground time is brief, doesn't that mean the spirit lives on, on another level? Kumin stays with the facts, choosing a deliberately neutral diction: "We gather speed for the last run / and lift off into the weather."

Such questions about our mortality grow out of the understanding that the body breaks down, as does everything we build and repair. Like weeds and brush, disorder encroaches, and the poet feels more acutely than anyone that language may be all we have for holding it at bay. What I like is the way Kumin's poetry confronts this entropy. She often chooses the well-

worn tools of traditional prosody—measured stanzas, rhyme, and meter—
adapting them to fit her needs.

In her interviews and essays, using a language that further underlines
the partnership between her physical and intellectual/creative work, Ku-
min explains her approach:

> there is also an order that a human can impose on the chaos of his emotions and
> the chaos of events . . . as you marshal your metaphors really, as you pound and
> hammer the poem into shape and into form, the order—the marvelous informing
> order emerges from it [*To Make a Prairie* 23]. . . . Maybe it's because I'm so com-
> pulsive that I need the shape to hold me together. The harder—that is the more
> psychically difficult—the poem is to write, the more likely I am to choose a difficult
> pattern to pound it into. (*MP* 50)

I think most readers would agree that Kumin's "tribal" poems draw on
material that is "psychically difficult," and they provide excellent examples
of the formal tools that she employs to hammer them into shape. In some
cases, "hammer" may seem too heavy a word. Her use of rhyme in "The
Thirties Revisited" provides a lighter touch of control:

> It's the thirties again, that dream. I'm assigned
> to remember laundry lifting like ghosts
> on the propped-up lines where step-ins blush,
> the cheeks of trousers fill, and skirts
> open their petals in the washday wind.
> But why just now must the horse go lame,
> drop in the shafts and be left behind
> struggling, struggling so to rise
> that blood pours from his nose?
> Why is he shot
> on this Monday noon of my queer pinched life
> as I watch from the parlor window seat?
> (*GT* 93)

Tenuous yet binding, the irregular patterns of slant rhyme in this poem
and in such others as "Life's Work" and "The Knot" from *House, Bridge,
Fountain, Gate* "hold together" the intense emotions of memory.

Kumin uses more regular patterns of formal design in poems like "For
My Son on the Highways of His Mind" and "For My Grandfather: A Mes-
sage Long Overdue." In "The Pawnbroker" one can see how they impose
a crucial order:

> On Saturday nights the lights stayed lit until ten.
> There were cops outside on regular duty to let
> the customers in and out.
> I have said that my father's feet were graceful and clean.
> They hurt when he turned the lock

on the cooks and chauffeurs and unlucky racetrack touts
and carwash attendants and laundresses and stock-
room boys and doormen in epaulets;

they hurt when he did up accounts in his head
at the bathroom sink
of the watches, cameras, typewriters, suitcases, guitars,
cheap diamond rings and thoroughbred
family silver, and matched them against the list
of hot goods from Headquarters,
meanwhile nailbrushing his knuckles and wrists
clean of the pawn-ticket stains of purple ink.

(*GT* 193–94)

Out of the chaos of the past, the demands of form in this poem have helped
Kumin select from what can be overwhelming choices of narrative detail.
They serve as their own "retrieval system."

Kumin uses rhymed stanzas to create darkly comic effects in the dream
poem "The Longing to Be Saved" from *Our Ground Time Here Will Be
Brief*:

Finally, they come to their senses and leap
but each time, the hoop holds my mother.
Her skin is as dry and papery
as a late onion. I take her
into my bed, an enormous baby
I do not especially want to keep.
Three nights of such disquiet
in and out of dreams as thin as acetate

until, last of all, it's you
trapped in the blazing fortress.
I hold the rope as you slide from danger.
It's tricky in high winds and drifting snow.
Your body swaying in space
grows heavier, older, stranger

and me in the same gunny sack
and the slamming sounds as the gutted building burns.
Now the family's out, there's no holding back.
I go in to get my turn.

(*GT* 46)

While the barn burns and events become more chaotic and surreal, the
narrator, like the poem itself, maintains order, keeping her poise.

So the poems depict actual tools, using them to explore the standard
though eternally compelling issues—life, death, sex, love, religion, ambi-
tion. And Kumin's poems add poetic form as a tool to make the most
difficult explorations of human experience possible, art and artifice fulfill-

ing their primary function. "To spend your life on such old premises is a privilege," Kumin's friend and fellow poet Mona Van Duyn says in one of her early poems.

What we have in "Ars Poetica," a "found" poem in *Looking for Luck* (p. 24), is an analysis of those premises. To articulate her theory, Kumin brings together two of her previous "tool" strategies and adds a third. First, the story includes practical tools like bolts and stalls, reins and bridles. Second, it is "hammered" into a set form that echoes the sonnet. In fact, its meaning depends on our attention to the way the lines move carefully toward a traditional pentameter. The third element is embodied in the poem's title. Here we have one of the most sophisticated linguistic tools: a poem as a tool to talk about poetry, art to understand art. As if to directly confront those critics who claim that her plain diction and domestic details limit her achievement, Kumin has chosen to adopt what was, in real life, a common, distinctly nonliterary voice and situation to make her case.

Using a colloquial, five-beat line, she re-creates out of the meetings between trainer and horse the extraordinary story of Pegasus, trusting that this voice will bring down to earth such high drama:

> Whenever I caught him down in the stall, I'd approach.
> At first, he jumped up the instant he heard me slide
> the bolt. Then I could get the door open while
> he stayed lying down, and I'd go in on my hands
> and knees and crawl over to him so that
> I wouldn't appear so threatening. It took
> six or eight months before I could simply walk in
> and sit with him, but I needed that kind of trust.

The speaker wants something from the horse. If she can only earn his trust, she can bridle and tame him and use him to serve her needs. What are the needs of the poet and poetry? How far will the winged horse take us?

Patiently, the poet learns her craft:

> I kept him on a long rein to encourage him
> to stretch out his neck and back. I danced with him
> over ten or fifteen acres of fields with a lot
> of flowing from one transition to another.

The poem, in its understatement, only implies an important part of the story—that the rider of Pegasus wanted him to serve the ultimate purpose and fly with him to the gods. But the further implication is clear: such poets, such riders, will likely find themselves, suddenly and rudely, earthbound.

"What I've learned is how to take the indirect route," the speaker tells us, an answer offered by the whole body of Kumin's work. The way to the gods, such as they are, must be located in the ordinary, especially in those bridges between the natural world and the human. And for Kumin, the art of poetry depends on one's understanding the connection between freedom and restraint, what Frost called "moving easy in harness:"

> That final day I felt I could have cut
> the bridle off, he went so well on his own.

One of the most poignant and resonant poems Kumin has given her readers is "Hay" (*LL* 25–29). It embodies all those successful elements of poetry that have characterized her work, bringing them together in this long (for Kumin), beautiful lyric. It is a poem about community, stewardship, memory, and mystery, all enveloped in a tone drawn from a line she quotes from Neruda: "[w]e are approaching a great and common tenderness."

The tools are here. We have the hay baler and aggie truck mentioned earlier and a pitchfork, wagon, and rope, but no handmade tool surpasses the grace in the hands of the speaker, who remembers herself as a girl with the cows:

> My four were: Lily, Martha, Grace and May.
> May had only three tits. I learned to say *tits*
> as it is written here. I learned to spend
> twenty minutes per cow and five more stripping,
> which you do by dipping your fingers in milk
> and then flattening the aforementioned tit
> again and again between forefinger and thumb
> as you slide down it in a firm and soothing motion.

Even the earth itself and its cycles of death and rebirth are presented as part of the machinery: "Perhaps in the last great turn of the wheel / I was some sort of grazing animal."

Kumin takes chances in this poem. She still employs the formal elements of stanza, slant rhyme, and a base iambic meter to shape the disparate elements of past and present narrative and exposition, but the narrator here seems more vulnerable and more open than most of Kumin's speakers. There is a secret in nature to which she may have once had access:

> We drank milk warm from the pail,
> thirsty and thoughtless of the mystery
> we drank from the cow's dark body. . . .

Perhaps that is why the meditation brought on and made possible by three days' hard work, cutting and baling, leads the speaker to a memory of the "old way," when the hay-filled barn "was alight with its radiant sun-dried manna." So this common hay becomes food sent from the gods, making possible her survival and deliverance.

For the speaker, looking back, the place and time seem also equivalent to Thoreau's "spring of springs." She rises to a higher and more ethereal life, and we are lucky enough as readers to be taken along:

> It was paradise up there with dusty sun motes
> you could write your name in as they skirled and drifted down.
> There were ropes we swung on and dropped from and shinnied up
> to some unknown plateau, tears standing up in my eyes
> and an ancient hunger in my throat, a hunger. . . .

Max's Garden: For Present and Future Consumption

The garden has me backed into a corner—the one by the stove—blanching veggies day & night & doing blueberry pies for present & future consumption. The sugar snap peas are an enormous success, 30 lbs worth in the freezer. Green beans have just come into their own, broccoli and cauliflower are imminent. Today I begin on the beets. Oi! Earth Mother!"—Letter to Author, 31 July 1979

During the twenty-three years of my friendship with Maxine Kumin, which began when she admitted me, then a housewife and mother of a three- and a four-year-old, to a workshop she was teaching at Newton College of the Sacred (or "Secret," as she called it) Heart, I've eaten richly from the actual New Hampshire garden, which grows through her poems like one of her sturdy Kentucky Wonder vines up the hill and beside the pond. A jar of maple syrup from her trees sits even now in my cabinet, having been opened as a treat just days ago when my son and his wife passed through. Therefore, when I was invited to write about an aspect of Max's poetry, that actual garden, so intertwined with the garden of her poetry, rose up before me.

I began with some general notions about the significance of the various gardens in the poems, from the first volume, *Halfway*, to the most recent, *Looking for Luck*. These responded to Maxine Kumin's own word, the "continuum" that appears both explicitly and implicitly in her work, and I set out to discern some of the particulars of the garden and its function in the poems. I expected to find it a source and sustenance, an earthly paradise, an emblem for the work of the poet. The very act of rereading all the poems together revealed some specific aspects of the garden and of the poet's uses of it that were made more vivid by a continuous reading. Further, especially in the last three volumes, the poet clearly indicates that the poems connect with each other as succeeding years' growth along that tough, fecund vine.

The present discussion of Kumin's poetic garden will weave in and out of the ten books of poems, though it is based on my predominantly chronological return to them. I will explore the garden as a vehicle for identity, the imagery of the garden and some of its various effects, and the observation strongly conveyed by my rereading: that an alteration in breadth and intensity manifested through uses of the garden (among other ways) comes with the last three books. The specific nature of that alteration will be suggested primarily through poems in these most recent collections, *The Long Approach*, *Nurture*, and *Looking for Luck*. Finally, to establish the parameters of the discussion, I assign several definitions to the garden in Kumin's poems. First, there is the New Hampshire garden or farm (i.e., a larger-scale garden), which her readers know well through their frequent visits. Other constructions of "garden" that figure occasionally in the present discussion concern field and forage—all manifestations of the wild garden and sharing the ability to provide sustenance for animals. These sources uncultivated by humans yield because it is their nature—with luck, without human obstruction—endlessly to die and revive. Garden qua farm, however, is most often the poet's domain. Over the whole of Kumin's work, a further distinction needs to be made between flower gardens and vegetable gardens. And this distinction we see clearly established from among her earliest poems.

Consider, for instance, how the early gardens of *The Privilege* are associated with female models provided to the speaker of these poems. The garden—literally, what women *grow* into—emerges in "The Spell," "Mother Rosarine," and "A Voice from the Roses." In "The Spell," the mother is seen as a powerful figure who "scolds" the common Stars of Bethlehem and "wrestles" the roses. By her magic, she speaks to the toads. She "infuses" the gingko, which rains long-stemmed fans fit for queens and drops "scrotal fruits"—thus acknowledged as the regal possessor of sexual power. In the background of this garden hover the fairy tales investing mothers with awesome and frightening potential. This duality or ambivalence, as well as the fact of the mother's absolute possession of the garden, is acknowledged explicitly by the poet when she points out "Notice I say my mother's garden / again and again advisedly!"—that is, deliberately, with careful consideration (*TP* 11). The poet's stance alters in two later poems—"The Fairest One of All," when she becomes "the middle-aged queen" to her own daughter, "fair / first born" (*The Nightmare Factory* 45–46), and "A Mortal Day of No Surprises," when she herself ordains and rules: "Out of here! I say / ripping the lime-green tendrils [of false strawberries] from / their pinchhold on my zucchini blossoms" (*The Retrieval System* 68).

"Mother Rosarine," resident of the convent that abuts the poet's mother's garden, presents a very different model but a mother powerful on her own terms. She, a "bristle-chinned queen," keeps the keys of the convent, and it is to her that the speaker of the poem comes "through the hedge" to plumb the secrets of the nuns. When the child takes away a rosary, she feels "the seeds [grow] wet in my palm"—a garden of mystery and otherness, if not faith, to be planted there.

"A Voice from the Roses," which may be read as a companion to "The Spell," establishes the speaker's wish to be free of the mother's magic. Again fairy-tale elements occur: spinning, vengeance, the thorn on which the speaker has lain thirty years and against which she is spinning her own messages. Yet the thorn is "rooted" in her, as witness the final plea, "Mother, Queen of the roses, / wearer of forks and petals, / when may I be free of you?" (*TP* 38). In the later poem, "Post-Op: Lying Flat," hardly coincidence that the recuperating speaker is "lying flat / as a blowzy rose and cultivating some / inner garden" where mums, peonies, crocuses, zinnias all bloom as the loci of pain, causing her to conclude, "Damn flowers and the tilling of such gardens" (*NF* 78).

I see these early poems as an origin for my journey through the subject of the garden in Kumin's work because they demonstrate the necessary and conscious separation of daughter from mother through the physical fact and symbolic value of the garden. The garden assumes multiple meanings in Kumin's poetry; but in terms of self-definition and her profound, continuing attachment to the gardens of her choosing, both in life and art, this formulation represents the staging area for other manifestations and characterizations of the garden.

Beside these poems stand the early ones pointing to New England literary forebears, Emerson and Thoreau, men who clearly represent a relationship between the individual and garden/farm/field at variance with the mother's. When the poet chooses her models, she travels far from the queen of the roses in space, time, and motive. In Kumin's first book, *Halfway*, she pays homage to Thoreau, admiring his "backbreak" work, his thoroughly understandable "curses on / all tillage that requires more / than a day's work for a month of bread" (*HW* 39). But her greatest praise is "I test / and love you for brave cowardice / in the graceless skiff, / in the tightening woodland, / in the tall bean patch, // in life near the bone, / almost true and gone" (*HW* 40). This "life near the bone" that she associates with Thoreau is a way she continues to follow in art and life, even as it disappears from the world at large. The permanence of her homage to Thoreau shows too in "Beans" (*Up Country* 26) and as late as 1985 in the epigraph to *The Long Approach* and a poem in that volume, "My Elusive Guest." Sometimes her quest after Thoreau's way only exacerbates the disparities between the nineteenth-century Americans' time and our own "chrome millennium" (*LL* 23). When the poet looks to Emerson in the face of contemporary events in "Weekend of Death" (*NF* 84), she keeps returning to his transcendental vision and the oversoul, addressing him ironically: "Waldo, pack the pickup / . . . So Waldo, rev the motor." Haunted by images of killing, war, inhuman atrocities, she closes with allusions to Vietnam—napalm, defoliated jungles, bombers:

> The villages go under.
> At night they glow like coal.
> Fire licks the paddies up
> and eats the oversoul.

Seeing the devastation in terms of destruction of the people and the paddies—gardens—that feed them, the poet identifies with that human suffering through a most elemental human need. The ideal vision is consumed simultaneously with the garden.

Returning finally to the mother in terms of the garden as vehicle of self-definition, Kumin writes "Surprises" in 1989 in *Nurture*. The poem leaps boundaries of time and space to reconcile the poet with her mother, who appears here once again with roses, spending all morning to "deal with her arrangements" (*N* 47). The surprises in the poem are several: the sudden yield of California peppers in the speaker's garden, after fifteen years of failure; the memory of the mother's enhancing term for leftovers; and best, the confluence of mother and daughter through the vegetable link, *peppers*. Here, as in other Kumin poems, the garden forms one element of the personal or family continuum. Many familiar subjects and objects reappear in "Surprises" as initiating moment, memory, diction, and metaphor all collaborate to bring mother and daughter into harmony. Only now, when the daughter "look[s] backward longer than forward," is she able to dethorn her mother's roses and to unorphan herself.

Looking both ways through Kumin's poems, I find that crossing over between animal and vegetable worlds consistently receives both explicit and implicit expression. Indeed, it could be argued that transmigrations are the essence of the poet's work. Kumin's tenth book, *Looking for Luck*, begins and ends with explicit crossovers from humans to other animals. Throughout her poems, however, figurative language has rendered permeable the usual convenient walls (Western, at least) between animal and vegetable worlds. No valves ordain movement just one way: sometimes vegetables are assigned human traits, sometimes the reverse. That Emerson's oversoul has operated from the start in Kumin's poetry is perhaps not surprising to her readers. Looking further into the specific language, I noticed some various effects of these crossings-over in the poems—sustaining, consoling, erotic, humorous, ominous, philosophical. Of these, the power to sustain or console seems most potent, primarily because crossover reaffirms Kumin's sense of the "continuum," and here enter her notions of the soul. How things go on is also expressed by the garden as source and repository of memories preserved "for future consumption."

Among the poems in which crossing over produces lighter effects, I count "Cows," with "eyes globed as green figs . . . / inside their irises fields of thought" (*NF* 13). The *Up Country* hermit evades a mosquito by lying "curled like a lima bean / still holding back its cotyledon" (*UC* 15), and a child's conception is the father's "plant[ing] you bald as an onion" (*House, Bridge, Fountain, Gate* 3). Parsnips become rabbis braiding their beards, beets are patients who submit to the scalpel and bleed, and perfection obtains via the onion, "God's first circle" (*HBFG* 41). Against frost, vegetables are like children being tucked in, peppers whimpering (*HBFG* 47); the rutabaga, which kept people alive through the most extreme conditions in World War II is apostrophized as "old swede, / strong-smelling Bigfoot" (*RS* 60). When "A New England Gardener Gets Personal," she describes her vegetables as humans—kale laughs; peppers with pectorals and green hips compare favorably to Greek statues; and the poem closes with a carrot that, like a poet, "puts down deep alone / its secret orange cone" (*LA* 71). Taken together, these images and others like them throughout the poems convey a tone of familiarity, amicability, unsentimental affection—a speaker in easy camaraderie with vegetable realms.

As indicated, I find the most significant effects of, imperatives for, crossover imagery of the animal and garden worlds in Kumin's poems to be those of consolation and sustenance, as these images locate people and events along the continuum, via the garden. Early examples of this use of animal/vegetable crossover surface in a poem such as "The Presence," in which bones become seeds in a burrow (*NF* 5). In "Making the Jam without You" Kumin wishes for her absent daughter berries that are plum size, "heavy as the eyes / of an honest dog," and a lover with whom to make the "annual jam" that has been the women's shared ritual. The "blood of the berries" colors this poem like the blood they share, even apart, when the mother finds comfort in faithful berries (*NF* 39).

Several poems focusing on the illness and death of a favorite brother provide moving examples of the power of the garden to reclaim, console, and continue. As the brother's illness progresses, the poet records how he bravely relinquishes more and more of his faculties yet maintains the capacity for joy. In "The Man of Many L's," as the siblings play "at being normal," the speaker wheels him through the streets of Palo Alto, where he writes for her "the name of every idiot flower / [she does] not know," his illness making him double the letter *L* wherever it appears. At last the brother himself becomes a flower—"The bottlebrush took fire / as you fought to hold your great head on its stem"—a momentary removal of his human pain and losses. The flower garden tour recalls early poems of the queen of the roses; it forges implicitly that connection between sister and brother. Closing with a reference to the brother's *spell* (a pun on spelling but magical power too), it echoes the spell their mother cast over her flora, with the distinction that brother casts one over his sister (*Our Ground Time Here Will Be Brief* 30). Another in the memorial sequence, "Retrospect in the Kitchen" portrays the poet at home in her kitchen, returned from her brother's funeral. Again a garden connects them, now her brother's, with the forty pounds of plums she has picked from his tree to cross space and time, even as he has crossed over, and to boil in her pot for preserves. Some of the most poignant words in the poem are "nine o'clock / your time" (*GT* 29).

Natural companions to these poems are several in which human souls are portrayed as vegetable. In "Our Ground Time Here Will Be Brief," the speaker waits for takeoff on the tarmac and thinks of the souls of the unborn aloft in the cloud-pack, personalized as her "children's children's children and their father . . . strewn / as loosely as parsnip / or celery seeds" (*GT* 3). Apart from the description of the planting of souls—"strewn" or scattered, an apparently inexact operation—are any characteristics of celery and parsnip relevant to this simile? My field guide informs me that both are perennial or biennial, that two ounces of celery seeds will fill an acre if grown in single rows three feet apart. Of the parsnip I learn that the young are delicate and that after harvest their quality improves with storage—to me, all satisfying attributes of soul.[1]

In other poems that sustain this view of soul, a month after the October death of Anne Sexton, Kumin writes "In my heart, a scatter like milkweed / a flinging from the pods of the soul" (*RS* 46). Again, my field guide helps with this entry for *milkweed*: "Pods stout, to 4 in. long, open

1. E. Laurence Palmer, *Fieldbook of Natural History* (New York: McGraw-Hill, 1949), 279–80.

to free many parachuted seeds sometimes throughout the winter."[2] This image from "How It Is" (*RS* 46) both links human soul with the garden and posits a journey of speaker's soul outward *throughout the winter*, perhaps toward her friend. The latter possibility is reinforced by lines from "Splitting Wood at Six Above," which address Sexton:

> your small round
> stubbornly airborne soul,
> that sun-yellow daisy heart
> slipping the noose of its pod
> (*RS* 48)

What does it mean that the soul made manifest derives from the garden? Clearly, the cycle of vegetable life may be continued apart from human will or intervention. Plants may go to seed, resowing themselves with the aid of the elements and other animals. For one whose view of the universe is not based on religious orthodoxy, this alternative seems natural and appropriate. Even if not a cog in a philosophical system, Kumin's notion of soul is fundamental to a worldview, her empirical response to the physical life of the gardens she either cultivates or observes, sometimes both. Later in this discussion I will turn to her direct and indirect comments on moral power and personal faith as they relate to the garden.

The relationship of soul and body is taken up in "Body & Soul: A Meditation," wherein the soul is sought (not found) in the body like a ball bearing in a pinball machine, yet remains "[s]till unlocated, drifting, my airmail half-ounce soul" and sounding like seeds burst from the milkweed pod (*RS* 43). In this poem, among several places the soul is sought are the erogenous zones. We may look there for crossover images of the garden too, considering some of the other effects of crossover imagery.

The identification of eros with the garden is another effect signaled in "The Spell," wherein the powerful mother "infuses" the gingko, which drops "scrotal fruits." When I began rereading, I expected to notice many such images as the description of fields that release "a sweet rancidness / warm as sperm" (*GT* 12) or the vegetables described in human terms in "In the Root Cellar" (*HBFG* 41). But as I examined more closely the language of poems in which products of the garden appear in an erotic context, I often found something short of what I had defined as crossover. Perhaps this linguistic distance defended against some of the lighter effects already mentioned (peppers with pectorals, etc.). For instance, in "The Ear," nuns are odalisques, buying from Tony the fruit man and eating "bold plums,"

2. Ibid., 294.

kumquats, currants, tangerines that "slip from their skins at the nick of a nail of a nun," and "dipping red berries in sugar and telling them, / like beads." Such delights they choose over their vow of "gristle and narrow beds"; hence (forbidden) fruits of the garden become emblems of the sexual enjoyment they have eschewed (*TP* 44). Peppers with pectorals and hips are erotically suggestive too, but the crossover between animal and vegetable in that poem is consummated by metaphor.

While these examples link through metaphor objects and events that transpire outside the poet, a later poem uses a metaphor that she inhabits. "Beans" opens with an epigraph from Thoreau ("making the earth say beans instead of grass—this was my daily work") and then addresses a lover, "You, my gardener . . . have raised me up / into hellos / expansive as / those everbearing rows . . . I say beans / at your touch" (*UC* 26). The speaker is the earth, fundamental to the garden and cultivated by a lover. To "say"—produce—beans, though, is not to be them. Here, the closing lines inevitably play off against the epigraph from Thoreau. More significant, it would be difficult for the speaker of a serious love poem to *be* beans at the lover's touch; hence, the speaker is earth, with all the acts of lovemaking suggested by its cultivation. Finally, a poem in which the crossover completes itself is "In the Pea Patch" (*GT* 11). Invested with human qualities, the peas are seducers who clack and speak, inviting observers to dance with them, to "do" them as they "dangle their intricate / nuggety scrota." Some peas are assigned female, or rather feminine, characteristics—"gauzy dress" and "tendrils of hair at her neck"—and the overall effect is of eros that crosses the ordinary boundaries. In this earthly Eden, all sexuality is one celebration of life, no shame or guilt for the dance.

If most of the crossover images in the poems comfort and sustain as I have seen, the garden and nature beyond are occasionally used to register discomfort, illness, or pain depending on the observer's condition. In this connection, I've already mentioned, for example, the depiction of postoperative physical pain in terms of flowers: mums "penetrate the bed. . . . Pain comes at the hips as peonies. . . . Common petunias malinger / to prick each foot" (*NF* 78). Similar figures occur when the broken leg removed from a cast is "my shrunken stalk" (*HBFG* 60), when the speaker is haunted by "puffball bellies / of the world's waifs" (*NF* 91), and when a thoroughly unsettling walk in "In the Pine Grove" includes this surreal image—"The floor is a sidewalk of fallen hair" (*HBFG* 43).

My examination of the sundry imagery of human or animal-vegetable crossover in Kumin's work, by no means exhaustive, may serve to suggest some of the ways in which these migrations function in her poems and to reinforce the integrity of her larger vision. As mentioned, I find that vision to alter perceptibly, in scale though not in essence, with the publication of the last three books. This shift I attribute to a number of extrapoetic circumstances, among them her term as poetry consultant to the Library of Congress, her daughter's international work, her own world travel, the predictable losses and illnesses accompanying even the most vigorous middle age, the grandmotherhood that puts her at a different place along the continuum, and the passage of time with all its human erosions. To call it a movement toward the public or "political" seems inadequate; furthermore, American literary criticism has not often valued highly the poetry it designates "political." I prefer to invoke some comments from Adrienne Rich (*What Is Found There* [New York: Norton, 1993]) to illuminate where I think Kumin's poetry has been moving:

. . . in a history of spiritual rupture, a social compact built on fantasy and collective secrets, poetry becomes more necessary than ever: it keeps the underground aquifers flowing; it is the liquid voice that can wear through stone. . . . What can it mean to say, in 1993, that we have no "emergency" situation here in North America, that because this is not Eastern Europe, South Africa, the Middle East, a poetry that doesn't assume a matrix of normality is inauthentic, melodramatic? (P. 122–23)

I believe that Kumin's latest poetry increasingly takes account of the emergency as Rich has defined it.

To enter these poems, I take as gateway "Lines Written in the Library of Congress after the Cleanth Brooks Lecture." This is a big poem, in which the poet straddles two lives, the public and the private, and uneasily attempts to reconcile them. The language shows polar oppositions between, for instance, the "warm stream" of D.C. traffic and "bad air / of rush hour" and the sap running in her maples in New Hampshire, where "[t]hough civilization crumble" her cows chew their cud (*GT* 36). The poem proceeds with observations about the life she lives at both poles, in its public stanzas ranging historically to include governments from Louis XIV to Alexander to contemporary Washington, the outrages of U.S. military support of tyrannical regimes that torture their citizens, and the violent episodes of U.S. history. The collision of worlds includes Lady Bird's two million flower bulbs flourishing beside the unemployed, the drug dealers. Anticipating return to her own garden—"[f]ive miles of beans to hoe"— she looks back on herself at eighteen, believing in "infinite perfectibility" and marching for justice. That innocent has been replaced by the realist: "Now I believe in infinite depravity." Another aspect of "all that is human" is the capacity to inflict suffering for political motive (*HBFG* 92).

But the sustaining force of her garden has not altered. A changed perspective on humanity does not preclude this poet's continuing to find joy and nurturance from the sources always present in her poems, from life at the bone. It does give that joy a profoundly bittersweet flavor. The imperfection of the world Kumin finds outside the garden is balanced by the perfection of the garden. Not the perfection of biblical Eden, to be sure, but innocence as a state in which survival and renewal are based on continuing, inevitable, reliable principles, free of humanity's guile. Her increasing awareness of the public, or outer, world is evident in a section of "After the Harvest" in *The Long Approach* (the next volume published), which I find self-referential as indication of her widening perspective: "To be snug / in spite of the world's world is the child-hermit's plan" (*LA* 76). Readers will recall that the persona of *Up Country* is the hermit. I give considerable attention to "Lines Written in the Library of Congress" because it stands as bellwether—in its historic sweep, its incorporation of public and private elements, its movements back and forth through time and space, its disappointments and consolations—for some of the latest poems I will examine now.

In an epigraph from Thoreau's *Maine Woods*, Kumin signals the ranging of her thought outward to primordial and eternal aspects of the earth and its inhabitants: "Here was no man's garden, but the unhandselled globe. It was not lawn, nor pasture, nor mead, nor woodland, nor lea, nor arable, nor waste-land. It was the fresh and natural surface of the planet Earth, as it was made for ever and ever" (*LA* x). I would stress the significance of Thoreau's qualifier, "man's." The possessive case underscores the distinction between owned and cultivated lands and those enduring, flourishing places on earth that belong to no one. The arcane word *unhandselled* visually underscores the absence of human hands buying and selling the land. Even as stewardship of earth begins to occupy a more prominent place in Kumin's thought and poetry, the pleasures of her own garden remain undiminished. Her observations and celebration of the wild (echoing Thoreau) become more numerous as well, seen mainly in terms of animals such as bear and moose.

Yet familiar gardens and links populate the poems. For example, the poet eats "wild red raspberries" in memory of her dead father—a treat he so enjoyed that he used to say "men kill for this" (*LA* 9). This ritual of connection echoes that of boiling, preserving plums from a recently gone brother's trees. "Expatriate" constructs a new bean fairy tale to connect the daughter and grandson in far-off Thailand with the poet as she harvests the beans they planted. "Today I am going up in the sky with these tendrils / . . . today I am / going up to cross over and seize you / . . . Down the broad green stem I will bear you home" (*LA* 14).

In "Shopping in Ferney with Voltaire," the poet's connection with her own garden provides an avenue into the lives of others beyond the members of her tribe. She imagines herself in the market with Voltaire, and in her meditation, cruelties of his age cross enlarged into ours, as surely as the poet crosses temporal and geographic borders for this encounter. The Enlightenment emerges as woeful misnomer for both ages; Voltaire disappears, carrying mushrooms, roots, and tangerines. Reiterating some of the juxtapositions in "Lines Written in the Library of Congress," as the poet attends a film showing in a gentrified D.C. brownstone, she is struck by the "[g]lass shards and daffodils / on alternate lawns" (*LA* 25). Here flower gardens throw into ironic relief the wreckage around them. She closes by wondering what purpose art serves amid the realities, a world in which the audience will "skulk out on this spring night / together, unsafe on Capitol Hill." Darker thoughts surface too in "How to Survive Nuclear War." This poem's speaker acknowledges the killer in herself, recalling the farmer who shoots woodchucks to keep them from raiding her garden (*UC* 28). She admits, "I kill to keep whatever / pleases me. Last summer / to save the raspberries / I immolated hundreds of coppery / Japanese beetles" (*LA* 51). This admission flows together with her reading of Ibuse's account of atomic devastation, her illness and fever, and her own dream of guilt, retribution, and renewal. It is noteworthy that "rescue" arrives via her dream invention of a festival "to mourn / the ritual maiming of the ginkgo" that crosses over into waking life as epiphany when she looks out her window at a row of "old ginkgos" and sees that "[t]he new sprouts that break from / their armless shoulders are / the enemies of despair." Other poems to be discussed from these last three books deliver similarly explicit statements of the power of the garden to heal a suffering humanity.

Here in this cozy backwater I am making jam, pickles, cole slaw & tomato sauces. Quite happily. It has been an extraordinary wild berry year. V. picked me 3+ gallons of blackberries (I froze them) for jam & I just made a fantastic batch of red raspberry jam. In spite of the drought the winter squashes—irrigated—have fruited prolifically. For some peculiar reason I associate this unusual fecundity with the coming of the end of the world. Would God send extra blackberries before pulling the plug? *My* God would.

—Letter to Author, 27 August 1988

"After the Harvest," penultimate poem in *The Long Approach*, is also shadowed by threat of nuclear disaster, "the firestorms that lurk in Overkill," and related thoughts initiated by the act of "[p]ulling the garden." Thus engaged, the poet always thinks "of starving to death, of how it would be to get by / on what the hard frost left untouched / at the end of the world" (*LA* 76–8). She moves in her thoughts between present and past, putting her experience into a perspective she feels "is ending, this cycle of saving and sprouting." Conventional religious views—the first and anticipated second coming of Christ, the Rapture—weave in and out of the poem, not offering any faith she chooses to join. Once again, the vegetables in her garden reliably link her to her tribe: "I lop the last purple cabbage, big / as a baby's head, big as my grandson's brain / who on the other side of the world is naming / a surfeit of tropical fruits in five-tone Thai." And thinking of him far away, she must think too of the larger world he inhabits, asking on behalf of those displaced and unwanted

> Who will put the wafer of survival on their tongues,
> lift them out of the camps, restore
> their villages, replant their fields, those gardens
> that want to bear twelve months of the year?

I cast a line from these questions back to "Weekend of Death" (*NF* 84), as well as forward to some of the poems from the two latest books that will soon occupy me, in the final pages of this discussion. Before turning to them, I want to note how one more poem from *The Long Approach*, "Shelling Jacobs Cattle Beans," relates to the subjects of past—and potentially impending—devastation and restorative faith that I have been exploring. As the poet shells beans on Rosh Hashanah, the Hebrew New Year, she contemplates her ancestors as well as other cultures. Her thoughts roam to ancient food preservation among the Hebrews, as well as to preservation by catastrophe in Pompeii. Contemporary catastrophes, Arab versus Jew, naturally appear in conjunction with other elements of the poem, leading to the plaintive "Where is the God of / my fathers . . . / That I may hand back my ticket?" (*LA* 73). The poet concludes: "[L]et me shell out the lot. / Let me put my faith in the bean," source of moral as well as physical strength. The beans are as individual as humans, perhaps as true faith, "[e]ach its own example" and "rare." It's noteworthy too that the beans assume a female identity—they "stand naked, old crones"—associated with magical power (as surely as the mother who once cast her spell over her roses). Rejecting the conventional religion that remains a divisive cause of suffering, the poet chooses faith in the garden.

The moral power of the garden has been explicitly noted in earlier poems too, for example, "Seeing the Bones" (*RS* 33). Comparing herself to a Canterbury pilgrim, "walking / on fallen apples like pebbles in the shoes" and keeping the garden up, the poet acknowledges how the daily rituals of garden and field "steady [her] against the wrong turn, / the closed-ward babel of anomie." This sense is echoed in the line "the power of the leaf runs the human brain" (*HBFG* 95). Similar force is present in "History Lesson" (*HBFG* 3), in which the intersections between personal and world history must be negotiated in order for the individual to grow freely. A boy conceived during the Korean War and tossed by disasters in the world around him is addressed, the final moral and psychological lesson presented in the last stanza of the poem:

> That a man may be free of his ghosts
> he must return to them like a garden.
> He must put his hands in the sweet rot
> uprooting the turnips, washing them
> tying them into bundles
> and shouldering the whole load to market.

As already noted in passing, Kumin's increasing preoccupation with wilder aspects of nature in the most recent volumes includes moose and bear, most often the latter. The earthly paradise she inhabits may involve a barter, such as occurs in "Encounter in August." Watching a black bear devour her beans, she comments wryly, "This is not Eden, which ran / unfenced and was not intercropped" (*N* 22). As representative of the ever-shrinking wilderness and ever more endangered wild creatures, the black bear is honored and respected. Further, poet/farmer identifies with bear, for as they stand ten yards from each other, they are both "omnivores / not much interested in flesh." The gardener who wielded a .22 against wood-chucks among broccoli and carrots now permits this black bear to eat every last Kentucky Wonder and finds "the trade-off fair: / beans and more beans for this hour of bear."

Time exacts trade-offs too, and this we see in the imagery of "Turn-ing the Garden in Middle Age," which I read primarily as a love poem— for the mates in an enduring marriage and for the earth in its flourishing. A male is seen as the bearded parsnip, his root grown around the female puddingstone with gold earring. The entwined pair that the speaker dis-covers leads to considerations on mortality, skulls underground and the balancing "gorgeous insurgency" of weeds, which "lure me once more / to set seeds in the loam" (*N* 50).

The lure of the garden convenes with the lure of poetry, as Kumin re-sponds to words of Georgia O'Keeffe that hang over her desk (*N* 49).

"Poetry is like farming. / It's a calling, it needs constancy, / the deep woods drumming of the grouse, / and long life, like Georgia's." Mortality themes and the renewals of the vegetable world echo and reecho in these most recent poems. Even contemplating the inevitable, Kumin is never without consolations. As she mows the field on a day near her birthday, she thinks of the deaths of parents, illnesses of friends, and finds comfort in presences that counter the accumulating absences. "I ought to be / melancholy . . . / but I take courage from a big wind . . . // ruffling and parting the grasses like a cougar . . . / I am thankful for what's left that's wild"—bears that venture into her swales one such creature (*N* 60). Courage, I see, also derives from the imaginative vision that can project a cougar into the scene, from the poetic imagination.

More personal aspects of the continuum as central to Kumin's worldview and her poetry flourish in poems to and about grandchildren, such as the final poem in *Nurture*, "A Game of Monopoly in Chavannes." Playing with her daughter and grandson in Switzerland, she remembers her own childhood, when she played the game in Atlantic City. Closing stanzas return to the present scene, the grandson as "our sole inheritor," and the terminology of the game resonates possessions and passages beyond the board. The poet concludes that "his ultimate task is to stay to usher us out." This stark recognition finds corresponding expression in the poet's embrace of "festoons of mushrooms" growing from the elms' decay earlier in the book (*N* 54).

The final poem of *Nurture*, in its designation of grandson as "this luxury of a child / who burst naked into our lives, like luck," moves smoothly into the beginning of Kumin's most recent book of poems, *Looking for Luck*, with its dedication to "Yann and Noah, lucky cousins." This title also asserts the dimension of experience contributed by the observer—the implication that we must look for good fortune in order to find some. We need to seek it in the ordinary circumstances of our lives and the planet we inhabit. Nothing new for Maxine Kumin, save perhaps the degree to which this becomes a conscious positioning, a direct and explicit witnessing.

The prologue poem to this volume states her beliefs: in some of the crossovers we've seen throughout the poems and in living in harmony— "respectful but not cowed"—with other creatures and with the earth and its provisions. "I believe in myself as their [the horses'] sanctuary / and the earth with its summer plumes of carrots. // its clamber of peas, beans, masses of tendrils // as mine" (*LL* 15). I attend to the word *sanctuary* as that most holy part of a sacred place.

"Allegiance to the land is tenderness," the poet proposes, a loyalty that defies what she calls "the chrome millennium." This commitment is echoed in her praise to the new filly and prayer that she and others may raise up and trot out "onto the long lazy unfenced fields / of heaven" (*LL* 23). Heaven is here and now, acutely seen by the poet looking for luck. Connecting to other times and places, she apostrophizes remarkable women as another lucky heritage. One of them, Helen Nearing, though she came late, at twenty-six, to the garden as a homesteader, at nearly ninety still kneeled to dig up potatoes for her lunch guests. The women of this poem, Beatrix Potter, Louisa May Alcott, and Helen Nearing, inspire Kumin with their "fevers"—those passions that moved them to literature or the land (*N* 78).

Return to her early identification with Thoreau is implicit in a poem depicting the speaker's reaction to the very different gardens of a friend in southern California. The life-at-the-bone New Englander is bound to look upon the exotic fruit that rains down in such profusion—"superfluous persimmons" and "messily fecund trees"—with some disfavor or, at best, suspicion. "God appears here a forgetful sloven." The economy of existence on the New England farm satisfies her sense of propriety through interconnection, use, nothing wasted or "superfluous."

Connecting the garden, history beyond the personal, and poetry in "The Poets' Garden," Kumin portrays the various uses of poets in China, through its twentieth-century revolution and counterrevolution to the present, when "it is still raining / in the poets' garden" and white moths are depositing eggs that will "hatch into green loopers / with fearsome jaws" (*LL* 63). Why portray the poets as gardeners? Perhaps because this poet is one; perhaps because during the cultural revolution, intellectuals forcibly became farmers; moreover, because the gardens as source of both physical and moral life convey power, the obvious goal of regimes over people. The situation of poetry is inextricably linked with the political regimes by which poets, threatening in their power to feed the people, must be coerced or silenced.

As register of the primacy of the personal life, the garden over the public life, stands the poem "The Geographic Center," clear in its reference to that place around which all else revolves. The poet is always and ever looking for luck, even in winter, even given the twentieth century's history of wars, atomic devastation, assassinations. Like the pair of pileated woodpeckers, the resident faithful couple remain "prisoners of hope." And the symbol of that hope, the moral exemplum provided by the garden, is "the flourishing bittersweet / we say we should but never will rip out" (*LL* 65).

The poignance and intensity of this bittersweet hope that triumphs over experience are only increased by the measure of disaster and disappointment, "human depravity," that the alert inhabitant of these times cannot help but take. The force of nature as comfort and delight increases proportionally to the decrease of hope in "all that is human." When the epilogue poem to this volume closes with bear and woman confronting each other in the forest—she unclothed to save herself by making him feel shame, of which he is reputedly capable; he unfurred for a rug—they are about to "prepare a new legend." This promises to rewrite the familiar fairy tales of female and bear, as well as recapitulate the poet's opening "Credo," "I believe in magic" (*LL* 15). The hope that this poet never will rip out demands re-creating the tales by which we have lived—the need for chrome, war, and power over others—the divisions between humans and other creatures, between animal and vegetable worlds, between humanity and the rest of life on the planet.

In making my way back and forward again through the poems, looking through the one lens of the garden, my sense of wholeness of the work, inextricable connections of the life and the art has been reinforced. I want to suggest finally that Kumin's poetry itself demonstrates the title "Continuum: A Love Poem" (*GT* 15). The love of earth and creatures and the cycles of the natural world both express the continuum and call up a continuing response in the poet. Whatever she finds to deplore, reject, rage, or sorrow at, love of the world in its merciful generations, its most innocent nonhuman forms, shapes her art as it does her life. To come full circle to spontaneous words from the poet, I choose this paragraph written shortly before her seventieth birthday, for which her family gave Maxine Kumin what she wanted most: raised beds in her garden.

Here, a heat wave! We are promised 94 tomorrow. If that doesn't galvanize the beans & corn into sprouting, I will be unpleasantly surprised. Actually, the garden is beginning to fill out & look orderly & serene. I really had no idea how much pleasure there would be in my daily visits to it, early morns, perching on the edge of one bed, plucking weeds from the adjacent one, all the while sorting out bird calls, squirrel rustles & ticks, the whole breathing landscape around me.

—Letter to Author, 31 May 1995

POEMS

ROBIN BECKER

Floating Farm

On summer nights
the horses sleep standing in the fields.
Their stalls are so empty your dream sweeps
like a good groom into the vacant rooms
to check the flooring of wood chips,
the salt licks attached to the walls
like magnified amulets.

Bales of hay cinched
at the waist fill the loft like tawny packages.
Saddles rest in their stands
like swans asleep on the pond.
And released from its duties
the scoop in the grain bin
is the ghost of your hand.

The horses are sleepwalking
in their designated fields.
Before dawn they'll drift —
one sleek shoulder at a time —
to the paddock, to the cool stillness
of the stable, while your dreaming lips
make the syllables of their names.

A Marriage

Diving nude into the pond they made—
the woman first, then the man.
Their dog barks. I am the friend,
I've come up the long driveway with my bottles of wine, good bread,
                    my persistent need for their table.
My friends swim slowly back and forth across the pond
                    across the diminishing shafts of light
lingering, lingering, like people at a table, unable
to let go. The good black-and-white dog shakes himself dry.

There is a sadness in our quiet walk
to the house, in the way he reminds her of some small chore
they must do after dinner. The dog finds her hand
and her palm rests on his spotted head. I watch them, loving them,
loving this trilogy of faithfulness renewing itself
with each attention to one thing, and the next.

WENDELL BERRY

Chicory

for Maxine Kumin

Raking hay on a rough slope,
when I was about sixteen,
I drove to the ridgetop and saw
in a neighbor's field on the other side
a pond in a swale, and around it
the whole field was filled
with chicory flowers in bloom, blue
as the sky reflected in the pond—
bluer, even, and somehow lighter,
though they belonged to gravity.
They were the morning's
blossoms and would not last.
But I go back now in my mind
to when I drew the long windrow
to the top of the rise, and I see
the blue-flowered field, holding
in its center the sky-reflecting pond.
It seems, as then, another world
in this world, such as a pilgrim
might travel days and years
to find, and find at last
on the morning of his return
by his mere being at home
awake—a moment seen, forever known.

PHILIP BOOTH

The Dive

for M., beginning analysis, 1961

You could, of course, see more with a mask,
stay down longer with air tanks, or surface
more surely with fins. But how you dive
will be what you hold up to the sun;
and will measure, better than amphora,
gold, or depth-gauge, where you have been.
Relics are not what you gasp to retrieve,
under such darkening pressures: you surface,
if barely, having recovered yourself.

NEAL BOWERS

Another Language

for Maxine Kumin

Where the toppled cottonwood
drags a limb and autographs the river,
a beaver swam out toward me—
his hair slicked down with water, his face
lifted like a kid's looking for a parent's approval—
swam directly under as I leaned over the footbridge
and then moved to the other side
just in time to see him tip and dive,
only my breathing
and the slow wash of the river
counting the minutes,
nothing but gray-green surface shine
and my shadow filling with minnows,
and the cottonwood signing its name.

ANNIE FINCH

Zaraf's Star

Walking changes as dusk starts to gather.
We're not able or sure anymore.
We don't know the path—and if we did know it,

we wouldn't go on. We're afraid of the dark
lowering its heavy, long familiarity
down on the grass. We're afraid of the night,

moonless, desert, California,
making us stumble. We shouldn't be lost,
out here like demons just at the border

that touches us solid, as if we were gone.
She's leading me on a path as narrow
as sisters can share. We pound back down the mesa.

Each of our feet finds its own way, delving
into the gulley whose trees never answer
until, with steps slapping soft as bandits,

I slow on the path, imagining horses.

Stretching necks right out of the stones,
out of the dusk where dark has achieved our
bodies, drawn by the strides that my sister

takes like a rider, Zaraf's Star,
Fashad, Kashmir, Arabian horses
raise her up with motionless shadow

so she can ride (like a rider, she walks),
cantering, encompassing the pace of the mountain.
Out in a landscape to curl or be curled in,

hunched like riders or curling like rides,
under the fairy-tale oaks of the mesa
that hide sleeping children or horses inside,

we talk about horses like hers who run carefully,
with thinner ankles, and mustangs, who, fast,
wild grown, wild on the path to blackness,

hunger like stars reaching down for dark leaves.

EMILY GROSHOLZ

Sidonie

Who's that in the garden? Halfway between
exclusive nature and the world of words.
The garden is a garden because she said
it is, and made it so:
what grows inside its lawful boundaries
is mostly what she thought to carry in,
rosier, laurier, sauge, ficelle de soie
up which the spiraled jut
of blind, light-seeking tendrils take the air.

Except for weeds, and trees already there,
and stones the fertile earth
keeps pushing towards the light, like frozen seeds.
She pries them up, expels them,
or makes them orderly as walls or borders.
Revenants she never entertained
come in by air or passing cat or simply
pop up out of the ground
to change the garden's soft geometry.

Trace of a larger order:
the cat's paw printing a rose
on squares of chocolate drying in the shade.
Aphids in the copper iris, blackfly
graying the lilacs, nettles by the hedges,
and fierce wisteria throttling the bower.
The tired, maternal gardener stands
and sighs, a trowel in one hand, and her silver
scissors, dangling idly, in the other.

CAROLYN KIZER

Parents' Pantoum

for Maxine Kumin

Where did these enormous children come from,
More ladylike than we have ever been?
Some of ours look older than we feel.
How did they appear in their long dresses

More ladylike than we have ever been?
But they moan about their aging more than we do,
In their fragile heels and long black dresses.
They say they admire our youthful spontaneity.

They moan about their aging more than we do,
A somber group—why don't they brighten up?
Though they say they admire our youthful spontaneity
They beg us to be dignified like them

As they ignore our pleas to brighten up.
Someday perhaps we'll capture their attention
Then we won't try to be dignified like them
Nor they to be so gently patronizing.

Someday perhaps we'll capture their attention.
Don't they know that we're supposed to be the stars?
Instead they are so gently patronizing.
It makes us feel like children—second-childish?

Perhaps we're too accustomed to be stars,
The famous flowers glowing in the garden,
So now we pout like children. Second-childish?
Quaint fragments of forgotten history?

Our daughters stroll together in the garden,
Chatting of news we've chosen to ignore,
Pausing to toss us morsels of their history,
Not questions to which only we know answers.

Eyes closed to news we've chosen to ignore,
We'd rather excavate old memories,
Disdaining age, ignoring pain, avoiding mirrors.
Why do they never listen to our stories?

Because they hate to excavate old memories
They don't believe our stories have an end.
They don't ask questions because they dread the answers.
They don't see that we've become their mirrors,

We offspring of our enormous children.

WESLEY MCNAIR

The Puppy

From down the road, starting up
and stopping once more, the sound
of a puppy on a chain who has not yet
discovered he will spend his life there.
Foolish dog, to forget where he is
and wander until he feels the collar
close fast around his throat, then cry
all over again about the little space
in which he finds himself. Soon,
when there is no grass left in it
and he understands it is all he has,
he will snarl and bark whenever
he senses a threat to it.
Who would believe this small
sorrow could lead to such fury
no one would ever come near him?

Why We Need Poetry

Everyone else is in bed, it being, after all,
three in the morning, and you can hear
how quiet the house has become each time
you pause in the conversation you are having
with your close friend to take a bite
of your sandwich. Is it getting the wallpaper
around you in the kitchen up at last
that makes cucumbers and white bread, the only
things you could find to eat, taste so good,
or is it the satisfaction of having discovered
a project that could carry the two of you
into this moment made for nobody else?
Either way, you're here in the pleasure
of the tongue, which continues after
you've finished your sandwich, for now
you are savoring the talk alone, how
by staring at the band of fluorescent light
over the sink or the pattern you hadn't
noticed in the wallpaper, you can see
where the sentence you've started, line
by line should go. Only love could lead you
to think this way, or to care so little
about how you speak, you end up saying
what you care most about exactly right,
each small allusion growing larger
in the light of your friend's eye.
And when the light itself grows larger,
it's not the next day coming through the windows
of that redone kitchen, but you,
changed by your hunger for the words
you listen to and speak, their taste
which you can never get enough of.

CAROLE SIMMONS OLES

Small Poem of Thanks

We are being ourselves at your pond's edge,
me taking swimsuit cover
you nude, shaving your legs.

While the sun beats time
we wash our woes in the lap lap
launching husbands, sons, daughters
toward the other shore.
Like two veteran schoolmarms
we take attendance by counting the absent

and I am in that other July we rested
among the antiquities at Gardner Museum
where we'd gone having sprung you
from Beth Israel Hospital.
Where we sat on the wall and wept
for what the experts would do to your heart
to your heart in twenty-four hours.

But you—we—still miraculously present,
have another summer full on our backs.

Friend, in these our bodies' light ships
some picture we must make:
me bound in embarrassing shame
and you taking off even your hair.

ALICIA OSTRIKER

Mid-February

for Maxine Kumin

The mare rears, she has almost thrown her rider.
It's the thaw, it's the scent of spring,
The animals know it before we do.
While we still shiver and fret
Over the ozone layer and the whale,
Incorrigibly peering forward and backward
In the manner of our species,
In the sickroom, the patient seems to heal.
Look at the way she kicks at her blanket.

Inside here, the windows are steaming up
But a path runs through the woods,
Half dirty snow, half mud
With the stones sticking through
And the snapped branches lying across, the ones
That were ready to die
And gave themselves to the wind.
Friend, it's a day for a walk.
Are we going to walk it?

HILDA RAZ

Family

The famous poet is sitting, she
is sitting in a wicker lawn chair
drawn down by her arms to the head
of her dalmatian, unnamed on this book jacket.

One could ask someone, a friend
of the poet, not—as I am—a friend of the work.
I don't know her nor am I likely to, except
through the clear language covering
breast and genitals in her poems.
Everything stirs, always, in the final stanza
but what comes before is static, passion
in disguise under a cotton tunic flushed
towards pink at the armholes. Her poems
have no flowers in their arms, don't tell us
hold on tight, won't call us names
we won't claim no matter how we want to;
our faces and noses reject the restraint
of high forehead, middle-German flesh
packed in fresh skin, just of heavy bone frame.

This woman cooks, she preserves, she leads horses
    by the reins
through the mushroom woods, makes rot into omelettes
redolent of basil, herbs grown not on the windowsill
but in their own plot behind the larger kitchen garden
where horse droppings are forked under
in service to what turns air to fire.

In the picture she sits, head lowered to the dog.
I love this woman and lower my head to her,
to rest on her text, rest my arms

(arms that flower into hands, on their center fingers
the pale mine-cut diamonds of my dead mother)
on the pink jacket of her new book.

ELEANOR WILNER

Postscript

to Maxine Kumin

Dear Max. I call you that because
two syllables are too much for the sharp
pain your poems cause, the ache
between the shoulder blades, from
what the older centuries called
heart. You're right
and there is something you can do, I can't:
say "I" and "love" and "gone" and
cut it right, neat as a split cord of wood,
the exact heft of the axe,
the straight, swift stroke.

Last week I tried to saw
a dead branch off the firethorn, and halfway
through I had to stop, not knowing
what I'd do when the damn thing started
falling . . . standing there, imagining
how it would pull down the power lines,
the wires for the phone, the healthy branch
below, and then, as it tore down
through all the wreckage of those lines
and ruined garden, it would hit me,
its thorns tear through my scalp,
put out my eyes and leave me bleeding
for the neighbors to discover. This sad
and total inability to cut
a simple branch down from the tree
when it was dead a year, this image
like some cheap disaster
film, makes me afraid
of scissors and of saw, of lighting fires,
of using "I," for fear I'll start

some mad striptease of art, tell all,
embarrass everyone, even the dog
and bring the gossip hounds to sniff
the ruins, the mess I made of it all,
like some baroque explosion in a clean
well-lighted room, and then climb out
onto the windowsill and hoot and
hoot like some demented owl, her feathers
damp from her own rain of tears,
trying to reel back the years—
and not the ones behind, that any fool
would not repeat—but those ahead
that speed up like a train
whose rails I'm tied to
like some poor, abandoned heroine
in a film that everyone is in
so no one wants to see it
over. And yet when you, refusing
both amnesia and the comfort of a myth
can talk as straight as one might
hold a saw to get the dead branch down,
somehow, you save the tree.

While I can't face
the amputation of a branch without
the towers of Troy beginning to go over
like Humpty Dumpty toppling through the years,
his scattered bits the Hittites, the Sumerians,
the Greeks, the Romans (row on row on row),
the French in the deep freeze of the Russian
snow, and don't forget the Jews, the Congolese,
the British Empire shrinking to
tin soldiers on the counterpane
and next America and all that now lives
with her, and then the planet like
a candle sputters out, and the sun
begins to fail in the heavens
and the cold sky fills
with an avalanche of angels, overweight,

falling through their feathers, with
burning hair like figures out of Blake,
and the planets break
their orbits and collide, the firmament
begins to crack and those old waters
that the Fathers said lay just beyond it
pour through the cracks in torrents,
close over everything (except this sonorous
voice-over, this announcer, who seems
to live out universal floods
and still not skip a beat, or miss
a comma)—

                    you see, I find myself
in a false position, and wish
some sanity would overtake me, like
Don Quijote unhorsed by the Knight
of Mirrors, and just say: dear,
could you just manage
to pull yourself together, take out
the trash and understand the universal
crash is not your business; your flight
from simply stating, from talking straight
as Max, is not being able
to do what Albrecht Dürer did
in just one simple drawing
in his notebook, shortly
before his own untimely death (for
whose death is not untimely?).
It was a portrait of himself, a naked man,
his right arm bent and pointing
at his middle, and written there
below it, just one line,
no easier in German:
"Here, it hurts."

Selected Bibliography

Works of Maxine Kumin

POETRY

Halfway. New York: Holt, Rinehart and Winston, 1961.
The Privilege. New York: Harper and Row, 1965.
The Nightmare Factory. New York, Evanston, and London: Harper and Row, 1970.
Up Country: Poems of New England. New York, Evanston, and London: Harper and Row, 1972.
House, Bridge, Fountain, Gate. New York: Viking Press, 1975.
The Retrieval System. New York: Viking Press and Penguin Books, 1978.
Our Ground Time Here Will Be Brief: New and Selected Poems. New York: Viking Press and Penguin Books, 1982.
The Long Approach. New York: Viking Press and Penguin Books, 1985.
Nurture. New York: Viking Penguin, 1989.
Looking for Luck. New York and London: W. W. Norton, 1992; paper, 1993.
Connecting the Dots. New York and London: W. W. Norton, 1996.

BOOKS OF ESSAYS

To Make a Prairie: Essays on Poets, Poetry, and Country Living. Ann Arbor: University of Michigan Press, 1979.
In Deep: Country Essays. New York: Viking Penguin, 1987; Boston: Beacon Press, 1988.
Women, Animals, and Vegetables: Essays and Stories. New York and London: W. W. Norton, 1994.

NOVELS

Through Dooms of Love. New York: Harper and Row, 1965. Republished as *A Daughter and Her Loves*. London: Gollancz/Hamilton, 1965.
The Passions of Uxport. New York: Harper and Row, 1968. Also published as *The Keeper of His Beasts*. New York: Harper and Row, 1968; Westport, Conn.: Greenwood Press, 1975.
The Abduction. New York: Harper and Row, 1971.
The Designated Heir. New York: Viking Press, 1974; Toronto: Macmillan Company of Canada, 1974; London: Deutsch, 1975.

SHORT STORIES

Why Can't We Live Together like Civilized Human Beings? New York: Viking Press, 1982.

SELECTED INTERVIEWS

Armitage, Shelley. "An Interview with Maxine Kumin." *Paintbrush* 7–8 (1980–1981):
George, Diana Hume. "An Interview with Maxine Kumin." *Associated Writing Programs Chronicle*, March–April 1993, 1–9.
———. "Kumin on Kumin and Sexton: An Interview." *Poesis: A Journal of Criticism* 6 (1985): 1–18.
Litwack, Georgia. "A Conversation with Maxine Kumin, Poet." *Harvard Magazine*, January–February 1977, 65–73.
Mapson, Jo-Ann. "An Interview with Maxine Kumin." *High Plains Literary Review* 7 (fall 1992): 69–86.
Showalter, Elaine, and Carol Smith, "A Nurturing Relationship: A Conversation with Anne Sexton and Maxine Kumin, April 14, 1974." *Women's Studies* 4 (1976): 115–36.

SELECTED UNCOLLECTED ESSAYS

"The Place of Poetry: A Symposium." *Georgia Review* 35 (winter 1981): 717–18.
"How It Was." Foreword to *The Complete Poems of Anne Sexton*. Boston: Houghton Mifflin, 1981.
"Stamping a Tiny Foot against God." *Quarterly Journal of the Library of Congress* 39 (winter 1982): 48–61.
"Custom, Birth, Food, Nature: A Perspective on Some Women Poets." *Georgia Review*, 39 (spring 1985): 169–81.
Introduction to *Rain*, by William Carpenter. Selected and edited by Maxine Kumin. Boston: Northeastern University Press, 1985.
"John Ciardi and the 'Witch of Fungi.'" In *John Ciardi: Measure of the Man*, edited by Vince Clemente. Fayetteville: University of Arkansas Press, 1987.
"On 'North Winter.'" In *In the Act: Essays on the Poetry of Hayden Carruth*. Geneva, N.Y.: H. and W. Smith Colleges Press, 1990.
Foreword to *Marianne Moore: The Art of a Modernist*, edited by Joseph Parisi. Ann Arbor/London: UMI Research Press, 1990.
"The Care-Givers." In *The Writer on Her Work*. Vol. 2, edited by Janet Sternburg. New York: W. W. Norton, 1991.
"Who and Where We Are." In *Miller Williams and the Poetry of the Particular*, edited by Michael Burns. Columbia and London: University of Missouri Press, 1991.
"Breaking the Mold." In *Where We Stand: Women Poets on Literary Tradition*, edited by Sharon Bryan. New York/London: W. W. Norton, 1993.

SELECTED BOOKS FOR CHILDREN

Sebastian and the Dragon. Eau Claire, Wis.: E. M. Hale, 1960.
Follow the Fall. New York: Putnam's, 1961.
A Winter Friend. New York: Putnam's, 1961.

Spring Things. New York: Putnam's, 1961.
Summer Story. New York: Putnam's, 1961.
Mittens in May. New York: Putnam's, 1962.
No One Writes a Letter to the Snail. New York: Putnam's, 1962.
Archibald the Traveling Poodle. New York: Putnam's, 1962.
Eggs of Things. With Anne Sexton. New York: Putnam's, 1963.
The Beach before Breakfast. New York: Putnam's, 1964.
More Eggs of Things. With Anne Sexton. New York: Putnam's, 1964.
Speedy Digs Downside Up. New York: Putnam's, 1964.
Paul Bunyan. New York: Putnam's, 1966.
Faraway Farm. New York: W. W. Norton, 1967.
The Wonderful Babies of 1809 and Other Years. New York: Putnam's, 1968.
When Grandmother Was Young. New York: Putnam's, 1969.
When Mother Was Young. New York: Putnam's, 1970.
Joey and the Birthday Present. With Anne Sexton. New York: McGraw-Hill, 1971.
When Great-Grandmother Was Young. New York: Putnam's, 1971.
The Wizard's Tears. With Anne Sexton. New York: McGraw-Hill, 1975.
What Color Is Caesar? New York: McGraw-Hill, 1978.

Recent Books on Women and Nature Writing, Kumin Reference or Reprint

Knowles, Karen, ed. *Celebrating the Land: Women's Nature Writings, 1850–1991*. Flagstaff, Ariz.: Northland, 1992.
Norwood, Vera. *Made from This Earth: American Women and Nature*. Chapel Hill: University of North Carolina Press, 1993.
Ostriker, Alicia. *Stealing the Language: The Emergence of Women's Poetry in America*. Boston: Beacon Press, 1986.

Articles and reviews

Booth, Philip. "Maxine Kumin's Survival." *American Poetry Review* (1978): 18–19.
Estess, Sybil P. "Past Halfway: *The Retrieval System* by Maxine Kumin." *Iowa Review* 10 (1979).
George, Diana Hume. " 'Keeping Our Working Distance': Maxine Kumin's Poetry of Loss and Survival." In *Aging and Gender in Literature: Studies in Creativity*. Edited by Anne M. Wyatt-Brown and Janice Rossen. Charlottesville and London: University Press of Virginia, 1993.
Oates, Joyce Carol. "One for Life, One for Death." Review of *Up Country* and Sylvia Plath's *Winter Trees*. *New York Times*, 19 November 1972.

Contributors

ROBIN BECKER is the author of four books of poetry, including *Giacometti's Dog*. She was a Bunting Institute Fellow in 1995–96 and teaches creative writing at the Pennsylvania State University.

WENDELL BERRY has written more than two dozen books of poetry, fiction, and essays. Recipient of Guggenheim Foundation and Rockefeller Foundation fellowships, he teaches at the University of Kentucky and lives and writes on his farm in Port Royal, Kentucky.

PHILIP BOOTH is the author of numerous books of poetry, including *Selected Poems 1950–85*. He is the recipient of fellowships from the Guggenheim Foundation, the Rockefeller Foundation, the National Endowment for the Arts, and the Academy of American Poets.

NEAL BOWERS is professor of English at Iowa State University. His three books of poems include *Night Vision*, and his books of criticism include works on Dickey and Roethke.

MICHAEL BURNS is professor of English at Southwest Missouri State University, and the recipient of a recent National Endowment for the Arts grant. The latest of his three books of poetry is *The Secret Names*.

ANNIE FINCH teaches creative writing at Miami University. She has published a book of poetry, *Changing Woman*, and a book of criticism, *The Ghost of Meter*. She has also edited a collection of formal poetry by women, *A Formal Feeling Comes*.

EMILY GROSHOLZ is professor of philosophy at the Pennsylvania State University. She has written four collections of poetry, including *Eden*, completed with the help of grants from the Guggenheim and the Ingram Merrill Foundations.

MARK JARMAN is professor of English at Vanderbilt University. He is the author of six books of poetry including *Iris*, a narrative poem, and has received grants from the National Endowment for the Arts and the Guggenheim Foundation.

CAROLYN KIZER won the Pulitzer Prize for Poetry in 1985 for her book *YIN: New Poems*. Author of seven books of poetry, she was recently elected to the Board of Chancellors of the Academy of American Poets.

WESLEY MCNAIR is the author of four books of poetry; *The Faces of Americans in 1853* won the Devins Award for Poetry. Professor of creative writing at the University of Maine at Farmington, he is also the editor of *The Quotable Moose: A Contemporary Maine Reader*.

CAROLE SIMMONS OLES runs the creative writing program at the California State University at Chico. Her five books of poetry include *Night Watches: Inventions on the Life of Maria Mitchell*.

ALICIA OSTRIKER has published seven books of poetry; *The Imaginary Lover* won the William Carlos Williams Award in 1986. A member of the English Department at Rutgers University, she has published two critical books on American women's poetry.

HILDA RAZ is editor of *Prairie Schooner* and has recently edited special issues on Canadian, Czech and Slovak, Chinese, and Australian writers. Her books of poetry include *What Is Good*.

HENRY TAYLOR won the Pulitzer Prize for Poetry in 1986 for *The Flying Change*. He has published many books of poetry and literary criticism, including *Compulsory Figures*, a collection of essays.

ELEANOR WILNER has written five books of poetry, including *Otherwise*. She teaches on the faculty of Warren Wilson College and is a MacArthur Foundation Fellow.

UNIVERSITY PRESS OF NEW ENGLAND
publishes books under its own imprint and is the publisher for Brandeis University
Press, Dartmouth College, Middlebury College Press, University of New Hamp-
shire, Tufts University, Wesleyan University Press, and Salzburg Seminar.

LIBRARY OF CONGRESS CATALOGING-IN-PUBLICATION DATA
Telling the barn swallow : poets on the poetry of Maxine Kumin / Emily
    Grosholz, editor.
        p.   cm.
    Includes bibliographical references (p.   ).
    ISBN 0-87451-784-2 (cl : alk. paper)
        1. Kumin, Maxine, 1925-   —Criticism and interpretation.
    I. Grosholz, Emily, 1950—   .
    PS3521.U638Z89   1997
    811'.54-dc20   96-24250